Four
Screenplays

APPLAUSE FOR SYD FIELD'S CRITICALLY ACCLAIMED BOOKS ON SCREENWRITING:

SCREENPLAY

"Quite simply the only manual to be taken seriously by aspiring screenwriters."

—Tony Bill, coproducer of *The Sting,*
director of *My Bodyguard*

"The complete primer, a step-by-step guide from the first glimmer of an idea to marketing the finished script."

—*New West*

"The basics of the craft in terms simple enough to enable any beginner to develop an idea into a submittable script."

—*American Cinematographer*

"A MUCH-NEEDED BOOK . . . straightforward and informed. . . . Facts and figures on markets, production details, layout of script, the nuts and bolts, are accurate and clear, and should be enormously helpful to novices."

—*Fade-In*

"Experienced advice on story development, creation and definition of characters, structure of action, and a direction of participants. Easy-to-follow guidelines and a commonsense approach mark this highly useful manual."

—*Video*

"Full of common sense, an uncommon commodity."

—*Esquire*

"IMPRESSIVE . . . His easy-to-follow step-by-step approaches are comforting and his emphasis on right attitude and motivation is uplifting."

—*Los Angeles Times Book Review*

SELLING A SCREENPLAY

"Syd Field is the preeminent analyzer in the study of American screenplays. Incredibly, he manages to remain idealistic while rendering practical 'how to' books."

—James L. Brooks, scriptwriter, *The Mary Tyler Moore Show, Terms of Endearment, Broadcast News*

"An informative, engaging look at this inside of the dream factory. This is a terrific aid for screenwriters who are trying to gain insight into the Hollywood system."

—David Kirkpatrick, producer, former head of Production, Paramount Pictures

"A wonderful book that should be in every filmmaker's library."

—Howard Kazanjian, producer, *Raiders of the Lost Ark, Return of the Jedi, More American Graffiti*

QUANTITY SALES

Most Dell books are available at special quantity discounts when purchased in bulk by corporations, organizations, or groups. Special imprints, messages, and excerpts can be produced to meet your needs. For more information, write to: Dell Publishing, 1540 Broadway, New York, NY 10036. Attention: Director, Special Markets.

INDIVIDUAL SALES

Are there any Dell books you want but cannot find in your local stores? If so, you can order them directly from us. You can get any Dell book currently in print. For a complete up-to-date listing of our books and information on how to order, write to: Dell Readers Service, Box DR, 1540 Broadway, New York, NY 10036.

Four Screenplays

Studies in the American Screenplay
Syd Field

A Dell Trade Paperback

A DELL TRADE PAPERBACK

Published by
Dell Publishing
a division of
Bantam Doubleday Dell Publishing Group, Inc.
1540 Broadway
New York, New York 10036

If you purchased this book without a cover you should be aware that this book is stolen property. It was reported as "unsold and destroyed" to the publisher and neither the author nor the publisher has received any payment for this "stripped book."

Copyright © 1994 by Syd Field

All rights reserved. No part of this book may be reproduced or transmitted in any form or by any means, electronic or mechanical, including photocopying, recording, or by any information storage and retrieval system, without the written permission of the Publisher, except where permitted by law.

The trademark Dell® is registered in the U.S. Patent and Trademark Office.

Library of Congress Cataloging in Publication Data
Field, Syd.
    Four screenplays : studies in the American screenplay / Syd Field.
        p.   cm.
    Includes index.
    ISBN 0-440-50490-2
    1. Motion picture plays—History and criticism.   2. Motion picture authorship.   I. Title.
    PN1997.A1F44   1994
    791.43′75′0973—dc20   93-49467
                                                                CIP

Printed in the United States of America

Published simultaneously in Canada

Book design by Susan Maksuta

September 1994

10 9 8 7 6 5 4 3 2 1

For all those
who love the movies . . .

WITH MUCH GRATITUDE

To all those who made this book possible—

To Michael Blake, James Cameron, Kevin Costner, Arlene Donovan, Thomas Harris, Callie Khouri, Dan Ostroff, Ted Tally, Jim Wilson, William Wisher;

To Margie, who transcribed all the interviews; and to Gabriele, Dan, Hugh, Jesse, Tony, and all the others at the Writer's Computer Store, who were always there when I needed them;

AND ESPECIALLY

To Baba and Gurumayi, who helped guide me along the path;

And, of course, to Aviva, who constantly teaches me that the heart is the most sacred place of all.

If it ain't on the page,
it ain't on the stage. . . .
—OLD HOLLYWOOD EXPRESSION

Contents

Introduction:
Four Themes, Four Screenplays

Screenwriting is a craft that occasionally rises to the level of an art. Like film, it is a unique and special form that is constantly shifting and changing, mirroring the needs and concerns of our time. As a result, each generation brings a new eye and a new sensibility to the screenplay.

It was during the '80s that screenwriters, weaned on the curricula of TV, film schools, and the computer, began to explore and elevate the language of screenwriting and explore new areas of our collective mythology and spirituality.

As a result, films today have literally become "more real." Scenes and situations once considered impossible to shoot are now depicted with "real reality": Look at *Boyz n' the Hood* (John Singleton), or *Menace II Society* (Tyger Williams), or *El Mariachi* (Robert Rodriguez and Carlos Gallardo). Locations once thought inaccessible to the filmmaker are now accessible: Look at *Cliffhanger* (Michael France and Stallone), where the real "star" of the movie is the breathtaking region in the Alps where the movie was shot. Look at special effects, at how much the field has expanded in just a few years, merging the art and science of computer graphics into films such as *Terminator 2: Judgment Day,* or *Jurassic Park* (Michael Crichton and David Koepp). The computer software created for *Terminator 2* allowed Dennis Murren, of George Lucas's Industrial Light and Magic unit, to create the software that made the "reality" of the dinosaurs in *Jurassic Park* so real.

At the same time, screenwriters discovered the work of the noted scholar/philosopher Joseph Campbell, who charted the vast oceans of mythology, presenting a contemporary perspective to a generation hungry for myth. His ideas of the story and structure of myth have influenced screenwriters everywhere.

For several years I've been traveling around the world, teaching seminars and workshops on screenwriting. And everywhere I've gone, I've analyzed and discussed the American screenplay—with foreign governments and their ministries of Culture, with screenwriters and filmmakers, with diplomats and businessmen, with actors and technicians. Everyone, no matter what country or culture, is interested in learning more about screenwriting.

Movies have become so much a part of our lives that sometimes we forget how much they can influence behavior, or our ways of thinking. The two most popular majors in colleges and universities across the land are business and film.

Movies are a form of contemporary myth, and our heroes set out on their adventures in front of a tremendous audience. Technology, contemporary spirituality, and the enormity of today's audience have changed the American screenplay and the way American screenwriters are telling their stories. Today's screenwriters are finding new ways to tell a story. The four films I've chosen to analyze all represent this change.

When I saw *Dances With Wolves,* I realized it was influenced by some of these cultural shifts. On the surface it was a Western, a "dust" picture, which, in Hollywood at the time, was taken for granted as being dead and buried. However, the journey of Lieutenant John Dunbar to the "farthest point of the frontier" embodied a mythic structure found in Joseph Campbell's work; Michael Blake dramatized the "hero's journey" with perception, wit, and understanding.

There was also a spiritual dimension in *Dances With Wolves* that I had not seen in another movie. It expressed the Native American point of view that we are all part of Mother Earth, that all living things are related. Today this is called the Gaia Principle.

A few months later I saw *Terminator 2: Judgment Day,* and as I walked out of the theater I sensed that I had just seen the future. The James Cameron and William Wisher sequel to the highly successful *The Terminator,* released in '84, was an amazing achievement in modern film: The screenplay utilized computer graphics as an integral part of the story line, and because the software had to be created for the movie, the science and technology of film took a giant leap forward.

Terminator 2 stayed with me several days after I had seen it. Why did this picture work so well? I knew it wasn't only the special effects that made it the top box office grossing film in the world for 1991. It was part of it, to be sure, but not all of it. And it wasn't only Arnold Schwarzenegger who made the film work so successfully, though we loved his portrayal of the robotic killing machine. What made the film work so well was that the writers took the original concept and characters, brought them seven years forward in their fictional world, and in the process changed the "bad" guy into the "good" guy. It was more than just a sequel; it was the original story with a new "twist," and it included special effects that had never been seen before.

Something else caught my eye in *Terminator 2:* As in *Dances With Wolves,* there was a spiritual awareness that resounded through the last act. A lot of writers laugh when I talk about that, but the Terminator embodied an awareness of human behavior and understanding that elevated him to the stature of a "hero." Even though he's a robot, he ends up sacrificing his life for the higher good of humankind. That makes him a character of heroic proportions. "And if a machine can learn the value of a human life, maybe we can, too," Sarah Connor comments over the last shot.

I had missed *Thelma and Louise* when it first opened, but when I did see it, I was knocked out by the characters and struck by the energy of the film. Traveling with these two women down the road of no return, I saw by their actions, by their behavior, who they were. I didn't need to hear an explanation of who they were—I saw it. A good film is behavior. In the language of screenwriting, action is character. What a person does is what he is.

That film is behavior is not really new; this kind of character portrayal has been done before, with skill and finesse. Look at *Ordinary People* or *Julia,* both Alvin Sargent screenplays, or Robert Rossen's *The Hustler,* or Robert Towne's script of *Chinatown,* and you'll see great examples of film as behavior. But Callie

Khouri's script of *Thelma and Louise* takes it to another level, a more stylized, visual, contemporary level.

Thelma and Louise is also a story of self-enlightenment, about two women learning to take responsibility for their actions. It is also a controversial film: To this day, when I talk about *Thelma and Louise* people seem to want to pick and claw it to pieces. It strikes a chord somewhere deep within ourselves. Yes, there are flaws in it. So what? Yes, people didn't like the ending. So what? Some of the action was carried too far. So what? It is a striking screenplay of both style and wit, visualized with a keen eye.

When I saw *The Silence of the Lambs* I walked out of the theater knowing I had just seen a great movie. As a movie experience it was more real than the other kind of mad slasher/demon/psycho/serial killer movies that are flooding the theaters. What made it so horrifying to me was that Hannibal Lecter could be my next-door neighbor. Sitting in the theater with that audience created the same kind of an emotional impact on me that *Psycho* must have had when it was first released. Remember the shower scene?

After I saw *The Silence of the Lambs,* I read the novel, then read the screenplay. It was a great novel that had been adapted into a great screenplay. That in itself is rare. And while I was reading the screenplay I saw that the visual transitions Ted Tally had woven through it were wonderful. A film transition is how the writer gets from one scene to the next, bridging time and action, using sound and image to weave a smooth flowing narrative line. Tally's transitions were stylized and inventive, and they expanded the craft of screenwriting.

The screenplay is a unique form; it is neither novel nor play but combines elements of both. A screenplay is a story told with pictures in dialogue and description placed within the context of dramatic structure.

Structure is the foundation of all screenwriting—it is the spine, the skeleton that "holds" it all together. My approach to these four screenplays is from a structural perspective.

Screenplay structure is like a road map through the desert, showing you all the necessary things you need to know before you begin the journey. It is both guide and support, and like a tree in the wind that bends but doesn't break, structure is flexible.

How do we create such a structure?

If we look at a screenplay as being a story told with pictures, the thing that all stories have in common is a beginning, middle, and end (though not necessarily in that order). In dramatic terms the beginning corresponds to Act I, the middle to Act II, and the end to Act III.

Act I is a unit of dramatic action and is about twenty or thirty pages long and held together within the dramatic context known as the *Set-Up*. Act I sets up the story, establishing who and what the story is about and defines the relationships among the characters and their needs.

Act II is a unit of dramatic action that is approximately fifty or sixty pages long and is held together within the dramatic context known as *Confrontation*. Here the main character confronts obstacle after obstacle on the way to achieving his or her dramatic need. Dramatic need is what the character wants to win, gain, get, or achieve during the course of the screenplay. If you know the dramatic need of your character, you can create obstacles to that need, and the story will be about your character overcoming (or not overcoming) those obstacles to achieve his or her dramatic need.

All drama is conflict. Without conflict there is no action; without action there is no character; without character there is no story. And without story there is no screenplay.

Act III is a unit of dramatic action that is about twenty or thirty pages long and is held together within the dramatic context known as *Resolution*. Resolution means solution. What happens at the end of your story? Does your character live or die, succeed or fail, win the race or not, get married or divorced?

Set-Up, Confrontation, Resolution; Acts I, II, and III. But how do we get from the beginning to the middle—from Act I to Act II—and then from Act II into Act III?

By creating a Plot Point. A Plot Point is any incident, episode, or event that "hooks" into the action and spins it into another direction, from Act I to Act II, Act II to Act III. There can be many Plot Points in a screenplay, but the ones that lock the story in place before you begin writing one word of screenplay are Plot Points I and II.

These incidents, episodes, or events—these Plot Points—"hold" the story in place, anchoring them to the story line. This is how it looks:

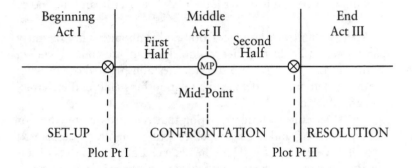

The Mid-Point connects the First Half of Act II with the Second Half of Act II; it is a link in the chain of dramatic action.

I call this the *Paradigm* of screenplay structure because it is a model, or example, or overview, of what a screenplay looks like if you could hang it on the wall and look at it like a painting. It is form, not formula.

Here, then, are four contemporary screenplays: *Thelma and Louise,* an original screenplay; *Terminator 2,* a sequel to an original screenplay; *The Silence of the Lambs,* a screenplay adapted from a novel; and *Dances With Wolves,* a screenplay adapted by the author from his own novel. Needless to say, these are films I liked, admired for their skill and craft, despite whatever holes or flaws they have.

All four films were released within a year of each other: *Dances With Wolves* in 1990, the three others in 1991. All four, taken together, stand above and apart from those that went before, poised on the threshold of a new decade of screenwriting.

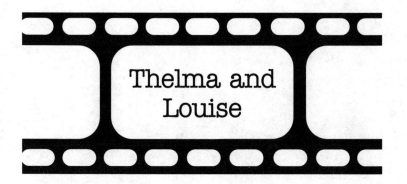

Thelma and Louise

1

The Phenomenon of
Thelma and Louise:

Callie Khouri

When *Thelma and Louise* was first released in the spring of 1991, I was conducting a screenwriting workshop for Austrian filmmakers in Vienna, a city of great beauty and culture, the home of Mozart, Beethoven, Goethe, Schiller, Strauss, Mahler, and Freud, to name just a few, and more recently, the homeland of Billy Wilder and Arnold Schwarzenegger.

That spring MGM was in financial turmoil and executive chaos, and it was possible that many films that were on the verge of release might be locked up in legal limbo until the traumatic events could play themselves out.

One of the films that was affected was a moderately budgeted film called *Thelma and Louise,* starring Susan Sarandon and Geena Davis, written by Callie Khouri, and directed by Ridley Scott, director of such highly stylized films as *Blade Runner, Black Rain,* and *Aliens.*

But after the legal hassles had been somewhat resolved and the film finally opened, everybody in the Austrian film industry was talking about *Thelma and Louise.* Word of mouth spread very quickly, and I was asked a million questions about it. I simply attributed the hype to Hollywood and promptly forgot about it.

When I returned home several weeks later, people were still

talking about *Thelma and Louise,* and it continued to be the subject of discussion and debate. It even made the cover of *Time.* I didn't know what the film was about, but it seemed everybody had an opinion about it, and nobody agreed about anything. I liked that.

So I finally went to see *Thelma and Louise.* I had no idea what to expect, so I put all my expectations on the seat beside me and spent the first ten minutes thoroughly enjoying myself. I thought it was a comedy.

Then came the scene with Harlan in the parking lot. He has Thelma spread out against a car, and he's going to rape her. It's starting to turn ugly. He shoves her face down on the hood of a car, spreads her legs open, shoves her dress roughly above her hips, and starts ripping her panties. Wait a minute, I thought, this is getting serious. I thought it was a comedy, and now this is happening.

When Louise comes out, gun in hand, and forces Harlan to stop, I was on the edge of my seat. And when she actually blows him away, shoots him in the chest, I was shocked.

As that green '66 T-Bird barrels out of the parking lot, I didn't know what to expect. I was set up to watch a comedy, and now this happens. But the great thing was that it worked! This film literally grabbed me by the scruff of the neck and forced my attention to be focused on the screen.

Suddenly I understood what everybody had been talking about. This film was fresh and funny, the relationships insightful, the humor laced believably through the dramatic situation. Every moment took me deeper and deeper into the characters and story. I experienced the film scene by scene by scene, and I trusted the screenwriter and director to take me where they wanted me to go —the ending.

I don't see too many films like that.

As the film progressed, I still thought it was a comedy, and it took me a while to realize that these two women had committed a murder, and somehow they were going to have to deal with the consequences of their actions.

How is this movie going to end? I asked myself. I can usually spot the ending within the first few minutes, but in *Thelma and*

Louise I didn't have a clue. It was only when Hal climbed into the police helicopter to join the chase that I knew how it was going to end. I knew they were going to die; I didn't know how it would happen, but I knew I didn't want it to happen. I wanted them to live. Somehow.

But I had to let go of my last shreds of hope as the two women said their good-byes on the lip of the Grand Canyon with a wall of police cars behind them. Only when Louise floored it and they sailed out over the eternity that is the Grand Canyon did I breathe easily. It worked. The whole film worked.

Over the next few days I kept thinking about the film. Moments of their relationship, the rape sequence, the truck driver sequence, little bits and pieces of visual memories flooded through me and kept replaying themselves in my head.

The more I thought about the film, the more I liked it. It was a script worth reading and studying, so when I decided to write this book, one of the first films I chose was *Thelma and Louise*.

At the time I was working with Roland Joffe (director of *The Killing Fields* and *The Mission*) on *City of Joy* (Mark Medoff), and one day when I was in the office, I saw a copy of the script of *Thelma and Louise*.

I found that it was a great read. From the very first page it had a strong visual style; it was truly a story told with pictures. It didn't matter to me whether there were unrealistic moments in the screenplay. You always have to suspend your disbelief when you read a script or see a movie. You must try to accept any story for what it is, regardless of whether it coincides with reality as you perceive it. When the unbelievability of the story punctures the willingness of your belief, the film doesn't work for you.

Who was this Callie Khouri person who had written this screenplay? I had never heard of her before, but I did manage to get hold of a videotape from a Writers Guild question-and-answer session with Callie Khouri, and the producer, Mimi Polk, and some of the production team. Callie Khouri was bright and articulate, and when she started talking about the film I was impressed by the way she spoke about her characters.

It was hard for me to believe that this was her first screenplay;

to be this good she must have had some writing experience. You just don't sit down and write this kind of screenplay.

When I started telling people that I was writing about *Thelma and Louise,* some of my writer friends went nuts. "The characters are stereotypes," said one. "It's antimen," said another. "I can't believe the relationship between the two women," said another. "She didn't have to kill him," the wife of a writer friend told me. "There were other ways she could have gotten out of that situation," she said. Everyone had an opinion. Even my aunt, an elderly woman who never goes to movies, went to see it. Somehow *Thelma and Louise* hit a common chord and jangled people's emotions. What was it that sparked so much emotion?

I did a little research. I went to the Academy of Motion Pictures Arts and Sciences Library and pulled out the review files of *Thelma and Louise.*

I was astonished.

It was classified "a crime movie of a different stripe," with headlines like "Desperadas," or "Girls just wanna have guns," and there were statements and judgments about two "strong women who have struck out on their own in a world full of men who are either pigs or hapless creatures who try to help and can't." It was labeled an "unabashedly feminist script" with "an explicit fascist theme," and it seemed to represent some kind of focal point in the "battle between the sexes."

It was branded a "pathetic stereotype of testosterone-crazed behavior," yet the movie launched a fashion spin-off on blouses and jeans that seemed to become a comment on the '90s. The distributors were amazed and said "it was defying gravity," and started selling the film as "an existential buddy movie."

Newsweek said the film was "exuberant, spontaneous, and brimful of social comment," and ranked it right up there with *Bonnie and Clyde* (Robert Benton and David Newman) and *Butch Cassidy and the Sundance Kid* (William Goldman).

The New York Times said that men "do not effect what Thelma and Louise do. The women become thoroughly independent in a way that is commonplace for male heroes. The freedom they embrace is remarkably complete and not even sexual."

The screenwriter was hardly mentioned. "It is a buddy movie,

with a script, sometimes funny, sometimes awkwardly polemical—
that serves mostly as an armature for two dazzling actresses, a
dazzling director, and a dazzling cinematographer." Everyone
seemed to forget that *Thelma and Louise* was a dazzling script by a
dazzling new writer whose approach to screenwriting was not limited by the old concepts of other road movies.

In other words, *Thelma and Louise* was fresh and original, with
a twist.

Who is this Callie Khouri? And where did she come from? I
tracked her down through one of my students who was working
for Geena Davis, called, and we set up an appointment.

It was a warm spring day when we met for lunch in Santa
Monica. She apologized for being late and said she was working
on a new script dealing with three generations of women; she was
very concerned because it was the exact opposite of *Thelma and
Louise*. Her biggest fear was that it was going to be all talking
heads and about four hours long. I thought she seemed nervous,
and then I realized the Academy Award nominations were going to
be announced the next day. She had every right to be nervous.
Being nominated for Best Original Screenplay on your first try does
not happen too often.

We chatted briefly, and I asked her about her background. She
was born in San Antonio, Texas, and since her father was in the
Army, she moved around a lot: first to El Paso, then to Paducah,
Kentucky. "The first eight years of school," she remembers, "were
basically a game of them trying to beat me into shape, and all I
wanted was to escape." Her father died when she was sixteen, and
his death affected her deeply. The next year found her leaving
home to attend Purdue University, majoring in drama.

"I always felt like a fish out of water," she says, "and it took me
a long time to find myself. The drama department seemed like a
game for people's egos, and that really bothered me. It seemed like
acting was such a powerful thing it didn't really have anything to
do with you. It seems so many people were pursuing acting careers
trying to get some kind of validation for their existence. And that's
backward, you know; it doesn't validate you, you validate it!"

Disenchanted with Purdue after three years, she moved to Nashville to be closer to her family. She worked at several odd jobs, and pursued her acting career as an apprentice at a community theater. "It was a great learning experience but basically unfulfilling," she says.

After the theater folded, she moved to Los Angeles. She studied acting at the Lee Strasberg Institute, then later with the noted acting coach Peggy Feury, who died tragically a few years ago. "People liked my work," Callie says, "but I couldn't get an agent to talk to me. I would meet them and they would look at me and say, 'Well, you're not beautiful enough,' or 'You need to wear more makeup.' I finally got a part at this little theater off Hollywood Boulevard. It was a horrible experience and it just rang the death knell for my acting desires, so I quit.

"I got a job working as a receptionist at a commercial production company, and they told me they wanted somebody for the job who doesn't want to be in production, who just wants to answer phones, somebody who has no desire. That was fine with me."

Just about that time they opened up a music video division, so "three or four months later I find myself working in production, and I worked my way up from being a runner to production assistant to production coordinator to production manager to producer."

I was very interested in how she made the switch from producing music videos to writing screenplays, so I asked if there were any movies that inspired her to write.

"Terms of Endearment" (James Brooks), she answered without hesitation. "The first time I saw it I went with a few friends and they thought it was the greatest thing they'd ever seen. And I walked out of it going, 'I don't know, I guess I missed it; I just didn't get it.' But I went back to see it again, I just fell to my knees. I couldn't believe it; it was like I didn't know where I was during that first screening. But when I went back and listened to that dialogue, I started to go nuts, it was so great.

"At first I had no desire to write screenplays," she continued. "I kind of wished I had because I was reaching the end of my time producing music videos. I was struggling so hard to figure out what it was that I was supposed to be doing. I kept thinking I'm supposed to be doing something creative. I can't believe I have such a knack for the vernacular and I don't have anywhere to apply it.

"I felt I had not found my true path. And then a series of events occurred that led me to the point where I didn't have anything to lose if I wrote a screenplay.

"So I started to write a sitcom with a friend of mine, somebody who ended up writing for *The Golden Girls.* He was a stand-up comedian, and we decided to write a spec script for some friends who had a show. We started writing together and he kept telling me how great it was, but I just kept thinking he's trying to be nice, to be encouraging.

"It felt so easy and so comfortable that I felt like I wasn't doing anything. So it was suspect to me. I'd always read so much when I was growing up and I have such a deep respect for the craft of writing, that I felt it was something that was going to be out of my reach. I know what an incredible art it is. So I completely underestimated myself in thinking it was out of the realm of possibility.

"I kept praying for an answer, contemplating and meditating, asking for help so I could be put on my proper path.

"And that's when I got this idea: 'Two women go on a crime spree.' As soon as I had the idea I felt this strange sense of euphoria.

"The more I thought about it, the more excited I became. I mean, what would make two seemingly normal women go on a crime spree? Why would they do that? Why would I go on a crime spree? I didn't want to do anything sexist, because I was producing music videos and my livelihood was dependent on exploiting women to sell records.

"I didn't want to write about two stupid women, or two evil women who go on a crime spree. I wanted to write about two normal women. The definition of women as presented in films and plays is so narrow, so limiting. I noticed that when I was acting: How many times did I play a prostitute? Dramatically, it seems one out of every four women is a prostitute.

"Where are the real people? Where are people that aren't prostitutes, that aren't selling themselves for sex? I wanted to write something with strong women in it. I wanted to write something that had I been an actress and read the script, I would have thought: I've gotta do this role or I'm gonna kill myself."

She paused for a moment, looking off into the distance. "I originally conceived of Louise as being this woman in Texas who works at a big oil company in one of those giant buildings," she continued, "and when you walk in somebody's sitting behind one of those big desks with a headset on directing people and taking calls and all that stuff. I pictured her as one of those people who never realized women could be executives until she saw one come in the front door. And then she started wondering how it was that this whole thing had gone on and she didn't know anything about it; she wasn't one of them, and she had an urge for power that's never going to be available to her. The way it had been explained to her when she was growing up was that because she was a woman her role was so narrow she couldn't even conceive of herself as being something like an executive.

"She was the kind of woman who wears makeup the way Dolly Parton wears makeup, or Naomi Judd; they have these beautiful features, but if you take all that stuff off, what do they really look like? I mean, could you recognize Dolly Parton without makeup? Would you even know who she is?

"That's how I thought of Louise. Now, I love to laugh and I love people who are funny. So I wanted it to be a movie that you were enjoying and having a good time with because in some ways you were watching these women get their lives back. Even though they lose their lives at the end, you watch them as society's convention is pulled further and pulled out of their grasp, so they become more and more themselves. These were great people to be with, and anybody would have loved to get to know them if they had a chance.

"But when I started writing I suddenly saw her clearing coffee cups into a bus tray and knew she was a waitress, working the night shift. It was like she said, 'I work in a coffee shop,' and she works the night shift because she's in a well-lit place all night, and not at home afraid.

"Then I asked myself what crime they had committed. I knew they were going to have to kill somebody because I needed it to be a crime from which there was no escape and for which there was no real justification. Though you couldn't justify it, you could understand it. You understand completely why this woman did what she did. That's another one of the things I've never seen dealt with in a film, the anger women feel about the way they're talked to. In that particular situation, it's almost a natural response.

"The idea that people can speak to you in such a way that if you had a gun you would kill them is something I think women experience every day. It's not that there's something wrong with the world in which we live, it's just that we haven't assimilated properly to understand that. Women don't know their place, because if we have to put up with this, then there really is no place, is there? So I knew the crime was going to have to be something like murder.

"Several years ago I was working as a waitress, and one day I was walking down the street, minding my business, when this old guy in a car starts talking to me. He's old enough to be my grandfather. I'm ignoring him, which is what you're supposed to do in that situation; you know, I can't hear you, I can't see you, you can say whatever you want, I'm not a human being. Then he said, 'I'd like to see you suck my dick,' and I just lost it for a second. I pulled my sunglasses off and I walked over to the car and said, 'And I'd like to shoot you in the fucking face.'

"That scared him. This guy doesn't know me from Adam, and this is the kind of thing he says to a total stranger on the street? I was so angry, yet I was glad I had ruined his day. That I scared him, maybe dissuaded him from ever speaking to another woman like that. There was a risk in what I did but I felt elated because I'd responded like a normal human being who *respected* myself. Because I not only allowed myself to feel anger, but expressed it. I put *him* at risk, making him deal with the consequences of his own words. I giggled to myself for the next block or so until I got back to my apartment. I'm so glad I did that. Most of the time people do those things to you, and if you're a woman, you're supposed to simply ignore it."

She looked off into the distance and asked the waitress for a cigarette, explaining that she doesn't smoke but she was nervous about the Academy nominations the next day. She took a drag and continued after a moment.

"What also appealed to me," she began, "was the idea that there is a side of you that you really don't know exists. And you don't know what the trigger for it is. You think you're a normal person and you have a normal life, but things can happen and you don't really know what's inside of you. That kind of tenuous relationship we have with our normal life was really intriguing to me. How one little thing can happen and your whole world can fall completely apart.

"I wanted to set up the screenplay where it was like dominoes falling. It had to be grounded in reality, so Thelma and Louise would never be in a situation that could never occur. Everything had to be real and believable.

"I liked the idea of this woman who's just trying to be normal, because that's all she wanted to be, but it was completely impossible."

She paused, gazing at a bird flying by, then shook her head slightly.

"I also wanted to deal with the idea of Louise feeling responsible for what happened," she continued. "She started out playing a game with Jimmy, that she wasn't going to be in town when he got back and this is what she gets for not being honest. So she feels like she precipitated the whole thing. If you find yourself holding back your feelings, or having to play games, nothing good ever really comes of it.

"Plus," she adds, "I knew something had happened to Louise, something she wasn't going to expose, and I didn't know what it was. I didn't know what had happened to her until about halfway through the screenplay. And she was never going to expose it, never going to open herself up like that again. Which is why she's sometimes hostile with Thelma, because she felt that if she had really tried, the whole thing could have been avoided, which is really how society feels."

This "something" that happened to Louise was that she was raped in Texas several years earlier. "I wouldn't let myself say she had been raped. I never said it in the screenplay. We added a reference to it toward the end because Ridley felt that people would come out of the movie going, 'Well, what did happen?'

"It doesn't really matter what happened to Louise," she continued. "What happened to her happened to her. There are thousands and thousands of women walking around that have something in their past we don't know about, and they deserve to be treated with respect, whether we had anything to do with it or not."

What happened to Louise in Texas is the structural backbone of the entire story line. It's because of this incident that Louise knows how to use a gun; it's because of this incident that she runs away from the murder. By the time she realizes what she's done, it's too late.

Because the "incident in Texas" is mentioned throughout the screenplay in a subtle and indirect way, we are forced to make our own discovery about these two women.

And good screenwriting is the art of discovery.

2

On the Road
to Liberation:

The First Ten Pages

The first ten pages of any screenplay are the most important. Almost everything you need to know about the movie is found in these first ten pages—that is, if you know what you're looking for. A good screenplay begins immediately, with page one, word one. You must grab the reader's attention, setting up crucial information that will pay off in the reader's and audience's immediate understanding of the film's opening situation.

In the seminars and lectures I teach around the world, most writers, no matter how professional, are totally unaware of how important the first ten pages are. You may read these pages and think nothing much is happening, but if the writer is doing his or her job, that person is carefully designing these pages to give us essential information about the story and characters.

A screenplay is a living thing, and each piece, even though separate and complete, is part of a whole. Structure, remember, is the relationship between the parts and the whole.

When the screenwriter sets out to write a screenplay, he or she must conceive of the first ten pages as a unit of dramatic action complete unto itself. Basically there are only two ways to open the screenplay effectively: with an action sequence, like *Terminator 2,* or with an expository, character-driven sequence, like those that open *Thelma and Louise* or *The Silence of the Lambs.* That's reducing it to the simplest terms; within these two parameters lie an infinite number of ways to open your screenplay combining both action *and* character.

It doesn't matter whether it's a European or an American film; it's got to be set up in the first ten pages.

That's why *Thelma and Louise* works so effectively. It's set up from page one, word one.

"Louise is a waitress in a coffee shop," and "Thelma is a house-wife."

That's the way the screenplay begins. Simple, right. From the very first words we know who these people are; more importantly, we *see* who they are.

In the first image we have Louise "slamming dirty coffee cups from the counter into a bus tray underneath the counter." At the same time, in a nice, visually matched cut, we see "Thelma slamming coffee cups from the breakfast table into the kitchen sink, which is full of dirty dishes anyway." The visual cuts, image to image, matching the slamming of the cups under the counter to the slamming of cups into the kitchen sink, indicate a writer who understands the value of the visual transition.

Khouri's visual transitions move the story forward, and as she cuts back and forth between her two main characters she gives us a chance to learn about her characters and see their relationship with each other.

These relatively simple actions in the first two paragraphs of the screenplay tell us a lot about these two characters. When a screenwriter sets-up the first ten pages of the screenplay, the reader must know immediately *what's going on*. To do that effectively, we have to see the behavior of these people.

"Film is behavior" is the way the great Italian film director Michelangelo Antonioni said it. Antonioni is a master of situation and puts his characters into emotionally charged situations, then charts their behavior. In film after film, from *L'Avventura* to *La Notte* to *L'Eclipse* to *Blowup* to *The Passenger,* Antonioni's characters are revealed to us by what they do, by their actions.

In *L'Avventura,* for example, a young engaged couple embarks on a weekend excursion to an isolated island off the Italian coast. The bride-to-be brings her best friend, Monica Vitti, with her.

They arrive on the island, and everyone goes exploring. Time passes. But when it's time to return to the mainland, the bride-to-be is missing. No one can find her; she is nowhere on the island and seems to have vanished into thin air.

Determined to find her, the future husband and the girl's best friend go searching for her.

Immediately they are attracted to each other but forcibly deny it, refusing even to acknowledge the possibility. Finally they give in to their desires and become lovers. Now, though they are still searching for his bride-to-be and her best friend, they dread the moment when they may actually find her.

It is this situation that drives the film forward. Act I sets up the situation, Act II explores it, and Act III resolves it. Once we set up the situation, all we have to do is follow the characters' behavior the rest of the way.

That's what happens in *Thelma and Louise*. In the very first line of dialogue Louise calls Thelma, saying, "I hope you're packed, little housewife, 'cause we're outta here tonight." They're supposed to go away for the weekend. But Thelma tells her she hasn't asked her husband if she can go away, and Louise freaks. Thelma doesn't know what to tell her husband, Darryl (Chris McDonald), so Louise tells her to tell him she's having "a nervous breakdown." But that's no big deal, Thelma replies, because "he already thinks you're out of your mind, Louise, that don't carry much weight with Darryl."

"Originally," says Callie Khouri, "Thelma had kids and stuff like that, but I realized she couldn't have kids. The idea that Darryl wanted her to wait because the kids would be a sacrifice for him financially, fit perfectly. And, of course, she's really a child herself.

"I had to set it up that way," she continued. "I love to laugh, and I wanted this to be a movie you were enjoying and having a good time with because you were watching these women get their lives. Even though they would lose them, they were becoming more and more themselves. It was a beautiful experience, a liberating experience to watch that."

Thelma decides to confront Darryl as he's getting ready to leave for work, but she can't go through with it. So, she decides not to ask his permission; she's just going to let him find out everything for himself. The scene, seemingly simple and irrelevant, is really a scene that reveals their relationship to us. Darryl is described as a man who "is dripping in men's jewelry. Polyester was made for this man. He manages a carpeteria." In other words, even though the character is described, we *see* their relationship. Darryl is set up as being self-absorbed, self-important, and righteous, a caricature; you can't really take someone like that too seriously. Callie Khouri is showing us that he's going to be a source of comic relief.

To get a better picture of Thelma, we see Darryl; what kind of person would build her life with a man like that? The answer is someone who's a "ditz" or an "airhead," and that sets up her character fast. We *see* who she is immediately, thus establishing the starting point of her emotional journey.

Though we've covered only the first three pages of screenplay, we already have enough visual information to glimpse an accurate portrait of Thelma and Louise.

We like them; we see who they are and find them funny and sympathetic; we might even know people like them.

As Thelma and Louise start packing for their little weekend adventure to the mountains, we get to see another aspect of their characters. Louise's suitcase is "perfectly ordered, with everything neatly folded and orderly. Three pairs of underwear, one pair of long underwear, two pairs of pants, two sweaters, one furry robe, one nightgown. She could be packing for camp. Reveal Louise. Her room is as orderly as the suitcase. Everything matches."

Thelma, on the other hand, throws in everything, her "bathing suits, wool socks, flannel pajamas, jeans, sweater, T-shirts, a couple of dresses, way too much stuff for a two-day trip. The room looks as if it was decorated from a Sears catalog."

Notice the contrast between the two women. We identify them by what they do, by actions as well as behavior. The simple act of packing a suitcase becomes a visual illustration of character.

Before she leaves, Thelma calls her boyfriend Jimmy. Again, this is a visual demonstration; she hesitates for a moment, then reaches down and dials, listens to the message, then "slams down the phone. A framed picture of Louise and Jimmy sits on the table next to the phone. She matter-of-factly slams that face down, too."

Jimmy becomes a significant character in the screenplay.

"Jimmy is a guy who's afraid to make a commitment," says Khouri, "for whatever the reason, even though Louise knows they're eventually going to end up together. 'What are you waiting for?' she would ask. She wants to get married, wants all the conventional things, yet she's being denied them because of the choice she's made in this man. Basically, his shortcoming is holding her back from what she really wants.

"Yes, she could leave him, but she loves him. I wanted to show her feelings because she feels responsible for everything that happens. She plays a game with him; when he comes back from his trip, she's not going to be in town, and this is what happens when she's not being honest."

The last thing Thelma does is rummage around the drawer of her nightstand and "we see a gun, one Darryl bought her for protection. It is unloaded, but there is a box of bullets. She picks up the gun like it's a rat by the tail and puts it in her purse. . . ." This, of course, is a key visual setup; we see she has the gun, but we also see she doesn't know how to use it.

By page six they're ready to go. Louise picks Thelma up in her green '66 T-Bird convertible, which is as clean and well cared for as the clothes in her suitcase. The car reflects her character. Whenever she gets "in trouble, this car always gets me out of it." Everything she says and does makes a statement about who she is.

When Thelma gets in the car, she has all her gear with her: "a suitcase that looks like it might explode, fishing gear, a cooler, a lantern." They jam everything into the trunk, take a picture of themselves, and pull away from the curb. The first thing Thelma does is "let out a long howl. She is laughing and sticks her arms straight up in the air." The journey to freedom and liberation has begun.

As they begin their adventure, there's a scene written that was partially omitted from the film. Whether Ridley Scott thought it too blatant, or too obvious, I don't know. As they're driving, Thelma reaches into her purse and hands Louise the gun. "You take care of this," she says. Louise is shocked at first, then takes the weapon and puts it away. That's where the scene in the film ends, but in the script the scene continues, and Louise "holds it in her hand, tests the weight of it, then puts it under the seat." In the script, we see that Louise has handled guns before; she is not like Thelma in that regard. How and where we have yet to find out.

Bit by bit, line by line, shot by shot, Callie Khouri is building her characters. Everything is a visual statement about who these characters are. The actions that are set up in these first few pages fashion a dramatic context for the actions that occur later in the story. Nothing is thrown in by chance, even though it may look like it.

When they're finally on the road, some exposition is needed, and we learn they're going to spend the weekend in a mountain cabin that belongs to the day manager where Louise works: "He's gettin' a divorce, so his wife's gettin' this place, so he's just lettin' all his friends use it till he has to turn over the keys."

The word "exposition" literally means "necessary information"; in creative writing, exposition is information necessary to further the action of the story. The trick in screenwriting is to try to find a way to present this exposition so it doesn't get in the way of the characters and story. Most screenwriters feel that exposition scenes always intrude in the development of the story; the scenes are usually too blatant, too obvious, and we constantly search for ways to present information that seems natural and unobtrusive. As they drive, we learn more about the two women.

>THELMA
>I've never had the chance to go out of town without Darryl.

>LOUISE
>How come he let you go?

>THELMA
>'Cause I didn't ask him.

>LOUISE
>Aw, shit, Thelma, he's gonna kill you.

>THELMA
>Well, he'd have never let me go. He never lets me do one goddamn thing that's any

> THELMA (cont'd.)
> fun. All he wants me to do is hang around
> the house the whole time while he's out do-
> ing God only knows what.
> (she pauses)
> I left him a note. I left him stuff to micro-
> wave.

She laughs. The way she tells him she's going away for the weekend is indicative of their marriage. She "left him a note," then explains she "left him stuff in the microwave," as if those made everything okay. Again, this says more about her marriage than a long exposition scene of trying to "explain" why she's doing what she's doing.

As they drive toward the mountains, the script presents the first visual setup of a truck driver who's driving a huge semitanker carrying gas; in the future we will recognize him by his signature mud flaps, which are the shiny silhouettes of naked women. "Lick you all over—ten cents." This scene was cut from the final film, but it shows how carefully Khouri sets up the action of the film now to pay it off later.

Thelma whines about being hungry, so they pull into a night spot called "The Silver Bullet," another little visual metaphor. This occurs at the bottom of page nine.

Most readers in Hollywood need only ten pages to know whether a script is working. They look for three things in this unit of dramatic, or comedic, action: the main character, the dramatic premise (what the story is about), and the dramatic situation (the circumstances surrounding the action). If you know what to do, then you can figure out how to do it, and the first ten pages give you plenty of time to set up the characters, premise, and situation.

These are the first ten pages of *Thelma and Louise*. You may think these pages are deceiving, that nothing significant is happening. It seems so simple. But the screenwriter is carefully designing these pages to reveal essential information about the story and characters for us to begin to identify with them and their situation.

3

Setting Up Character:

The Second Ten Pages

The great nineteenth-century American novelist Henry James had a theory of fiction that stated one of the great fundamental truths about the nature of literary character: "What is character," he wrote, "but the determination of incident? And what is incident but the illumination of character?"

Sometimes there are events in our lives that bring out the best in us. At other times, how we act, and react, or deal with a particular situation tells us who we really are. The events in a screenplay are specifically designed to bring out the truth about the characters so that we, reader and audience, can transcend ordinary life and achieve a connection, or bond, between "them and us." We see ourselves in them, and perhaps enjoy a moment of recognition and understanding.

As James says in his theory of fiction, the incidents you create for your characters are the best ways to illustrate the nature of who they are—their *character*. How they respond, what they do, what they say, how they act or react in a particular situation are what really define their character.

Film is behavior.

Thelma's casual remark about getting something to eat is one of those remarks that is totally incidental, except in the context of this particular situation. In this screenplay, Thelma's remark sparks the entire screenplay into being. It starts the second ten pages of the screenplay. In these pages, the screenwriter must focus on revealing the main characters.

Louise reluctantly pulls into the parking lot of a club called "The Silver Bullet." This begins the dramatic hook, or inciting incident of the story. What happens here, in this club, is what springs the entire screenplay into motion.

"The place is jumpin'," the script reads. The first words out of Louise's mouth are "I haven't seen a place like this since I left Texas." This may seem like a throwaway line, but when you go back and reread the script, you realize it's the start of one of those important plot threads that weaves itself through the entire story line. What happened to Louise in Texas? It's not long before we see that, whatever it was, it had a major, profound effect on her. It is her reaction in this situation that sparks the entire story, that puts it into overdrive. History does repeat itself, we're going to find out, and the two women will be swept up in the swirling emotions that drive them to their ultimate destiny.

They grab a table, and Louise is a little surprised when Thelma orders a "Wild Turkey straight up with a Coke back." When Louise tries to restrain her, Thelma retorts, "Is this my vacation or isn't it? I mean, God, you're as bad as Darryl . . . you said you and me was gonna get outta town, and for once really let our hair down."

Louise laughs then orders a "marguerita, with a shot of Chevo on the side." Another little piece that fits into the puzzle of character. What someone orders in a script can be a solid reflection of character.

Two women sitting alone at a table early on a Friday night lures the "shark" to their table. Harlan, a man in his "late 40s, heavyset, his face shining, pulls up a chair and straddles it backward."

"What are a couple of Kewpie dolls like you doin' in a place like this?" he asks. Louise tells him to shove off, but Thelma continues rattling on about their weekend trip until Louise kicks her under the table.

It's obvious that Harlan is known here because the waitress makes a snide remark about him when she brings the women their drinks.

Louise picks up the dialogue after Harlan leaves. "Can't you tell when somebody's hittin' on you?" Louise says, turning on Thelma. "Well, so what if he was?" Thelma replies. "It's just all your years of waitin' tables has made you jaded, that's all."

That says a mouthful about Louise.

As a matter of fact, one of the ways Khouri defines her characters is by what other people say about them. This is a technique discussed by Henry James in his theory of illumination. James imagined a main character occupying the center of a circle. In this circle, surrounding the main character, are the characters that he or she interacts with. James felt that every interchange between the characters should "illuminate" different aspects of the main character, just as various lamps illuminate different aspects of a dark room. You "illuminate" the room just the way other characters should illuminate the main character.

Callie Khouri uses this technique throughout the screenplay. I asked her how she goes about getting in touch with her characters, and she hesitated a moment before replying: "I think it's something like preparing the soil for planting," she says. "What I'll do is go out in the backyard in the morning, and just sit there and try to open myself up and let the characters come to me; let them talk to me. So much of writing is about getting quiet enough so you can hear your characters talking. Sometimes I feel they choose you because they know you're listening. You just have to shut up and listen.

"My greatest challenge was not to impose myself on them," she continues, "and just let them say what they've got to say. If I'm in turmoil about what a character is doing, I have to be careful not to let my own turmoil destroy what's happening. It's very much like a miscommunication between me and them. The same way it would be with a real person.

"As far as I'm concerned, Thelma and Louise are real people. One time I read something Geena Davis said in an interview. She said, 'I knew if I wanted to know what kind of toothpaste Thelma used I could call Callie and she would know.' And when I read that, I thought, Well, she uses the kind with red, green, and blue stripes, whatever has the most color in it."

I asked her why she chose to set the story in Arkansas, when they seem to be more "Texan" in attitude and behavior. She laughed, then explained that "At first, I was thinking of having them in Texas, but then I realized I had to have them in Arkansas, because when I looked at a map I realized their journey was going to have to take place over a certain period of time. So I had to ask myself where a good place for them to start would be so they can end up at the Grand Canyon.

"All the time I was writing," says Khouri, "I felt like I was telling a true story. And all I had to do was wait until somebody told me the next part."

If you look at the characters of Thelma and Louise, they are two distinct, individual people, yet from the standpoint of creating character, they are really two parts of the same whole. They are different aspects of each other, so together they could be considered to be the main character. They share everything—their life, their death. There is no real conflict between them other than the ordinary personality differences that plague any friendship.

Everything Thelma and Louise say to each other during the second ten pages reflects a certain aspect of their character. Even though they are in the midst of a wild bar on a Friday night, it is a very intimate scene, and we begin to sense the relationship between these two women and the men in their lives.

THELMA
Jimmy still hasn't called yet?

LOUISE
Givin' him a taste of his own medicine. Asshole.

THELMA
I'm sorry, Louise. I know you're all upset.
It's just I'm so excited to be out of the house,
I guess.
(pause)
I wonder if Darryl's home yet.

> LOUISE
> I wonder if Jimmy's gotten back.
>
> THELMA
> Why don't you tell him to just get lost, once
> and for all?
>
> LOUISE
> Why don't you ditch that loser husband of
> yours?

They both drift off momentarily, contemplating their domestic problems.

It's a very revealing interchange. Thelma, thinking she's upset Louise, tells her not to worry; when they get back, "Jimmy'll be kissing the ground you walk on."

Following this exchange between Thelma and Louise, Khouri cuts to Thelma dancing with Harlan, which shows the passage of time within the sequence. Harlan appears to be a nice guy, even if he is a "womanizer," and he's obviously taken with Thelma. The script describes Thelma as "breathless, drunk, and giggly. She holds a beer bottle in one hand. She is laughing a lot about nothing, and Harlan is studying her closely."

Louise sees this and knows it's time to leave. She tells Thelma that after she goes to the ladies' room, "we're gonna hit the road."

It is here that Khouri sets up the Plot Point at the end of Act I. A Plot Point is an incident, episode, or event that hooks into the action and spins it around into another direction—in this case, Act II. A Plot Point is very important in the progression of the story. Its function is simple: to move the story forward. It is the result of the actions of the main character. There could be as many as nine or ten Plot Points during a screenplay. But the two most important come at the end of Act I and the end of Act II. They are the anchors of your story line, the stitches that hold everything together. Before you can write one word of the screenplay, you must know your structure: the ending, beginning, Plot Point I, and Plot Point II. The screenwriter builds his or her story around these four elements.

In *Thelma and Louise* the Plot Point at the end of Act I is the culmination of Act I, and concludes the Set-Up portion of the script. In most screenplays the real story begins at Plot Point I.

Thelma doesn't feel so good and tries to follow Louise into the ladies' room, but Harlan interferes and forcibly steers her toward the door to "get some fresh air."

Thelma, dizzy, knowing she shouldn't be where she is, wants to go back in, but Harlan forcefully prevents her. He tells her that "you're startin' to feel pretty good to me," and he tries to put his arms around her. She pulls away.

Cut to Louise walking out of the bathroom, and like the opening of the script, we now intercut between Thelma in the parking lot with Harlan, and Louise looking for Thelma around the club. Harlan moves Thelma to the far end of the parking lot and tries to kiss her, but she resists.

"Don't. I'm married. I don't feel good. I've been sick," she says.

That's okay, he replies: "I'm married, too."

When I asked Callie Khouri about the genesis of Harlan, she explained that "the character of Harlan is a very typical profile of a rapist." I asked her to explain that a little. She took a sip of coffee, inhaled deeply on her cigarette.

"Violence against women has always been a subject that has troubled me greatly," she began, "and I've had so many friends that have been raped, I've always made myself aware of those things. I've read books on criminal behavior, and when I started writing about Harlan I knew he's a guy who's very nice and then turns on you."

That's exactly what he does. Not satisfied with Thelma's reaction, he begins using force. He pins her against the car and begins kissing her. "He has her ass in his hands," reads the stage directions. "He's beginning to hump her. She is pushing him away as hard as she can, but he is relentless."

Harlan starts pulling at her clothes, and "Thelma gets one of her arms free and hits him hard in the face. He hits her back and grabs her face, squeezing it hard. 'Don't you hit me! Don't you fucking hit me!' he yells at her.

"There is no trace of friendliness in his face now," the script reads. "He looks mean and dangerous, and he tells her to shut up."

He turns her around, pushing her face down onto the back of the car. He holds both her arms in one hand and continues pulling her dress up over her hips. He starts to undo his pants as we hear the CRUNCH of gravel, and we hear Louise offstage.

"Let her go," she says.

"Get lost."

"Louise!" Thelma yells, and then we see a "TIGHT SHOT of the barrel of Thelma's gun being pressed into the nape of Harlan's neck. Louise's finger pulls back the hammer."

"Let her go, you fat fucking asshole, or I'm going to splatter your ugly face all over this nice car." Harlan raises his hand and tells her to relax: "We were just havin' a little fun." She replies that it "Looks like you've got a real fucked-up idea of fun."

Louise backs away as the tension releases, and then she tells him, "Just for the future, when a woman's crying like that, she's not having any fun."

Angry and pissed off, Harlan calls her a "bitch," and then, "I should have gone ahead and fucked her."

Louise stops in her tracks and turns. "What did you say?"

"I said suck my cock."

That does it. Louise totally loses it. "She takes two long strides back toward him, raises the gun, and FIRES a bullet into his face. We hear his body HIT the gravel parking lot. . . . We hear the SOUND of the nightclub in the distance."

Plot Point I.

This incident swings the story around into Act II. From here on, Thelma and Louise are on the run, and as they race down this highway, like so many other characters in so many other movies, they come to grips with themselves, find out who they really are, and ultimately end up taking responsibility for their lives and actions. *Thelma and Louise* is a road movie, yes, but it's really a journey of enlightenment.

"What is character but the determination of incident?" asks Henry James. "And what is incident but the illumination of character?"

4

On the Run:

The First Half of Act II

When I was making television documentaries for David L. Wolper I was a staff writer-producer on a series called *Hollywood and the Stars*. One of my assignments was pulling film clips from the great Hollywood movies for the half-hour show that aired on NBC. The show would trace the careers of Hollywood's greatest stars by showing film clips, still photographs, personal interviews, sometimes home movies, anything we could use to document the lives of the stars. It was a very free-flowing, creative time, and we broke a lot of rules about what could be seen on network television.

For me it was an education. I would sit in that darkened editing room viewing all these great movies. If we were doing a show on Hollywood's great lovers, my job would be to isolate and clip together all the great love scenes, then make up an outline based on the material we had, go over the outline with my executive producer, then make up a cutting outline, give the scenes I had pulled to the film editor, and structure a show around those scenes. It was a wonderful introduction to the great films of Hollywood.

As I was thinking about this, I remembered a film John Garfield made in 1939, called *Dust Be My Destiny*. And for some reason, the more I thought about *Thelma and Louise* the more I kept thinking about *Dust Be My Destiny*.

The script was written by Robert Rossen, one of the great forgotten geniuses of Hollywood: *The Hustler,* with Paul Newman and George C. Scott, *Lilith,* and *All the King's Men,* to name a few.

In *Dust Be My Destiny,* Garfield plays an ex-convict hunted by the police for a crime he didn't commit. Only the woman, played by Priscilla Lane, believes in him and knows he's telling the truth.

The film has a typically melodramatic plot, padded with a series of contrived incidents. Garfield's journey, like Thelma and Louise's, is what Joseph Campbell describes as the "initiation ritual," where the "hero" of the story, the main character, is placed into a situation where he must overcome a series of obstacles on the road to achieve his "manhood," or sense of spiritual enlightenment. It is a physical as well as a spiritual journey, for it is on the road that the hero experiences his symbolic transformation of death and resurrection; he must cast off all the old parts of his life and move up the ladder to another level, the "birth" of his new self. It is a journey of acceptance; the hero must accept his fate, his destiny, no matter what it is, whether it's life or death.

The thing both films have in common is that the plight of the characters gradually evolves into a journey of personal transformation. As the green T-Bird races away from the scene of the murder, the two women begin their journey, and their flight becomes a journey of self-enlightenment.

"Louise, where are we going?" Thelma asks.

"I don't know, Thelma! I don't know! Just shut up a minute so I can think."

That's the beginning of the first half of Act II. They can't go to the police, because "about a hundred people saw you cheek to goddamn cheek with him all night, Thelma! Who's gonna believe that!? We just don't live in that kind of a world," Louise argues.

Louise is "jaded," which is what Thelma pointed out to us in the previous scene before the murder. Even if they commit a murder, no matter what the extenuating circumstances are, they can't turn themselves in; the only alternative is to be on the run. They are "outlaws" who don't really belong.

The outlaw theme is the dramatic subtext of the first half of Act II. Each action, each reaction affects the story and their growth in character as outlaws. As Newton says in his Third Law of Motion, "For every action there is an equal and opposite reaction."

Louise pulls into a late-night truck stop to buy some time. "We have to think this through," she says. "We have to be smart. . . . If we panic now, we're done for. Nobody saw it. Nobody knows it was us. . . . Now all we have to do is just figure out our next move."

To this Thelma sardonically responds, "I'll say one thing, Louise. This is some vacation. I sure am having a good time. This is really fun."

"If you weren't so concerned with having a good time, we wouldn't be here right now."

"Just what is that supposed to mean?" Thelma replies. And the two women stare at each other in silence, the subtext of blame and accusation strong and unspoken. Thelma abruptly stands up and shatters her coffee cup.

At this point we cut back to the club. It's 4:00 A.M., and police cars are all over the parking lot. Hal, the detective in charge, is asking the waitress if she can identify Thelma and Louise.

"What I was trying to do with Hal," Khouri observes, "is go against the stereotype of the cop. I wanted to show the cop as a human being. You always see movies with cops in them and they're always guys that shoot guys and they have a problem with their wife and so on. I wanted the cop to be a real family man; I wanted a cop that was somehow smarter and more aware. He knew there was more here than met the eye. That something here had happened underneath everything, something that would explain how this happened. He knows there's got to be some answer, and he wants to figure it out. These weren't two crazy bitches from hell."

The scene begins with the waitress trying to convince Hal that these two women were not the type to "off" Harlan in a parking lot. When he questions her judgment, she retorts, "If waitin' tables in a bar don't make you an expert on human nature, then nothin' will, and I could've told you that Harlan Puckett would end up buyin' it in a parkin' lot. I'm just surprised it didn't happen before now."

This speech allows us to know our sympathies should not be

with Harlan; we, the reader, the audience, know Harlan was asking for it, and it was just a matter of time before he "bought it."

If we look at the screenplay at this point, the entire story has been completely set up. We know the characters, and we know the situation. The style of the film has been set up, cross-cutting among the different elements that comprise the action. The only thing we don't know is what will happen and how it will end.

"The story lent itself to a perfect structure because you have a straight line," says Khouri. "You have a limited period of time, and you have a journey, with a beginning point and an end point, so everything just fell together."

Thelma calls home, but Darryl is not there, and we see that the food is still in the microwave. Louise looks at herself closely in the mirror, and freaks out when she sees blood on her cheek. She grabs Thelma and they jump in the car and head down the road.

All drama is conflict. Without conflict, you have no character; without character, you have no action. Without action, you have no story, and without story, you have no screenplay. Thelma and Louise must now confront the first obstacle in their quest for freedom: If they are going to escape and make it to safety, they have to have enough money to get them where they're going. Wherever that is.

When Louise asks Thelma how much money she has, she takes out her money, says sixty-four dollars, then watches as a twenty-dollar bill flies out of her hand; "Shit. Forty-four dollars." And then the stage directions: "Thelma's not that good at handling money." It's a nice little touch.

They pull into a motel, disturbed, distracted, on edge. They're still reacting to each other: "You could help me try and figure it out!" pleads Louise. "I gotta figure out what to do, and you could *try* and help me."

"I suggested we go to the police," Thelma replies, "but you didn't like that. So, frankly, Louise, I'm all out of ideas."

Louise tells Thelma to go out to the pool while she tries to figure out what to do. When Thelma asks for the car keys to get her stuff out of the trunk, Louise overreacts and says no. At this point Thelma reveals a little truth about Louise: "God! You care more about that car than you do about most people."

"Most people just cause me trouble," Louise replies, "but that car always gets me out of it."

Another little bit of character revelation. This is what Henry James meant when he said that character can be brought out by incident. Therefore, the more details you know about your people, the more substance and dimension you add to the screenplay.

Louise "watches herself in the mirror. She stares as if she's trying to see into herself, see through herself." It's a necessary pause in the action, time to let her take a few deep breaths and settle down, time for us to digest the situation with her.

What to do? What to do?

After a moment she picks up the receiver and calls Jimmy. The machine picks up, but just as she's ready to hang up, Jimmy picks up the receiver. Again, Act II is a unit of action that is held together with the dramatic context of Confrontation. Your character will confront obstacle after obstacle after obstacle to achieve his or her dramatic need. For Louise it's simple: She's just committed a murder, so her dramatic need is to escape, and flee to safety. To do that she needs help. There's only one person to help her, the one person who is the very reason why Thelma and Louise are in this predicament: Jimmy.

"I wanted to deal with the idea of Louise feeling responsible for what happened," Khouri says. "She started out to play a game with Jimmy so she wasn't going to be in town when he got back. She was playing a game and this is what she gets for not being honest. She feels she precipitated the whole thing. If you find yourself holding back your feelings, or having to play games, nothing good ever really comes of it."

At the beginning of the conversation, Jimmy is light and loose. But as soon as he hears the solemn tone in her voice, he gets serious. "Louise, honey . . . where are you? You sound funny."

Before she answers, she "is still looking at herself in the mirror, as if she's never seen herself before."

LOUISE
I'm in . . . I'm in real deep shit, Jimmy.
Deep shit Arkansas.

JIMMY (VO)
Louise, just tell me what the hell is going on
here! I come back, nobody knows where you
are. Is Thelma with you? Darryl's been callin' here every half hour sayin' he's gonna
kill you both when you get back. He's goin'
nuts. I don't envy her if she is.

She deftly avoids his questions about where she is. Instead, she
asks him to loan her sixty-seven hundred dollars, the exact amount
she has in her savings account. "What the fuck is goin' on?" he
asks.

"Something real bad has happened and I can't tell you what,
just that it's bad and I did it and I can't undo it. Can you help me?"

Straight, direct, to the point.

Jimmy agrees to send the money, but insists on knowing where
it's going to be sent. "Western Union in Oklahoma City," she says.
Jimmy won't accept that; he says there has to be a specific Western
Union, and a code word to release the money to her.

She can't handle that right now. She tells him she'll call him
back in about an hour. Struck by the gravity of her tone, he tells
her he loves her and hangs up.

Louise grabs Thelma and they're on the road again.

Notice how the action in the screenplay keeps moving forward.
Even though the first obstacle, needing money, has just been introduced, the story is always active, moving forward, so the tension
can mount.

At this point the screenwriter has to buy time until Jimmy can
raise the sixty-seven hundred dollars, at least an hour, so this is
a natural transition point where we can cut back to see what
progress the police have made.

At the police station, Hal is talking with his superior about the
two women who were seen speeding out of the parking lot at the
time of the murder. They were in a green T-Bird. The Major, as
he's called, tells Hal to put "out an APB with a description and see
what comes back." And then, as an afterthought, "Somebody's
butt is gonna bar-b-que."

Part of the reason this script works so well is that it relies on a film convention called cross-cutting. Two story threads are being woven together: the women trying to escape, and the police tracking them down. This technique lets us condense our time frame (you cut away from one action to another action, and condense time).

In screenwriting, where you enter the scene becomes important, and the general rule is "to enter late and get out early." Every scene has a beginning, middle, and end. If you design the scene in this way, then you can enter the scene at the last possible moment, just before the purpose of the scene is established. Then you can end the scene literally before it's ended. In that way the tension leads us into the next scene and becomes a good method of transition between one scene and another.

The next scene picks up Thelma and Louise in the car heading toward Oklahoma City. We don't have to explain where they are or how they got there. The scene opens right in the middle of their conversation, when Louise tells Thelma, "Jimmy's gonna wire me some money. . . ." Thelma, surprised, breaks in and asks if he's mad, and if she told him.

"No, I didn't tell him," Louise replies. "And that's something we gotta get straight. Darryl was callin', mad as a hornet, makin' all kinds of noise. When you talk to him, you *cannot* say anything about this. You gotta make everything sound normal."

Thelma replies, "I called the asshole at four in the morning and he wasn't even home. I don't know what he's got to be mad about. I'm the one who should be mad."

"I've been tellin' you that for the last ten years," Louise says.

"Do you think Darryl's having an affair?"

"I don't think Darryl is mature enough to conduct an affair."

"But you think he fools around," Thelma wonders out loud. This is the setup line that is going to pay off at the end of the scene.

Louise ignores her and tells her that she's going to Mexico and she's got to know what Thelma is going to do.

> LOUISE
> Goddammit, Thelma. Every time we get in
> trouble, you go blank or plead insanity or

LOUISE (cont'd.)
some such shit, and this time . . . not this
time. Everything's changed now. . . . Now
you can do whatever you want. . . . Are
you coming with me?

"Thelma is staring down the road. She does not answer."

Then she pays off her earlier question: "I think he does. Fool around."

And we're out. The bigger question is still not answered.

We pick up the action as they pull into a small country store. Louise goes to a pay phone and calls Jimmy. He's got the money, and tells her to go to a place called Shaw's Siesta Motel in Oklahoma City; the money will be there. But, he adds, there is a code word.

"And what's the mysterious code word?" Louise asks.

"Peaches," he tells her. "That's the code word. I miss you, Peaches."

"Louise rolls her eyes and tries not to melt."

It's a nice little touch for the reader.

Thelma is in the store, buying some gum and beef jerky when she picks up a little bottle of Wild Turkey "and puts it on the counter. The old man rings it up. She takes another one and puts it on the counter." Then she takes all the little bottles they have on the counter. And when the man asks her if she wouldn't like the large, economy size, she shakes her head.

Another little illumination of character.

Louise tells her to call Darryl and "tell him you're having a wonderful time and you'll be back home tomorrow night."

"Will I be?" she answers.

"I don't know. I won't be," Louise replies.

They look at each other for a moment as this sinks in.

Thelma calls Darryl, who's in the middle of watching a football game. And in this situation, he's presented as a total idiot, more interested in his football game and being right than in the safety and well-being of his wife. His caricature brings back the comedic aspect of the movie and gives us some breathing room.

In this conversation Thelma takes her first step toward personal growth and freedom: "You're my husband, not my father, Darryl," she says, "go fuck yourself."

What does Thelma have to go back to? Darryl is a self-righteous asshole, something she's known and accepted and agreed to in the context of their relationship. This conversation makes us see that Thelma really is on the brink of change: Either she goes with Louise to Mexico and shares whatever the consequences are, or she goes back to her life with Darryl. It's up to her.

On the journey toward personal growth and transformation, it's a new beginning for both of them.

And that brings us to Pinch I.

5

The Con Man and the Thief:

J.D.—The Die Is Cast

Pinch I is an event that occurs midway through the First Half of Act II. It is usually a sequence—a series of scenes with a beginning, middle, and end connected by one single idea. Remember the fight sequence at the end of the five *Rocky* movies? Or the wedding sequence at the end of *Father of the Bride*? Or the shoot-out that is the entire third act of *Witness*? A sequence can be any event you want it to be. When the screenwriter confronts those sixty blank sheets of paper that make up Act II, it is very easy to get lost without the guiding light of structure.

The pinch really keeps the story on track, literally "holds" it together. Its primary function is to move the story forward.

In *Thelma and Louise*, Pinch I is when Thelma and Louise meet and pick up the hitchhiker J.D. It occurs at about page forty-seven in the screenplay and is the event that keeps the story moving forward and on track. That's the dramatic function of J.D.

J.D. is a charming hustler and small-town armed robber who has just been released from prison. That he is hitching his way out of the state, thus breaking the terms of his parole, is a deliberate choice by the screenwriter.

Khouri says she created J.D. "because I wanted Thelma to have a romantic experience. J.D. just kind of grew as the screenplay grew. I knew they were going to have to commit a robbery to get some money, but J.D. was just one of those things that 'happened' while I was writing the script. I thought, This is perfect, this character who's a con man and a thief. I just thought it was so great for Thelma to do something crazy like that."

After telling Darryl to "go fuck yourself," Thelma has tears running down her face when she turns around and literally "slams into someone that she does not see." The hitchhiker (J.D.) apologizes, and in the script, Thelma can't help but "notice how blue his eyes are." Khouri immediately lets us know that we should pay more attention to this character.

J.D. debates with himself, then turns and walks toward the car as Thelma watches his every step in the mirror. "He looks good. Really good."

"Would you mind me asking which direction you and your friend are going?" he asks courteously. Then, as if to explain, "I'm trying to get back to school and my ride fell through, so I'm kind of stuck. Are you going my way?"

Thelma doesn't know what to say except to ask Louise. But we know, or we can guess, how Thelma feels: She would definitely like to give this "nice young man a ride."

Act II deals with obstacles—either overcoming them, removing them, or being overcome by them. So the first dramatic function of J.D. is to be an obstacle for the two women. A romantic fling, or a comedic one-night stand, provides a nice change of pace at this point in the story. But it's not what Thelma and Louise need at this moment in the screenplay. From their point of view, J.D. is the worst thing they could deal with right now. Most of us are victims of our own desires, and Thelma and Louise are no different from any of us. Callie Khouri remarks that she "had to keep pushing them further and further, burning their bridges behind them, so they could only go forward."

With the introduction of J.D., the "whole story began to fall into place," says Khouri. "I began to see that the idea of having anything onscreen that is superfluous to the forward motion of the story is absolute torture to the audience. Knowing that you have to get this image on film and this image on film and this image on film is essential if you want the audience to know what's going on. And if you want to verify that, just watch some movies that aren't like that and it really drives it home with a sledgehammer. If you have information on the screen that doesn't move the story forward, you are taking moments away from people's lives."

When Louise returns from talking to Jimmy, Thelma tells her that "this young man is on his way back to school and needs a ride, and I thought since . . ."

Louise looks "like she might kill Thelma" and doesn't let her finish the sentence: "It's probably not a good idea," she says sweetly.

The hitchhiker picks up the message immediately, tells them both to have a nice day, and walks away. Thelma won't let it go so easily. "See how polite he is? He was really nice." Louise doesn't reply. They get into the car and drive away, passing the hitchhiker, who yells to Thelma to "cheer up now."

This little incident is really the Set-Up for a much longer incident later. Good screenwriting plays against the grain, plays against the obvious, plays against the way you would expect things to happen. Introducing J.D. gives the screenwriter a choice here; J.D. could be introduced simply as a minor, irritating obstacle to get in the way and pump up the tension a little, or she could set him up now and then pay him off later as a character who plays a pivotal role in the story. In this screenplay, Callie Khouri makes the more interesting choice—the latter.

As they get into the car, Louise asks Thelma what happened with Darryl. She replies by asking, "How long before we're in goddamn Mexico?"

That's the only answer we need. We don't need any explanation. From now on, the two women are united in their dramatic need: escape to Mexico and freedom. The only conflicts they exhibit now are in matters of personality and point of view. This is why they must be considered together as the main character: They are two totally different aspects of the same character, the exact opposite of each other, who share the same goal, the same dramatic need.

But Thelma will not let J.D. go. "She's like a dog with a bone," say the stage directions. "I just don't see what it would hurt just to give somebody a ride. Did you see his butt? You could park a car in the shadow of his ass."

But Louise is not in the mood for company; she knows what she has to do, so her priority is simple. "I need you to find all the secondary roads to Mexico from Oklahoma City," she tells Thelma. As an afterthought, she casually mentions that Thelma should "find a way where we don't have to go through Texas . . . you know how I feel about Texas."

This is the second time she mentions Texas. When Thelma asks why, Louise tells her to shut up. "Louise is completely unreasonable on this subject," the script reads, "and Thelma is totally puzzled by Louise's reaction but is reluctant to press her further." Louise continues, "If you blow a guy's head off with his pants down, believe me, Texas is the last place you wanna get caught! Trust me!" Louise declares.

Even thinking about it, she "looks very shaken up. She keeps her eyes on the road but she's holding the steering wheel so tightly her knuckles are white."

In a scene that was not included in the final film, two bikers pass the T-Bird, and "the hitchhiker is on the back of one, and he waves as they go by. Thelma waves back enthusiastically."

"I'll tell you what. He is gooood-lookin'," she comments. Louise doesn't reply. She pops a tape into the cassette player.

After a few cutaways of Hal tracking down Louise, we see the hitchhiker standing along the side of the road. As they pass him "Thelma looks at Louise pleadingly." In the film Geena Davis does a great bit panting like a dog going for a goodie, and Louise finally gives in and they pick him up.

Simple and effective. Setup and payoff. Pinch I.

Now we can begin the relationship with J.D., integrate him into the story, and let him fulfill his dramatic function of moving the story forward. An animated Thelma turns around backward in the front seat to face him. "So what are you studying in school?" Thelma asks. "Human nature," J.D. replies. "I'm majoring in behavioral science." "And whaddya wanna be when ya grow up?" Louise asks. "A waiter," he responds.

"Louise laughs. He has charmed her, too."

Once we've established their initial response to each other, we can cut back and forth anytime we want; Khouri now begins to build the subplot that deals with the police who are tracking

Thelma and Louise. Between each scene with Thelma and Louise, she intercuts scenes of Hal searching for them finding out things about the two women. One interchange in particular is an example of good cinematic writing: When Hal tells Darryl that Thelma and Louise are somehow implicated in the murder, here is the reaction:

INT. THELMA'S HOUSE—DAY

Hal and Darryl in den. The TV DRONES in the b.g. Pictures and papers are on the table. TIGHT SHOT of Darryl's face.

DARRYL

What!?

EXTREME CLOSE-UP of Darryl's face.

DARRYL

What?!

Enter late and get out early. We don't need any explanation. You can play like that in a screenplay when the characters and situation have been set up so well you don't need more than a word or two to see Darryl's reaction to the news. Dramatically, it also lets us concentrate on the relationships among Thelma, Louise, and now J.D.

J.D. asks Thelma why she doesn't "have any kids," and she replies that "Darryl, that's my husband, he says he's not ready. He's still too much of a kid himself. He prides himself on being infantile." To which Louise retorts, "He's got a lot to be proud of."

Here's another example of Henry James's theory of illumination. J.D. becomes the ideal vehicle for us to find out more about these two women; who they are, where they come from, where they're going.

J.D. casually mentions that there's a cop car on the other side of the road, and Louise immediately veers off the road to avoid it. This little visual threat jolts Louise back to reality. Fast. "We'll take you on to Oklahoma City," she says to J.D. "Then you'd best be on your way."

At this point in the screenplay we're running two parallel lines of action: Thelma and Louise on the run is the major line of action, and the other line of action, the subplot, is Hal tracking them down, step by step, scene by scene. Cross-cutting between these two story points heightens the tension and rhythm of the story. The screenwriter usually details a subplot in a complete line of action from beginning to end, then weaves it through the story line to achieve maximum dramatic value.

We see Hal finding Louise's house, then see him, along with the FBI and other policemen, roaming through Thelma's house, Darryl watching helplessly. After this has been set up, we're ready to move the story another step forward.

Louise pulls into Shaw's Siesta Motel in Oklahoma City. She gets out, looks at Thelma and J.D., pauses, then reaches back and takes the keys out of the ignition. "You two better go on and say your good-byes."

She enters the motel and asks if there's anything for Louise Elizabeth Sawyer. No. Anything "for Peaches"? The woman says no. At this point Jimmy steps up behind her and cups his hands over her eyes and surprises her.

Now there are two different elements developing in the Thelma and Louise plot thread. One is the relationship between Jimmy and Louise, and the other is the relationship between Thelma and J.D. Just as Thelma and Louise are two halves of the same character, so their relationships with these two men mirror each other. The movement of the sequence, like the film, is structured by following one action with both characters, and intercutting one with the other. So as Jimmy and Louise are defining their relationship to us, Thelma and J.D. are seducing each other. One is tender and emotional; the other is fresh, vigorous, and erotic.

And when it's over, the two women have been fucked—in more ways than one.

The Mid-Point of the screenplay occurs halfway through Act II. It is the incident, episode, or event that links the First Half of Act II with the Second Half of Act II. It is a "link" in the chain of dramatic action. The subcontext of the First Half of Act II is "what to do," because the action focuses on what they have to do to get away.

Now we've reached a point in the script where we have to set up and prepare the story line for what's going to happen during the Second Half of Act II. Jimmy and J.D. will be the catalysts used to tighten the screws and heighten the action.

When Louise returns, Thelma remarks, "I don't care what you say about Jimmy. The boy has got it bad." Louise responds with the essential truth about their relationship: "He's always got it bad as long as I'm running in the other direction," she says. "Don't be fooled, he's no different than any other guy. He knows how to chase, and that's it. Once he's caught you, he doesn't know what to do. So he runs away."

It's a wonderful observation, something I think most men and women can relate to.

The true test of good screenwriting is the chord of truth it touches within each of us. A universal truth goes beyond culture, race, age, or geographic location.

Louise is very clear she's not going to get Jimmy involved. She did what she did, and she knows she has to accept the responsibility for it. The first step of her transformation has begun.

Jimmy has brought the sixty-seven hundred dollars as Louise had requested, and she gives it to Thelma to keep while she goes with Jimmy to his room. Thelma says she's not going to wait up for her.

While Jimmy and Louise are getting reacquainted, we cut back to Thelma, alone in the room. There's a knock at the door. It's J.D. Because of the rain, he can't get a ride. Thelma is happy to see him, and offers him the use of the shower.

Jimmy thinks Louise has met someone else, but she is quick to tell him that that's not the case. Puzzled, hurt, anxious, he gives her an engagement ring. "Louise is flabbergasted."

Cut to: J.D. has finished his shower and the two of them are eyeing each other; both are beginning to feel the strains of passion.

Louise and Jimmy are having a "heart to heart."

Notice the subtext of this scene; the subtext is what is *not* said during the course of the scene. The forces working on Louise are getting stronger now, and though she is caught in the whirlpool of her emotions, the one thing she cannot do is involve Jimmy. Notice what is *not said* during this scene.

> JIMMY
>
> So, whaddya think? I mean . . . I could
> . . . uh . . . get a job. Of some kind. I
> mean you've been telling me that for years,
> right?

> LOUISE
>
> Why now, Jimmy?

> JIMMY
>
> (this is hard for him)
> 'Cause, Louise. I don't want to lose you.
> And for some reason I get the feelin' you're
> about to split. Permanently.

Louise doesn't know how to respond. She struggles for a reply.

> LOUISE
>
> Jimmy, we've gone all these years . . . we
> never made it work. . . . We're not gonna
> be able to just . . . I'm not . . . What
> kind of job, honey? Can you see it? I can't.

Jimmy doesn't answer right away. He's trying to see it.

> JIMMY
>
> I'm the one . . . I never made it work. I
> just . . . it's not that I don't love you. It's
> not that. I just never thought I'd be thirty-six
> years old and I never thought . . . I don't
> know what I thought. What do you want,
> darlin'? What do you want me to do?

> LOUISE
>
> I don't know. It doesn't even matter any-
> more. I just want you to be happy. . . . It's
> not that I don't love you either. But Jimmy,
> your timing couldn't be worse.

Jimmy does not really understand why this is happening.

JIMMY
Are you just doin' this to punish me?

LOUISE
Believe me, the last thing I want is for you to
get punished.

This is a beautiful little scene. It illustrates the relationship between the two of them. Louise says she doesn't want to "punish" Jimmy, but the whole reason for their weekend trip to the mountains was precisely to "punish" him. And he's afraid of losing her, even though he never wanted to be tied down in any kind of permanent or committed relationship.

Not only are the emotional elements presented in these scenes, but also notice how the visual transitions of the next few scenes are steadily moving the action forward, culminating in the sex scene. In continuous action, J.D. is "playing with Thelma's wedding ring. He takes it off and drops it in his drink. Then he kisses her hand." Cut to:

Jimmy's room as he takes Louise's hand and puts the engagement ring he has just given her on her finger. "It does look good," he tells her. Cut to:

Thelma and J.D. having a good time. During the course of their dialogue he tells her he's a robber. She's totally infatuated with him and "demands" that he tell her how he goes about robbing people. It's a real show for both of them. They respond to each other and kiss passionately. Cut to Louise and Jimmy making love. Cut to Thelma and J.D. in their foreplay. We hold on this erotic sex scene.

The next morning Louise and Jimmy are having breakfast. He is sincere and concerned, and she says, "Damn, Jimmy, did you take a pill that makes you say all the right stuff?" "I'm choking on it," he replies. When he asks, "Do you want me to come with you?" she knows it's impossible. "It's probably not such a good idea right now. . . . I'll . . . catch up with you later, on down the road," she lies.

He makes her keep the ring; then his taxi pulls up outside. They say their good-byes, and then he's out the door, leaving Louise staring wistfully into her coffee cup.

At this point the screenplay presents a scene with Hal and his wife, also in bed. It is a transition-of-time scene. He holds her in his arms and asks if "you could ever think of a set of circumstances that would just cause you to haul off and shoot someone." It is an odd place to insert this kind of a scene, because it diminishes the intensity of the action, and Ridley Scott was wise not to include it in the film.

Louise is still sitting in the booth as Thelma joins her for coffee. "Her energy and volume is several notches higher than the rest of the people in the coffee shop," the script reads, and we know it must have been fantastic for her. She can't wait to share it with Louise. "I don't think I wanna hear what you're gonna tell me," Louise tells her. Thelma is totally into it: "I can't believe it! I just can't believe it! I mean I finally understand what all the fuss is about. This is just a whole 'nother ball game!"

Louise is too wrapped up in her own feelings to be ecstatic for Thelma. When she asks where J.D. is, Thelma replies that he's in the room, "taking a shower."

"You left that guy alone in the room?"

"Where's the money, Thelma?" Thelma looks at her, comprehending. "On the table. It's okay," she says.

But it's not okay, and both of them know it. "As they hit the door they both break into a full run."

When they reach the room, he's gone, and so is the money. They're too late. "That little sonofabitch burgled me," Thelma cries.

That's the Mid-Point of the second act. The money is gone, along with their hopes of escape and freedom.

Louise falls apart. "It's not okay, Thelma. None of this is okay. What are we going to do for money? What are we gonna buy gas with?"

But now we see a new side of Thelma. Suddenly taking responsibility for her actions and their predicament, she leaps into action. "Come on! Stand up. Don't worry about it. I'll take care of it. Just don't you worry about it . . . dammit, get your stuff and let's get out of here!"

It is a shift in character identities, and while it's a little hard to believe that this would happen so fast, it works within the parameters of the story line. It's the second step along the road of transformation.

There's only one way for Thelma and Louise to go now—down the long highway toward freedom, and beyond.

6

No Turning Back:

The Second Half of Act II

Sitting in that motel room, their dreams of escape and freedom gone, there's not a whole lot Thelma and Louise can do except react to this new situation. Louise, still in shock, sits obediently as Thelma shifts into a new dimension of her character and takes over.

There are many people who tell me that Thelma's shift of character happens too fast, that it's not set up anywhere in the screenplay and thus is unbelievable. That may be true, but so what? Thelma has already told Darryl to "fuck off," her first major step toward liberation, and this becomes her second step. In the larger context of the story, it doesn't matter at all. Storywise there has to be a shift at this point because things are starting to close in, heat up. The stage directions say the two women are "both looking a little rougher than we've seen so far."

The Mid-Point, that link in the chain of dramatic action that connects the First Half of Act II with the Second Half of Act II, is what moves the action forward and creates a new dramatic subtext.

The new subtext of the Second Half of Act II is "turning up the heat" for the forces of the Law are relentlessly bearing down on them. This theme powers *Thelma and Louise* through the next thirty-page unit of dramatic action, from the Mid-Point to Plot Point II. The overall dramatic context of Act II, Confrontation, is still in effect, and the emphasis remains on the main characters overcoming obstacles to achieve their dramatic need. For both Thelma and Louise their dramatic need, as mentioned, is to escape.

Says Callie Khouri: "I knew I had to keep pushing them so they could only go forward. There was a time when I wanted to direct this, and the way I envisioned it being shot was that you only saw what was in front of them. Somehow I wanted to find a way to rig a camera in the backseat so their heads are always in frame and we're sitting between them so when they take off we would feel the momentum, the G-force of the car speeding forward. At this point when I was writing it, I was getting into the idea of the cinema of it; it was cinematic because there was so much of it you could tell with no dialogue."

And that is really the art of screenwriting: finding places where silence works better than words, a story told with pictures.

After the Mid-Point, entering the Second Half of Act II, they still need money to get away, and Oklahoma City is a long way from Mexico, especially when you don't want to go through Texas.

As they get back on the road, we cut to Hal and the FBI moving into Darryl's house. They have tapped the phone and literally moved in. This particular scene really summarizes the action in a visual way. Because the characters have been set up so clearly from the beginning, we don't need to communicate much information to the reader or viewer. The action moves forward by itself, and the characters' portraits are drawn by the incidents and the situation.

Look at the following scene. In terms of scene construction, this scene begins at the very last moment ("enter late and get out early").

A screenwriter prepares each scene by going through a mental process of breaking the scene down into beginning, middle, and end. For example, in the beginning, we could show Hal, the police, and the FBI pulling up in front of Thelma's house, knocking on the door, coming in, sitting Darryl down, and explaining that they're tapping his phones. That is the opening, the beginning event of a series of events that would have Darryl watching as the FBI scurries around laying wires, taking the phones apart, planting microphones, and so on. At the end of the scene the authorities would give Darryl specific instructions about what to do, and then Hal and the others would leave.

But look at where the scene begins—right at the end, immediately before Hal leaves:

INT. THELMA'S HOUSE—DAY

Police are tapping the phones, dusting for prints, etc., while Darryl sits motionless in his recliner with a dull expression on his face.

> HAL
>
> (to Darryl)
> As you know, we've tapped your phone. In the event that she calls in.

Max [the FBI man] comes up and joins them as they walk down the hallway.

> MAX
>
> We're going to leave someone here at the house in the event that she calls in. Someone will be here until we find them.

> HAL
>
> The important thing is not to let on that you know anything. We want to try and find out where they are. Now, I don't want to get personal, but do you have a good relationship with your wife? Are you close to her?

> DARRYL
>
> Yeah, I guess. I mean, I'm as close as I can be with a nut case like that.

> MAX
>
> Well, if she calls, just be gentle. Like you're happy to hear from her. You know, like you really miss her. Women love that shit.

Khouri enters the scene after the explanation and action have happened; Hal tells Darryl what they've already done. No explanation is needed; all the screenwriter has to do is summarize what they've done and why they've done it. We don't have to see Hal walk out of the house or drive away. The main point of the scene is to tell us that the phones have been tapped, and to illustrate Darryl's character to provide some comedy relief. Many writer friends of mine have complained about the male characters in *Thelma and Louise* being caricatures or stereotypes, not real people. Most of that was in Scott's direction, not in the screenplay. But what must be remembered is that Darryl is always *consistent* in his portrayal. As are all the other characters. That consistency is the key to the screenwriter developing his or her characters. If we accept Darryl as he really is, he becomes what he is—comic relief.

"I've had positive as well as negative experiences with men," says Khouri. "No matter what anyone says, I am not antimale. I could never hate a gender, because it goes against everything I stand for. The idea that it would be perceived that way was astonishing. I mean, my brothers and I laughed about it.

"Whether you like it or not," she continues, "that husband is a real guy, that boyfriend is a real guy; that cop is a real guy; that truck driver is a real guy; that rapist is a real guy; I'm not antimale, I am anti-idiot."

After Hal taps Thelma's phone, we cut back to Thelma and Louise sitting outside a convenience store. They don't have very much money. Thelma, with a determination we've not seen before, tells Louise not to worry and marches into the store. The stage directions read: "Louise takes her lipstick out and is about to put it on. She makes eye contact with herself and, instead, throws it out the window, closes her eyes, and leans her head back on the seat. She's in a world of shit."

After a beat, Thelma races out of the store holding a bag. She's just robbed the store. Of the many scenes in this movie I love, I think I love this one the most. Thelma's robbing the convenience store is cinematic, funny, and shows great style and a great understanding of the craft of screenwriting. What makes this scene so great is that we see the *result* of the action before we actually *see* the action.

Here's the scene in its entirety:

Thelma comes trotting out of the store and jumps into the car.

THELMA

(breathless)
Drive!

Louise looks at her.

THELMA (cont'd.)

Drive! Drive away!

LOUISE

(driving away)
What happened?

Thelma opens her purse and exposes a bagful of bills.

LOUISE (cont'd.)

What? You robbed the store? You robbed
the goddamn store!?

Thelma shrieks with excitement. Louise is completely stunned.

THELMA

Well! We need the money! It's not like I
killed anybody, for God's sake!

Louise shoots her a look. She puts the car in gear and FLOORS it out of the parking lot. She is still looking at Thelma as if she has completely lost her mind.

THELMA (cont'd.)

I'm sorry. Well, we need the money. Now
we have it.

LOUISE
Oh, shit, Thelma! Shit! Shit! Shit!

THELMA
Now you get a grip, Louise! Just drive us to goddamn Mexico, will ya!

LOUISE
Okay. Shit, Thelma! What'd you do? I mean, what did you say?

THELMA
Well, I just . . .

INT. POLICE STATION/INTERROGATION ROOM—DAY

Hal, Max, various other cops, and Darryl all watch as the TV plays back VCR TAPE of Thelma in the convenience store pulling a gun. In perfect lip sync is:

THELMA (VO)
All right, ladies and gentlemen, let's see who'll win the prize for keepin' their cool. Everybody lie down on the floor. If nobody loses their head, then nobody loses their head. . . .

TIGHT SHOT of Darryl's face going deeper and deeper into a state of shock. TIGHT SHOTS of Hal, Max, etc., all looking at the screen.

VIDEOTAPE IMAGE of Thelma boldly ordering the cashier to fill her purse with money. As he's loading the purse with bills, she's taking beef jerky from the display and putting it in there, too, while she points the gun at the cashier.

THELMA (VO cont'd.)
You, sir . . . you do the honors. Just empty that cash into this bag and you'll have an

>   THELMA (VO cont'd.)
>   amazing story to tell all your friends. If not,
>   you'll have a tag on your toe. You decide.

INT. CAR—DAY

Thelma and Louise in car, driving.

>   LOUISE
>   (incredulous)
>   Holy shit.

>   CUT TO:

INT. POLICE STATION/INTERROGATION ROOM—DAY

TIGHT SHOT:

>   DARRYL
>   Jesus Christ.

TIGHT SHOT:

>   MAX
>   Good God.

TIGHT SHOT:

>   HAL
>   (wearily)
>   My Lord.

EXT. DRIVING SHOT—DAY

>   LOUISE
>   Holy shit.

>   THELMA
>   Lemme see the map.

*Louise throws the map across the front seat at Thelma and
FLOORS it.*

This is screenwriting at its best: There is an enormous amount of information conveyed to the reader here. Three things are seen: Louise's reaction; Hal, Darryl, and the police seeing the crime on the VCR; then everybody's reaction to it. The scene is humorous, bridges time and distance, and moves the story forward. All this in less than two pages.

Notice we don't have Thelma *tell* us what she's done; we *see* it in such a way that we know everything that happened. A screenplay is a story *told* in *pictures,* with dialogue and description. That must never be forgotten.

Structurally, this incident is a reaction to the Mid-Point. By seeing the result, then the action, then the reaction to the entire incident, we've expanded our visual perception. Strictly from a story point, they now have armed robbery to deal with in addition to murder.

Louise and Thelma speed down a country road, Louise pissed, Thelma elated: "Oooooweeee! You shoulda seen me! Like I'd been doin' it all my life! Nobody would ever believe it."

"You think you've found your calling?" Louise asks sarcastically. "Thelma howls like a dog and drinks a little bottle of Wild Turkey."

"You're disturbed," says Louise.

"Yes! I believe I am!" she responds.

These little moments are scattered throughout the screenplay and are absolutely wonderful. No matter what the circumstances or conflicts, Thelma and Louise are bonded together in terms of their actions, their deeds, and their consequences. Their journey to enlightenment and realization can move forward only if they keep burning their bridges. In mythic terms, the first part of any journey of initiation must deal with the death of the old self and the resurrection of the new; the hero, or heroic figure, "moves not into outer space but into inward space, to the place from which all being comes, into the consciousness that is the source of all things, the kingdom of heaven within. The images are outward, but their reflection is inward," says Joseph Campbell.

The journey itself is inward as well as outward. The visual metaphors reflect the inward state. In *Witness,* in the second half of Act II, after the wonderful "raising of the barn" sequence, Harrison Ford is sitting staring at the burning lantern in Rachel's room while outside, the storm rages. Inside reflects the outside.

Everything is connected. Many of the ancient Hindu scriptures say we should consider the "outside and inside as one." What's inside our heads—our thoughts, feelings, memories, and emotions —are reflected outside, in our everyday life. Our mind creates our experience. The inside and the outside are the same.

As time passes and the pressure builds, we start cutting more and more to the police, who are making steady progress in tracking Thelma and Louise. Some of these scenes were omitted from the film, but this is really an editing decision about building tension and rhythm visually. Hal questions Jimmy, who swears Louise did not tell him anything, but did see "the kid that was with 'em." "Find that fucking kid," Jimmy pleads. "He probably knows something."

Every scene now begins to connect with each other. The Thelma and Louise plot line has now overlapped with the Hal and police plot line. Henry James says that all art "is a living thing, one and continuous, and like any other organism, in each of the parts there will be something of the other parts."

The thread of action that shows Hal tracking down the two women is a continuous line with a beginning, middle, and end, and is then intercut into the main story line. *Thelma and Louise* is a fine example of crafting and integrating a subplot into the story line.

I tell writers that the best way to construct this type of subplot is to write each line of action separately. Once the progression of events is laid out from beginning to end, each thread, or scene, can be intercut and woven into the story.

This particular style of screenwriting builds and tightens the action; and to turn up the volume, to make it more exciting, we cut from one scene to the other, back and forth, each scene getting shorter and shorter, building a certain rhythm into the story line.

That's what good screenwriting is all about. The line of action, the characters, the reactions, the structure—everything is connected with everything else. Over and over again, in screenwriting workshops and seminars all over the world, I stress that everything in a screenplay is related. Structure is the relationship between the parts and the whole. Nothing is thrown in by chance, or written to pad or lengthen a scene or sequence.

For example, one of these cutaways deals with the truck driver who "flicks his tongue at them." It's a scene that's introduced only to set us up. The entire incident takes only two short paragraphs, but it's of major importance to the entire story line.

In the next scene, the police have picked up J.D., and we learn the hitchhiker was found with "about six grand on him."

Here's where screenplay and movie begin to differ slightly as a few scenes have been removed in the editorial process. No matter what the reason—whether creative differences, budget considerations, inclement weather, studio interference, illness, or whatever —production decisions have to be made on a creative as well as a realistic level. So while the screenplay and the movie diverge slightly at this point, the tone and the intention of the finished film are the same.

This takes us up to Pinch II, where J.D. is picked up, questioned, and finally confesses that he took Louise's money. Then he tells Hal the two women are heading for Mexico. The net is being drawn tighter and tighter.

In *Thelma and Louise* there is a connection between Pinch I and Pinch II. It does not always work out this way. At Pinch I J.D. is picked up by the girls, and at Pinch II J.D. is in police custody and confesses he was with the two women.

In the next scene Louise tells Thelma to call Darryl to find out whether the phone is tapped. "You think so?" Thelma asks. "Oh, come on! Murder one and armed robbery, Thelma!" "Can't we even say it was self-defense?" Thelma asks. Louise replies that it won't work because there's "no physical evidence. We can't prove he did it. We probably can't even prove he touched you by now." We suspect Louise is making another reference to the incident that happened in Texas.

They pause for a moment. "God. The law is some tricky shit, isn't it?" Thelma concludes.

Cut to Hal questioning J.D., with Darryl present. Hal is polite but firm: "Son, I gotta feelin' about somethin' and I just wanna ask your opinion. Do you think Thelma Dickinson would have committed armed robbery if you hadn't taken all their money?" J.D.

doesn't answer. "Those two girls out there had a chance, they had a chance . . . ! And you blew it for 'em."

Just the threat of going back to prison is enough for J.D. He decides to tell Hal everything, even though we don't see him confessing. We don't have to. We've seen the action, we don't need the explanation.

Pinch II. It's that little "pinch" in the action that keeps the story moving forward.

Thelma and Louise pull into a small gas station to use the phone. Louise wants Thelma to call Darryl to see what's going on and "if you *think* he knows, even if you're not sure, hang up."

So when Thelma calls Darryl it is a wonderful scene, funny and touching.

INT. THELMA'S HOUSE—NIGHT

The TV is ON and the place is a mess.

Darryl, Hal, Max, and other cops spring into action as the phone RINGS, putting on headsets, turning on tape recorders. Darryl picks up the phone.

> DARRYL
> Hello.

EXT. PAY PHONE—NIGHT

> THELMA
> Darryl. It's me.

INT. THELMA'S HOUSE—NIGHT

Hal, Max, etc., are gesticulating wildly.

> DARRYL
> (really friendly)
> Thelma! Hello!

EXT. PAY PHONE—NIGHT

Thelma hangs up the receiver.

> THELMA
> (matter-of-factly)
> He knows.

It's a great little scene. Not only is it humorous, it also lets us know that reality is starting to intrude and things are getting heavy. The way the scene is structured, first showing us the beginning of the action, then showing us the reaction, is wonderful.

Louise calls Darryl back and asks if "the police are there." He denies it, but the police forcefully take the receiver away from him, and for the first time, hunter and hunted speak.

"I'm Hal Slocumbe, chief investigator, homicide, Arkansas State Police. How are you? You wanna tell me what happened?" he asks. "Sure." Louise replies flippantly. "Maybe over coffee sometime. I'll buy."

"I just want you to know, neither one of you are charged with murder yet," Hal continues. "You're still just wanted for questioning. Although now Mrs. Dickinson's wanted in Oklahoma for armed robbery." Then he pleads with her: "Miss Sawyer, I don't think y'all are gonna make it to Mexico. We should talk. Please. I wanna help you."

She doesn't know what to say, so she bangs down the receiver, leaving the police frantically trying to trace the call. Louise storms back to Thelma. "How'd they find out we're going to Mexico, Thelma? How do they know that? You told that thievin' little shit [J.D.] where we were goin'?"

"I just told him if he ever gets to Mexico to look us up. . . . I didn't think he'd tell anybody."

Now we know that it's only a matter of time before the forces of society find and crush Thelma and Louise. At this point, when I first saw the film, I had the sinking feeling that the film was going to end in a way I really didn't want it to end. I liked these women. I didn't want them to die, especially at the hands of the police. Until this point I wasn't sure about the ending. After all, I thought, this is a comedy, a humorous "buddy" film. It couldn't turn serious, could it? From now on I watched the film with mixed feelings, torn between hope and fear even though I knew, intellectually at least, that the "forces of society" always win in this situation.

Now what?

Everyone waits. We see Hal and the police, waiting. Thelma and Louise in the car, driving, silent under the spell of night. Jimmy waiting. There is a break in the action, a time to pause and breathe a little between the peaks of tension. Even though these scenes are only a line or a paragraph long, they open up the action and add another dimension that enriches our experience.

The next scene in the screenplay is, at least to my mind, one of the most essential scenes in the film, and a scene that was partially cut from the film. Only the first half has been included. I think it should have been kept in. It's the scene that sets us up for Plot Point II and the ending.

INT. CAR—NIGHT

Thelma is sipping on a little Wild Turkey.

> THELMA
> Now what?

> LOUISE
> Now what what?

> THELMA
> Whaddo we do?

> LOUISE
> Oh, I don't know, Thelma. I guess maybe we could turn ourselves in and spend our lives trading cigarettes for mascara so we look nice when our families come to visit on Saturdays. Maybe we could have children with the prison guards.

> THELMA
> I'm not suggestin' that! I'm *not* goin' back. No matter what happens. So don't worry about me.

Louise speeds up.

Thelma hands Louise a little bottle of Wild Turkey and she drinks it down. Thelma has one, too. [And they cut to the next scene. The rest of the scene has been cut from the final movie.]

THELMA (cont'd.)
Can I ask you kind of a weird question?

LOUISE
Yeah.

THELMA
Of all the things in the world that scare you, what's the worst thing that scares you the most?

LOUISE
You mean now or before?

THELMA
Before.

LOUISE
I guess I always thought the worst thing that could happen would be to end up old and alone in some crummy apartment with one of those little dogs.

THELMA
What little dogs?

LOUISE
You know those little dogs you see people with?

THELMA
Like a chihuahua?

LOUISE
Those, too, but you know those little hairy

LOUISE (cont'd.)
ones? Those flat-faced little fuckers with those ugly goddamned teeth?

THELMA
Oh, yeah. You mean peek-a-poos.

LOUISE
Yeah. Those. That always put the fear of God in me. What about you?

THELMA
Well, to be honest, the idea of getting old with Darryl was kinda startin' to get to me.

LOUISE
I can see that.

THELMA
I mean, look how different he looks since high school. It's bad enough I have to get old, but doin' it with Darryl around is only gonna make it worse.
    (quieter)
I mean, I don't think he's gonna be very nice about it.

LOUISE
Well, now, maybe you won't have to.

THELMA
Always lookin' on the bright side, aren't ya?

EXT. MOONLIT DESERT HIGHWAY—NIGHT

They are driving through Monument Valley. The T-Bird speeds through the beautifully moonlit desert. It is almost like daylight.

MONTAGE of silhouettes of cacti, huge rock formations, desert beauty SHOTS, etc.

INT. CAR—LOUISE AND THELMA'S POV [POINT OF VIEW] THROUGH THE WINDSHIELD—NIGHT

The sky is bright and expansive and the road goes on forever.

> THELMA
> This is so beautiful.

> LOUISE
> Gosh. It sure is.

> THELMA
> I always wanted to travel. I just never got the opportunity.

> LOUISE
> Well, you got it now.

They both look forward for another moment. And then, at the same time, they look at each other, each taking the other one in completely, in this moment.

They're saying everything to each other in this moment, but their expressions don't change and they don't say a word. MUSIC plays on the RADIO.

Then we cut and we're out.

It's a beautiful moment. In silence, underneath a blanket of stars, in a place that exists beyond time, they accept themselves and their destiny. For the first time they understand there may be no way back. However, Khouri does not state the obvious. The silence of the scene is the pause before the storm, and that silence works better and more effectively than words ever could.

This particular moment is the Plot Point at the end of Act II. In the screenplay it takes place on page 94 (the final shooting draft is 129 pages), but in the movie it occurs approximately 88 minutes into the action. It should be noted that a Plot Point does not have to be a dramatic moment, or a major scene or sequence. A Plot Point can be a quiet moment or an exciting action sequence. A

Plot Point is whatever you choose it to be—long, short, a moment of silence or of action, depending on the script you're writing. It's the choice of the screenwriter, but it is always an incident, episode, or event that is dictated by the needs of the story.

From here on, there's no turning back. There are no options left: It's death or it's death.

And that takes us into Act III: The Resolution.

7

Journey's End:

Act III: The Resolution

Resolution means *solution:* How is the screenplay going to be re-solved? What is the solution of the story? Do the characters live or die? Succeed or fail?

Figuring out the Resolution is really the first creative decision the screenwriter has to make before he or she sits down to write the screenplay. When Callie Khouri sat down to write *Thelma and Louise* she knew only two things: "Two women go on a crime spree," and they die at the end. That's it.

The events that propel them to that end have to be worked out by the screenwriter. The writer knows what's going to happen but has to figure out *how* it's going to happen. In this figuring-out process, the Plot Point at the end of Act II brings the writer to a position of resolving the story.

For Thelma and Louise the journey's end leads to death, but not before there is enlightenment and inner transformation, and that can be accomplished only by overcoming the trials and obstacles of the mythic journey. "To lose yourself is to find yourself" is the way Joseph Campbell puts it. In the case of Thelma and Louise, they must kill the past before they can transcend the obstacles in their path to transformation. Thelma and Louise kill their pasts in Plot Point II. The obstacle Thelma and Louise now face is society, which dictates that the guilty must be punished.

In other words, there's no way back.

As Act III begins at dawn, the two women are surrounded by silence as they drive through the splendor of Monument Valley. The silence cements the bond between them: "They both look forward for another moment," reads the script. "And then, at the same time, they look at each other, each taking the other one in completely.

"They're saying everything to each other in this moment, but their expressions don't change and they don't say a word. MUSIC."

This serious moment is followed by a humorous episode. Shakespeare knew that when you have a very serious, perhaps tragic scene, it is best to follow it with a humorous scene. After Macbeth and Lady Macbeth kill King Duncan, the screams of death and murder take us to the scene at the gate with the gatekeeper, drunk out of his head, rambling on about the vagaries of alcohol. A high tragic moment followed by laughter.

Here Khouri reintroduces the semi-gas tanker for a moment of humor. They pass the semi-gas tanker "with the same mud flaps. . . ." As they pass, once again the driver lewdly points to his lap. "Oh, Christ. I hate this guy," Louise says.

This sets us up for the next scene, when Thelma starts laughing convulsively, thinking about the look on Harlan's face when he was shot. "Boy, he wasn't expectin' that! . . . Suck my dick. . . . *Boom!!*"

"Thelma has just crossed the line from laughing to crying," the stage directions read, and they pause for a moment. Then "Thelma leans back just watching Louise. She studies her as if she's never really seen her before. All of a sudden a look of shocked realization comes over Thelma's face. She jerks upright and startles Louise: 'It happened to you . . . didn't it?' "

"I don't want to talk about it," Louise replies. "I'm warning you, Thelma, you better drop it right now! I don't want to talk about it." This, of course, refers to the incident in Texas. In my opinion, it's not really necessary here because it's an explanation of character that tries to justify the killing. It's the kind of scene a writer struggles with: Should I write it or shouldn't I? Do I really need to explain what happened to her, or not? I tell my writers that if you don't know whether to write a scene or not, write the scene. It's always easier to cut it out than it is to put it in. Later it could become a structural problem. If you decide not to write the scene, then decide later that you really need it, you have to write it; but then you have to find a way to pry it into the existing structure. More often than not it's very difficult.

At this point in the story we have a pretty good idea what's going to happen. Khouri manages to keep the material from getting too heavy while introducing two sequences that are written for the specific purpose of making sure the chase scene at the end is justified.

The first sequence concerns the New Mexico cop who stops them for speeding. It increases the tension and intensifies the action, as well as adding a note of humor to the proceedings. As the cop sits in his car and runs a check on Louise, Thelma appears and "puts a gun to his head. Officer," she explains, "I am so sorry about this. . . . I really, really apologize, but please put your hands on the steering wheel." Louise apologizes for what's happening as well, while Thelma goes on to explain: "I swear, before yesterday, neither one of us would have ever pulled a stunt like this. But if you ever met my husband, you'd know why. . . ."

Louise dismantles the police radios, then Thelma fires two shots into the trunk—"air holes," she explains—and they force him inside. "Ma'am, please . . . I've got kids . . . a wife."

"You do," Thelma replies. "Well, you're lucky. You be sweet to 'em. Especially your wife. My husband wasn't sweet to me and look how I turned out."

Again, they are doing something they have to do, even apologizing for doing it. As they speed away, the two women yell back, "Sorry!" and they're back on the road again. As they drive away, Thelma can hardly believe what she's done: "I know it's crazy, Louise, but I just feel like I've got a knack for this shit."

A little later in the film, Ridley Scott added a Rastafarian, stoned out of his head, bicycling through Monument Valley. When he hears the shouts of the policeman, he takes a giant hit on a massive joint and blows it into the trunk. It's a little bit much.

We cut back to Hal and Max: "I can't figure out if they're real smart or just really, really lucky," says Max. To this Hal replies, in a great line, "It don't matter. Brains will only get you so far and luck always runs out."

In the stage directions a cop walks into the kitchen and hands Hal a file that says "Louise Elizabeth Sawyer" on the outside. Inside there is "a case file from Texas containing an incident report of a rape. Stamped across it are the words 'charges dropped.' " This lets us know that Louise indeed was raped, a piece of information Callie Khouri thought necessary to include. Ridley Scott wisely omitted it from the final cut.

In the next scene Louise picks an argument with Thelma over the smell of beef jerky, but that only hides the real issue. "I think I've really fucked up," Louise confesses. "I think I've got us in a situation where we could both get killed."

But Thelma, speaking now with her own voice, her transformation complete, resolves the event for both of them: "That guy was hurtin' me," she says. "And if you hadn't come out when you did, he'da hurt me a lot worse. And probably nothin' woulda ever happened to him. 'Cause everybody did see me dancin' with him all night. And they woulda made out like I asked for it. And my life woulda been ruined a whole lot worse than it is now. At least I'm havin' fun. And I'm not sorry that sonofabitch is dead. I'm only sorry that it was you that did it and not me. And if I haven't, I wanna take this time to thank you, Louise. Thank you for savin' my ass."

This confession is a reflection of the change that has evolved in her character. From this point on, whatever happens, happens. She has risen above her beginnings at the start of the film and accepted herself for who and what she is. She can do anything she wants, free from all limitations and restraints. She is free to be herself. The journey of transformation is complete.

In the next scene, Louise is on the phone to Hal, trying to figure out their options. Hal is kind and gentle as he tries to assess the situation:

"How are things goin' out there?" he asks.

"Weird," Louise answers. "Got some kind of a snowball effect goin' here or somethin'."

"You're still with us, though," Hal says, trying to be friendly. "You're somewhere on the face of the earth."

"Well, we're not in the middle of nowhere, but we can see it from here," she replies.

"You're gettin' in deeper every moment you're gone," Hal states.

Louise agrees. "Would you believe me if I told you this whole thing is an accident?"

"I do believe you," Hal replies. "That's what I want everybody to believe. Trouble is, it doesn't look like an accident and you're not here to tell me about it. . . . I need you to help me here." Silence.

"Do you want to come on in?" Hal asks after a moment.

"I don't think so," Louise says firmly, sealing her fate.

"Then I'm sorry. We're gonna have to charge you with murder. Now, do you want to come out of this alive?" he asks, keeping the conversation going. In the background the police are working frantically, trying to trace the call.

We hear what she's thinking. "You know, certain words and phrases keep floating through my mind, things like 'incarceration,' 'cavity search,' 'life imprisonment,' 'death by electrocution,' that sort of thing. So, come out alive? I don't know. Let us think about that."

Hal pleads with her, telling her, "I know what's makin' you run. I know what happened to you in Texas." And here at last is the final confrontation of that incident in Texas that has been driving Louise since Plot Point I.

At this point Thelma takes over by hanging up the receiver. "Come on, Louise. Don't blow it. Let's go." Louise stands there, unable to move. Thelma's change in character allows her to take charge of the situation.

"Louise, you're not gonna give up on me, are ya?" Thelma asks, in Callie Khouri's favorite scene. "You're not gonna make some deal with that guy, are you?"

> THELMA
> I can understand if you're thinkin' about it. I
> mean, in a way, you've got something to go
> back for. I mean, Jimmy and everything.

Louise is surprised to be hearing this from Thelma.

> LOUISE
> Thelma, that is not an option.

> THELMA
> But I don't know . . . something's crossed
> over in me and I can't go back. I mean, I just
> couldn't live . . .

> LOUISE
> I know. I know what you mean. I don't
> wanna end up on the damn *Geraldo* show.

They are both quiet for a moment.

> LOUISE (cont'd.)
> He said they're gonna charge us with mur-
> der.

> THELMA
> (making a face)
> Eeuww.

> LOUISE
> And we have to decide whether we want to
> come out of this dead or alive.

> THELMA
> Gosh, didn't he say anything positive at all?

*Louise starts the car. They lurch into reverse, then SCREECH for-
ward as they tear off down the road.*

After we see Hal and Max getting into a helicopter, we see a
MONTAGE of Thelma and Louise "driving through the intense
beauty of the Arizona desert."

This little moment allows us to assimilate what's going on.
Things have been happening so fast that we need to slow down
and get some "breathing room." This sets us up for the next scene,

which is very important, and one of the last where the two women will be able to communicate with each other before the final chase sequence.

Thelma asks Louise if she's awake. "You could call it that," she replies. "My eyes are open."

"I feel awake," Thelma shares. "Wide awake. I don't remember ever feelin' this awake. Everything looks different. You know what I mean. I know you know what I mean. Everything looks new. Do you feel like that? Like you've got something to look forward to?"

It is one of their last moments together, and this little exchange reveals how much Thelma has transcended her "old self." They try not to get too serious, so they start pushing their dreams as far as they'll go. "We'll be drinkin' margaritas by the sea, Mamasita," Louise says. "We can change our names . . . live in a hacienda. . . . I wanna get a job. . . . I wanna work at Club Med," Thelma states. "Yes! Yes!" says Louise. "Now, what kind of deal do you think that cop can come up with to beat that?" she asks. "It'd have to be pretty good. It would have to be pretty damn good."

"They are both laughing. The car is flying down the road. The sun is coming up higher in the sky now."

That's when they "come roaring up on the semi-tanker, the same one they have seen before."

They really have nothing to lose at this point, and this guy is so obnoxious, so repulsive, they want to do something. In terms of the screenplay, it's the last moment something humorous *can* happen. So Callie Khouri and Ridley Scott go for it all. In my opinion it's a sequence that's not needed, and even though it's overindulgent, we can at least get a good laugh before we cry. But Callie disagrees. She feels it's totally necessary because it's the only active revenge in the whole film and is totally delightful to the women in the audience. It would be better if they kept the lines "You know what's happened, don't you. We've gone totally insane." It's true; at this moment they are beyond the realm of normal human response.

They motion for the truck to pull over. The driver gets out, and they vocalize everything they feel about the driver's repulsive behavior. They do it openly, without remorse or regret.

Thelma confronts him immediately: "You probably even called us beavers on your CB radio, didn't you?" "Are you going to apologize or not?" Louise demands. The trucker's only answer to both is "Fuck you."

So Louise "points the gun" at his truck, then "SHOOTS two of the tires flat." The trucker screams, then Louise fires at the truck and the whole thing explodes into a huge ball of fire. Thelma and Louise are like two kids playing under a hose on a hot day; they drive around the trucker, "both howling at the top of their lungs," then take off.

The next scene in the screenplay was omitted from the film. Thelma asks Louise where she learned to shoot like that, and she replies "Texas."

Khouri now tries to resolve all those little things in the story line. The script contains a few written scenes that were omitted in the film. One is a scene where an old man rescues the New Mexico cop who was locked in the trunk. We cut to Hal and Max flying over the burning truck. The forces of society are closing in. Then, we cut to a:

WIDE SHOT of the car speeding through the desert on an empty highway heading west. DRIVING SHOT—Thelma has her face to the sun with her eyes closed. Louise is driving with a fierce intensity. They hardly resemble the two women who started out for a weekend in the mountains two days earlier. Although their faces are tanned and lined and their hair is blowing wildly there is a sense of serenity that pervades.

"A sense of serenity that pervades." Everything before has led to this moment, which brings them to their final understanding; there is no going back, the only certainty is death, and they have reached that point of acceptance and understanding. They are at peace with themselves; whatever happens, happens.

And that brings us to the end. Many people I've talked to, both writers and nonwriters, "didn't like the end." When I asked what they didn't like about it, they shrugged and did not respond. When I asked how they would have liked it to end, they didn't answer that, either.

How does the screenwriter approach the ending? In Hollywood, changing the screenwriter's ending is very common. In some cases the studio, or production executive, has a different idea than the writer. So they change it regardless of whether it works, or whether the writer approves or disapproves.

In other cases, the ending has been written, but when the director is on the set shooting, he or she suddenly thinks of a better, more visual ending, so they change it.

Sometimes the director shoots an ending as written, but in the preview screenings the ending does not work with the audience, so they change it. This happened with *Fatal Attraction,* and they had to shoot three different endings (at a very high cost) before they were satisfied.

In the case of *Thelma and Louise* there is only one ending possible. The dramatic options the screenwriter has to deal with at this point are few: either they escape to Mexico, get caught and go to prison, or get killed. These are the only three dramatic choices the writer has. If they escape, society is not satisfied. Someone has to pay: A crime has been committed. This is a serious film, remember, laced with comedy and funny moments, to be sure, but Thelma and Louise have murdered someone, committed armed robbery, and are considered dangerous. A price has to be paid. A getaway and escape would not be in keeping with the integrity of the story; it would be unsatisfying as well.

Should they get captured? Or watch as they surrender? Do we see them getting out of the battered and dusty green '66 T-Bird, walking back to the long row of police cars, their hands raised, watch them being cuffed and driven off into the sun as the end credits roll?

Is that a better ending? No; it is not a satisfactory solution; it would leave us with a sad, bitter feeling.

There's only one other option: They die. It's the only ending that logically fits and is emotionally correct. But how they die becomes the next question. What does the writer do? Show them firing three shots with their puny little pistol against an army of sharpshooters? Have an ending like *Bonnie and Clyde*? All slow motion and bullets bursting flesh at 160 frames a second? Does that fit into the story line as it's been presented so far?

Or, should the end be like that of *Butch Cassidy and the Sundance Kid*—surrounded by the law, wounded, struggling with pain, almost out of ammunition (I think they have one, possibly two bullets left), "making a break for it," which is funny because it's so impossible, in other words, they're going to die. But we don't have to *see* bullets riddling their bodies; we can *imagine* it. So, screenwriter Goldman has Butch and Sundance get off the floor to make their break, and then *we freeze;* we hear shots exploding everywhere, but the last image we see is a heartwarming, sympathetic, compassionate picture with maybe a smile on Butch's face.

It's effective. It works.

So how do we end *Thelma and Louise*?

With a good feeling. If they're stepping out of life, then let them do it with class—with humor, dignity. When Callie Khouri won the Academy Award for best original screenplay, she raised the Oscar and declared, "This is the happy ending that everybody wanted."

An Arizona police car passes them going in the other direction. The first thing Louise says is, "Is your seat belt on?" Typical Louise remark. Then Thelma remarks, "We shoulda made some kinda plan for what to do if we get caught." Yeah, Louise agrees, but "we're not gonna get caught."

That determination drives them forward in an exciting chase sequence. A line of police cars sweeps across the Arizona desert after them, dust flying everywhere.

Louise mentions, "We probably shoulda filled up the car before we blew up that truck." Thelma states, "I know this whole thing is my fault. I know it is." And Louise counters, "There's one thing you oughta understand by now, Thelma: It's not your fault." This little interchange leads to the final moments of their wild adventure.

"You're a good friend," Thelma says. "You, too, sweetie, the best."

"I guess I went a little crazy, huh?" Thelma asks.

"No . . . you've always been crazy," Louise responds. "This is just the first chance you've had to really express yourself."

This dialogue *plays against the grain of the scene.* They are in the middle of a giant chase scene, the dust swirling, sirens roaring, lines of police cars following them, and *this* is what they talk about! It's totally unexpected, and that's what makes it work so well.

Thelma says, "I guess everything from here on in is gonna be pretty shitty." "Unbearable, I'd imagine," Louise answers. "I guess everything we've got to lose is already gone anyway," Thelma says. "How do you stay so positive?" Louise asks with a smile.

Again, even though the lines work well, they are not needed.

Behind them "it looks like an Army. More police cars have joined, and from every direction, police cars are swarming across the desert, although none are in front of them. Way off in the distance, a helicopter joins the chase."

That's when they see it.

"What is it?" Thelma asks. "Louise starts to laugh and cry at the same time."

"It's the goddamn Grand Canyon!"

"Isn't it beautiful!" Thelma exclaims.

Louise has tears streaming down her face as she realizes there is absolutely no escape. Louise slams on the brakes about twenty yards from the edge, and the police cars stop behind them, the authorities pulling out their guns and taking cover.

A wave of silence sweeps over the area.

Then the helicopter with Hal and Max arrives. "Hal sees Thelma and Louise for the first time."

"God! It looks like the Army!" Thelma says.

"All this for us?" Louise jokes.

Now the focus shifts to Hal. "Hey!" he says to Max. "Don't let them shoot those girls. This is too much."

It is too much. We know that, Hal knows that, but the authorities, the "forces of society," are taking no chances.

Thelma and Louise sit in the car, the Grand Canyon in front of them, the police behind them. "Now what?" Thelma asks.

"Then let's not get caught," Thelma says. "Go." "Go?" Louise asks. Thelma smiles at her.

"Go."

"They look at each other, look back at the wall of police cars, and then look back at each other. They smile."

Somehow Hal knows what's going to happen: "How many

times has that woman gotta be fucked over?" he asks, speaking for all of us. Suddenly he starts running toward the car.

And then, in the script as written, B. B. King's song " 'Better Not Look Down' begins. It is very upbeat." (In the film they used the Glenn Fry song "Part of You, Part of Me" over the end credits.)

Louise looks at Thelma and asks, "Are you sure?" Thelma nods. "Hit it," she says. "And Louise puts the car in gear and FLOORS it."

The cops lower their guns in bewilderment as the song begins. The lyrics say it all:

> Better not look down, if you wanna keep on
> flyin'.
> Put the hammer down, keep it full speed ahead.
> Better not look back or you might just wind up
> cryin'.
> You can keep it movin' if you don't look
> down. . . .

"A cloud of dust blows THROUGH THE FRAME as the speeding car sails over the edge of the cliff." And we freeze.

It is the perfect image to end the film. Thelma and Louise have literally run out of world.

They are free spirits. "I did not want them to be pulled down," says Callie Khouri.

The same could be said for Callie Khouri. "When I was sitting in that room," she says, "it was just me and the screenplay and it was the most perfect experience in my life. Regardless of how anybody else feels about it, regardless of anybody else's perception of it, when I was alone with those characters it was the perfect experience.

"Writing *Thelma and Louise* was the first real love affair I ever had with myself. It was the first time I was happy to be who I was, the first time I ever really loved myself completely.

"That experience can never be taken away from me, can never be changed."

I think Thelma and Louise would feel the same way.

Terminator 2:
Judgment Day

8

The Hero's Journey:

Terminator 2: Judgment Day

The eighteenth-century English poet Samuel Taylor Coleridge declared that when you approach a work of art, you must leave your perception of reality behind and approach the work on its own merits, its own level. He described it as "the willing suspension of disbelief." We must willingly suspend our disbelief no matter how far the subject matter strays from what we know to be true, or not true. No matter how outrageous the premise, no matter how unpredictable the characters, situations, reactions, or plot developments are, all have to be left behind when we approach "the work."

I thought about this when I was considering the films for this book. In 1991 there were 424 movies released in Hollywood; 150 were made and distributed by the major studios, and the other 274 were made and released by the independents. Of all those films, roughly a third were action/adventure.

Action is big business in Hollywood, and creates a very large market internationally. Not to include an action film in this book would be like trying to ignore an elephant in a closet.

The only trouble is that I find most of the action films produced and released in Hollywood totally unbelievable. The situations are absurd, and most of the characters are one-dimensional and predictable. Of course, you don't go to an action film to see a good character study. If you look at the "good" action films released in the past few years, *Lethal Weapon 1, 2,* or *3,* or *Die Hard,* or *The Last Boy Scout,* all are exciting with big and spectacular action sequences, but the characters are usually flat and one-dimensional. In short, it's very difficult for me to "suspend my disbelief" willingly.

Then I went to see *Terminator 2.* I wasn't expecting very much. I had seen *The Terminator,* and while the premise was different and original, I didn't think too much of the film. But *Terminator 2* was a different story. I was totally engrossed, literally glued to the edge of my seat, and in those two plus hours in that darkened theater I willingly suspended my disbelief. I mean, how could I not accept the premise that the world had self-destructed in August 1997, and the ruling machines of an epoch beyond the apocalypse had sent back a "terminator" to destroy the one person who could possibly change that particular future?

I sat watching these spectacular action sequences unfold, utterly absorbed in the most amazing special effects I had ever seen, and I *knew* this was a film of the "future." The story concept was unique and original (which you usually don't find, especially in a sequel), and I found that I liked the characters: they were engaging and sympathetic, even though they were becoming "machines" dedicated to altering the future. But what I found the most interesting was the Terminator, the Arnold Schwarzenegger "character," a machine, a cyborg.

When I started thinking about this I found myself confronting a real dichotomy: Number one, how could I willingly suspend my disbelief and accept this robot as a real, living character? And two, how could I be so emotionally moved by his sacrifice, by his very commitment to life? For this is no ordinary man-in-a-suit robot; this is a robot who acquires the highest human values, who willingly gives up his life to save his comrades and humanity from the devastation of the future. His action transforms the future. Action is character; what a person does, not what he says, is what he is. Joseph Campbell declares, "A hero is someone who has given his or her life to something bigger than oneself," like Oedipus and Hamlet. And "if a machine can learn the value of a human life,"

Sarah Connor states in the last line of the movie, "maybe we can, too." That line reverberated in my mind for days after I heard it.

It's a thoughtful, provocative way to end the film. If you think about it, it is the Terminator "character" who embodies the classic values of Aristotelian tragedy and undertakes the hero's journey. Was this intentional? I asked myself. Can this robot, this cyborg, played by an Austrian actor, be the prototype of the new American hero?

The more I thought about it, the more intrigued I became. I didn't know too much about James Cameron except that I was impressed with his innovative skill as a filmmaker. It seemed he always had an interesting premise, whether it was *Aliens, The Terminator,* or *The Abyss. Aliens* was a masterpiece of shock and suspense. I had heard so much about it that I found myself deliberately holding back my emotions, constantly reminding myself that this was only a movie so I wouldn't get too freaked out. Of course, it didn't help too much. I jumped as high as everybody else. Yes, I was very impressed with the way he created suspense, the way he crafted his films.

Creating suspense on film is a special art. Very few filmmakers have the talent really to pull it off. Hitchcock, of course, was the master, and it was the hub of almost all his films. Val Lewton was another who could pull it off. *Cat Woman of Paris* is a classic exercise in film terror: The suspense comes when you least expect it. Jim Cameron is one of those natural filmmakers—like Hitchcock, Welles, Lewton, or Stanley Kubrick, to name a few—who are masters at generating terror and suspense in their movies.

In addition to being an artistic success, *Terminator 2* was also a financial success. It was the highest-grossing film in the world when it was released. It grossed more than $497 million worldwide, of which $205 million was the domestic return; the rest came from the foreign market. It's easy to see that, in the near future, the foreign marketplace will be a key factor in determining which films will be selected for production in Hollywood. *Terminator 2* was definitely a film I wanted to analyze for this book.

I wanted to find out more about Jim Cameron, so I called his office, spoke to his very capable assistant, and we set up an interview. But it was not going to be that easy. After a series of broken and rescheduled appointments—because of "Jim's new deal," it was explained—we finally agreed on a day and time.

It was a long ride to the far end of the San Fernando Valley, where Jim Cameron's company, Lightstorm Entertainment, was located at the time. I pulled up to the nondescript building that looked like any other office warehouse, parked in the visitors' parking lot, and walked inside. It was cool and efficient. "Jim hasn't arrived yet," I was told (I arrived some ten minutes early), so I sat down to wait. The phones were ringing off the hook, and there was a sense of energy and excitement in the air that I couldn't quite identify.

When I opened *Daily Variety* and the *Hollywood Reporter,* the industry's trade papers, and read the headlines, I suddenly understood all the previously canceled appointments. Spread across the top of the page, in big, bold headlines, I read: "CAMERON TAKES FOX BY STORM," and underneath, "Director Signs for $500 Million!"

The article explained that James Cameron had signed a deal with 20th Century Fox to produce some twelve movies over the next five years. It's an extraordinary deal—$500 million for twelve movies! Even the most jaded Hollywood executives have to think about that one. For the people at Fox, however, it made a lot of sense. Cameron is one of the "most talented and commercial directors working in the marketplace," says Joe Roth, the former studio chairman. Together, *Aliens, The Terminator, The Abyss,* and most recently *Terminator 2: Judgment Day* have grossed more than $652 million worldwide.

The deal gives Cameron creative control over his pictures. He has earned it. *Terminator 2* reflects Cameron's uncanny ability to combine creative thinking with scientific technology.

I had just finished reading about "the deal" when Jim Cameron drove up in a black, late-model Corvette. Tall, lean, and friendly, Cameron briefly introduced himself, asked for five minutes to check things out, and disappeared. He had just shaved his beard, and he looked much younger than he did in the pictures I had seen of him.

I was ushered upstairs into the large conference room, very plush and very high-tech, dominated by a beautiful conference table. On the walls were posters of Jim Cameron's films, and along one wall was a long oak table displaying five small silver alloy models of the Terminator 1000. Right next to these models, and totally contrary to the "look" of the room, was a beat-up and obviously well-used diving helmet: "I spent some 560 hours in that 40-pound diving helmet," Cameron later explained, talking about *The Abyss*. Along the far wall were two pinball machines, both based on the *Terminator* movies, and a beautiful, polished oak bar surrounded by plush and comfortable chairs. The entire room was magnificently decorated, and everything was expertly arranged under a sloping wood beam ceiling. It was beautiful.

We sat at one end of the large conference table, had coffee and coffee cakes, and began talking about *Terminator 2*. The more Cameron talked, the more impressed I became. Immediately, through our conversation, I saw that this man is a natural filmmaker, a man of science and art, with a passion for research and detail.

Jim Cameron grew up in Kapuskasing, a little town just outside Niagara Falls in Ontario, Canada. When he was fifteen, he saw Kubrick's *2001: A Space Odyssey*. "As soon as I saw that," he recalls, "I knew I wanted to be a filmmaker. It hit me on a lot of different levels. I just couldn't figure out how he did all that stuff, and I just had to learn.

"So I borrowed my dad's Super-8 camera and would try to shoot things with different frame rates just to see how it looked." This, of course, is much different from picking up a Super-8 in a high school in a large city like L.A. or New York. "If you pick up a Super-8 camera there, it's because you're going to film school," he said. "For me, it was completely innocent. I had a fascination with it, but I couldn't see myself as a future film director. In fact, there was a definite feeling on my part that those people were somehow born into it, almost like a caste system. Little kids from a small town in Canada didn't get to direct movies."

When he was in his teens his family moved to Orange County in Southern California, and "from a pragmatic standpoint, I could have been in Montana. There is no film industry in Orange County, and since I didn't have a driver's license, it made Hollywood as far away as another state.

"I liked science," he continued, "and thought I might want to be a marine biologist, or physicist. But I also liked to write, so I was pulled in a lot of different directions. I liked the idea of an ocean, even though I'd never seen or been in one. But I had been certified as a scuba diver when I was sixteen in a swimming pool in Buffalo, and I dived in the local rivers and lakes.

"I loved the idea of being in another world, and anything that could transport me to another world is what I was interested in. To me, scuba diving was a quick ticket to another land."

He continued talking about his fascination with other worlds, and as he was speaking I could see the evolution of his films: The two *Terminators, Aliens, The Abyss,* all deal with other worlds.

"I enrolled in junior college and studied physics," he continued, "along with all the math: calculus, chemistry, physics, astronomy, which I loved. And while I made good grades, I knew that's not what I wanted to do with my life, so I switched to being an English major and studied literature for a while. Even so, I couldn't make up my mind what I wanted to do, so I simply dropped out. I worked in a machine shop for a while, then as a truck driver, a school bus driver, and painted pictures and wrote stories at night."

Gradually he began to see that the medium of film could accommodate his interests in both science and art, and with the help of a little book called *Screenplay* he "figured out how to write a screenplay, just like all the big guys, so a friend and I sat down and wrote a little ten-minute script. We raised the money to make it and shot it in 35mm; it was all effects and models and matte shots, all this wild kind of stuff.

"It was a bit like a doctor doing his first appendectomy after having only read about it. We spent the first half day of the shoot just trying to figure out how to get the camera running. We rented all this equipment—the lenses, the camera, the film stocks, everything—then took all the gear back to this little studio we had rented in Orange County.

"Now, I knew in theory how the threading path worked, but we couldn't get the camera to run to save our lives. There were three of us, and one of the guys was an engineer, so we simply took the camera apart, figured out how it worked, traced the circuitry, and then realized there was something in the camera that shut the camera off in case the film buckled. Later, when we returned the equipment, we were talking to the rental guys and they said something about 'a buckle trip,' and I said, yeah, yeah, I know about that, not telling them that we had disassembled their camera and spread it out on the table and figured it all out. It was like the Japanese doing reverse engineering."

I asked him about his background in special effects and he told me he "was completely self-taught in special effects. I'd go down to the USC library and pull any theses that graduate students had written about optical printing, or front screen projection, or dye transfers, anything that related to film technology. That way I could sit down and read it, and if they'd let me photocopy it, I would. If not, I'd make notes. I literally put myself into a graduate course on film technology—for free. I didn't have to enroll in school, it was all there in the library. I'd set it up to go in like I was on a tactical mission, find out what I needed to know, take it all back. I just had files and files stacked on my desk of how all this stuff was done."

It is this kind of analytical approach to film projects that separates Jim Cameron from other filmmakers. "I've always felt that people seek out the information and knowledge they need," he said. "They seek it out and find it. It's like a divining rod to water; nobody will give you the pathway. It's something you have to find yourself."

It's so true. In seminar after seminar, workshop after workshop, people all over the world tell me that success in Hollywood is based on "who you know," not what you do. I tell them that's not true at all.

"People ask me how do you get to be a film director," Cameron continued, "and I tell them that no two people will ever do it the same way, and there is nothing I can say that will help you. Whatever your talents are, whatever your strengths and weaknesses, you have to find the path that's going to work for you. The film industry is about saying 'no' to people, and inherently you cannot take 'no' for an answer.

"If you have to ask somebody how to be a film director, you'll probably never do it. I say, probably. If that pisses you off, and then you go out and say, 'I'm going to show that Jim Cameron; I am going to be a director,' that gives you the kind of true grit you need to have in order to go through with it. And if you do become a film director, then you should send me a bottle of champagne and thank me."

There is no "one" way to find your true path in Hollywood. Whether you're a screenwriter, director, actor, producer, whatever, each person has to find his or her way. Success in Hollywood is not measured on talent alone. Persistence and determination are the keys to success; then comes talent.

Cameron got a job working for Roger Corman's New World Pictures, building miniatures. He was the art director and special effects cameraman on *Battle Beyond the Stars,* and was production designer and second-unit director on *Galaxy of Terror* (1981).

Corman's "frantic, frenzied," high-energy school of filmmaking was "like being air-dropped into a battle zone," Cameron recalls. "It was the best, fastest, strongest injection into filmmaking I could have gotten."

He became special effects supervisor on John Carpenter's *Escape from New York* (1981), then directed *Piranha II: The Spawning,* filmed in 1981, though not released until 1983.

After that he wrote and directed *The Terminator.* When I asked how it came into being, Cameron paused for a moment, looked at the pinball machine against the far wall, and smiled slightly. "If you want to know the truth, the evolution of *The Terminator* is somewhat dishonest. I had just directed my first movie, *Piranha II,* but the truth is that I'd actually gotten fired from the shoot after a couple of weeks. Officially my friends knew I was a film director, but that really wasn't true within the industry because I couldn't get my phone calls returned, even from the people at Warner Bros., and they were the ones who put up the negative costs of *Piranha II.* I couldn't get a call back from anybody. I was absolutely dead in the water. I knew that if I was ever going to direct a movie again, I was going to have to create something for myself. So writing a screenplay became a means to an end, a way of visualizing what the movie would be.

"I had to contour whatever I wanted to do into how I could sell myself," he continued. "I have a strong background in special effects. So my natural inclination would be to go toward science fiction. But realistically, I knew the most money I could probably raise to make a picture would be $3 million or $4 million. So I knew it would have to be contemporary, had to have a contemporary location, and I would have to shoot it nonunion. So I started putting things together. I've got effects, I want it to be science fiction, but I want it to be a contemporary story. So how do I inject the fantastic element into a contemporary story? I didn't want to make a fantasy, like a magic mirror communicating with another dimension. I wanted it to be gritty realistic, kind of hardware-based, true science fiction, as opposed to fantasy science fiction.

"I'd always liked robots, so essentially I came up with the idea of time travel and catching glimpses of the future. From a budget standpoint that would be controllable. But if I thrust myself entirely into that world, then I was suddenly talking about a $15 million, $20 million, or $30 million picture. If I kept it limited in terms of what I saw through flashbacks or dream sequences or whatever, and I injected one element from that world into our own, I felt it was controllable.

"Then I hit on the idea of the future being determined by something that's happening now; someone who's unaware of the results of their actions finds out they have to answer for those actions—in the future. So what's the most extreme example of that I can think of? If the world has been devastated by nuclear war, if global events are predicated on one person, who is the least likely person you can imagine? A nineteen-year-old waitress who works at Bob's Big Boy (a fast-food restaurant in Southern California).

"That was the premise, and it started to unfold from that. The easiest way to undo what she had done would just be to kill her, just erase her existence, which is not the most subtle approach to the story. It's true that the future could come back and tell her what was going to happen, but being they were machines, they were thinking in a very binary mode.

"So I started creating some juxtapositions that seemed interesting to me. This incredible nightmare would be glimpsed through little windows of contemporary reality.

"The story evolved from that."

What about *The Terminator*? I asked.

He paused a moment, reflecting. "I first started thinking about the film in two stages," he continued. "In the first stage the future sends back a mechanical guy, essentially what *The Terminator* became, and the good guys send back their warrior. In the end, the mechanical guy is destroyed; but up in the future, they say, well, wait a minute, that didn't work, what do we have left? And the answer is something terrible, something even they're afraid of. Something they've created that they keep locked up, hidden away in a box, something they're terrified to unleash because even they don't know what the consequences will be—they being the machines, or computers, whoever's in charge.

"And that thing in the box becomes a total wild card; it could go anywhere, do anything, a polymorphic metal robot that is nothing more than a kind of blob. I saw it as this mercury blob that could form into anything. Its powers were almost unlimited, and they couldn't control it.

"That scared me. Just sitting there writing the story scared me.

"That's what *The Terminator* was going to be about. But already I could see that it was starting to slop over the boundaries I had set for myself. And I thought, no, I'll get killed. If I try this now it'll be too ambitious; I'll get creamed. I've got to scale back, got to go for something tighter, simpler. So I took out the liquid metal robot.

"Besides, there was no way I could accomplish something like that. In all my effects experience, nobody had really come up with a way of doing it. Maybe in a future film context you could advance that technology and get it looking better, but at that time, in 1983, the answer was a definite no. So I decided against it."

That was the first major creative choice Cameron had to make before he could move forward with his idea. The next key decision he had to confront was that "I didn't want the robot to look like a man in a suit. If this robot was something that was supposed to fit inside a human form, we could not accomplish that visual by putting it outside a human form, then trying to imagine that it was also inside. It just wouldn't work. Nobody had ever created a robot that wasn't a suit. *Star Wars* [George Lucas] had been done a few years earlier, and since then there had been a whole history of film robots that were basically guy-in-suit robots. So for me, the special effects challenge was getting something believable that could have existed inside a human form. That was the real challenge."

The Terminator was filmed and released and became "a sleeper hit." It literally made Arnold Schwarzenegger a superstar and paved the way for the sequel, which took seven years to come to the screen.

It was a hero's journey.

9

Approaching the Sequel:

Where the Writer Begins

Writing a film sequel is always difficult. If you think about the sequels that are successful—the *Rocky* series, *Lethal Weapon,* or *Aliens,* to name just a few recent examples—they always start with the same characters and generate a new story line. They break new ground.

Most film sequels are not successful because they try to put the characters into the same, or similar situations. Look at *Die Hard 2.* Basically it was the same type of story, but instead of setting it in a building like *Die Hard,* they set it in an airport. The action, with only a few modifications, was exactly the same. I'm sure the template of structure was identical. "If it works well," the old Hollywood saying goes, "do it again."

How did Cameron approach the sequel to *Terminator 2*? After all, there were seven years of intense legal battles between *The Terminator* in 1984 and *Terminator 2.* Carolco, the producing company, and Orion, the distributing company, both claimed they owned the sequel rights, and fought for years until they reached an agreement. How did you bridge that kind of gap? I asked him.

He paused for a moment, took a sip of coffee, and said that "from a writing standpoint, the things that interested me the most were the characters. When I was writing Ripley for *Aliens* there were certain things known about her and her experience, but then we lost track of her. In the sequel I was picking her up at a later point and seeing what the effects of those earlier traumas were. With Ripley there was a discontinuity of time, but experientially it was continuous for her because she just went to sleep, and when she woke up, time had gone by.

"It was much different, much more interesting with Sarah. I had to backfill those intervening nine years, so I had to find efficient ways of dramatically evoking what had happened to her. The tricky part was having it all make sense to a member of the audience who didn't remember or hadn't seen the first film. Basically, I had a character popping onto the screen in a certain way, and therefore had to create a back story for that character. I told myself I had to write the script just like there had never been a first film. The sequel had to be a story about someone who encountered something nobody else believes, like the opening scene of *Invasion of the Body Snatchers,* where Kevin McCarthy swears he's seen something shocking, and nobody believes him; then he starts telling the story.

"In *Terminator 2,* the first time we meet Sarah, she's locked up in a mental institution, but the real question is, Is she crazy? The advantage of a sequel is that you can play games you can't play in the original. For example, I know the audience knows the Terminator is real. So they're not going to think she's crazy. But the question still remains: Is she crazy? Has the past ordeal made her nuts? I wanted to push her character very far.

"The strange thing that happened in the wake of the film is that a lot of people made the mistake of thinking I was presenting Sarah Connor as a role model for women. Nothing could be farther from the truth. I wanted people to invest in her emotionally, to feel sorry for her, because she had been through such hell. And people made a straight-line extrapolation from Ripley to Sarah.

"They're very different characters. Ripley's been through a trauma, but she has certain innate characteristics of leadership and wisdom under fire; she's a true hero. Sarah's not really a hero. She's an ordinary person who's been put under extreme pressure, and that makes her warped and twisted, yet strengthened, in a sad way. It's like you don't want this to happen to her. The initial image of her had a big scar running down the side of her face, and we actually did makeup tests with scars, but it would have been a real nightmare to deal with a scar like that in production on a day-to-day basis. I really wanted her to look like Tom Beringer in *Platoon* (Oliver Stone). And Linda was up for it, because the last thing she had done was play Beauty in *Beauty and the Beast* for three years. It's a tribute to her as an actor that she was able to pull off that severity without the help of any makeup whatsoever."

In theater the main ingredient of modern tragedy is an ordinary person who is in an extraordinary circumstance; the situation creates the potential for tragedy. Sarah Connor is no hero; she's an ordinary person who just happens to be placed in extraordinary circumstances. The situation has the potential for tragedy, but in this case, the Terminator, the Schwarzenegger "character," becomes the hero.

That was another major problem Cameron had to confront in the sequel. "There's a strange history that happened with the first film," he explains. "A year or two after *The Terminator* came out, people remembered the film fondly. They remembered Schwarzenegger from the other roles he had played, like *Commando* or *Predator,* (Jim Thomas, John Thomas) where he was running around with a machine gun in his hand, spraying bullets everywhere, like he had in *The Terminator*. But there was this curious blurring of distinction that he was the bad guy in *The Terminator*.

"That made me very nervous," he says. "I knew the 'bad guy being the hero' could get me into some pretty dangerous territory, morally and ethically. I absolutely refused to do another film where Arnold Schwarzenegger kicks in the door and shoots everybody in sight and then walks away," he said, choosing his words carefully. "I thought there must be a way to deflect this image of bad guy as hero, and use what's great about the character. I didn't know exactly what to do, but I thought the only way to deal with it would be to address the moral issues head-on."

For the screenwriter, the challenge is to find a way to deal with this situation so it springs out of the story context and is based on the reaction of character. The dramatic need, the dramatic function of the Terminator is to terminate, to kill anybody or anything that gets in its way. Because he is a cyborg, a computer, he cannot change his nature; only a human or another robot can change the program. So to change the bad guy into a good guy requires changing the dramatic situation, the circumstances surrounding the action. Cameron had to find a way to change the context yet keep Terminator's dramatic need intact.

"The key was the kid," Cameron explains. "Because it's never really explained why John Connor has such a strong moral template.

"For me, John was pushed by the situation where he sees the Terminator almost shoot the guy in the parking lot. I think everybody invents their own moral code for themselves, and it usually happens in your teens based on what you've been taught, what you've seen in the world, what you've read, and your own inherent makeup."

John Connor intuitively knows what's right "but can't articulate it," Cameron continued. "John says, 'You can't go around killing people,' and the Terminator says, 'Why not?' And the kid can't answer the question. He gets into a kind of ethical, philosophical question that could go on and on. But all he says is, 'You just can't.'

"I thought the best way to deal with this was not be coy about it and hope it slides by, but to tackle it head-on, make this a story about why you can't kill people," continued Cameron.

He paused a moment, stared at the blinking light on the telephone. "What is it that makes us human?" he asked. "Part of what makes us human is our moral code. But what is it that distinguishes us from a hypothetical machine that looks and acts like a human being but is not?

"Essentially you've got a character associated with being the quintessential killing machine; that is his purpose in life. Devoid of any emotion, remorse, or any kind of human social code, he suddenly finds himself in the strangest dilemma of his career. He can't kill anybody, and he doesn't even know why. He's got to figure it out. He's got to, because he's half human. And he figures it out at the end. The Tin Man gets his heart.

"Once I clicked into that, I saw what the whole movie was going to be about."

Every screenwriter knows that there are four major elements that make up the visual dynamics of screen character. One, the main character or characters must embody a strong *dramatic need*. Dramatic need is what your main character wants to win, gain, get, or achieve during the screenplay. What drives your character through the obstacles of the story line, through the conflicts of plot? In the case of Sarah Connor, John Connor, and the Terminator, the dramatic need is to destroy the future by destroying the one vital computer chip that will determine that future. To destroy that computer chip they will have to destroy the creator of that chip, Miles Dyson, along with the manufacturing entity, Cyberdyne. They will also have to destroy the Terminator 1000, sent back from the past to protect the future. It is this dramatic need that pushes the entire story line through to its completion.

In some screenplays a character's dramatic need will remain constant throughout the entire story, as it does in *Terminator 2*. In other screenplays, the dramatic need will change based on the function of the story. In *Witness,* for example, the dramatic need of John Book changes after Plot Point I. The same thing happens in *Thelma and Louise,* as mentioned in Chapter Four. If the dramatic need of the character changes, it usually will occur after the Plot Point at the end of Act I.

The second element that makes good character is a strong *point of view,* the way your character views the world. Point of view is really a belief system. "I believe in God," for example, is a point of view. So is "I don't believe in God." So is "I don't know whether there is a God." All these are belief systems.

What we believe to be true is true. For Sarah, nothing can alter her belief that the future is already here. On August 29, 1997, the nuclear holocaust will be unleashed and sweep across the planet like some wild wind destroying everything in its path. That we know from *The Terminator.* This inevitability defines Sarah's point of view and motivates everything she does.

The third thing that makes good character is *attitude*—a manner, or an opinion. People express their attitudes, or their opinions, and then act on them: Dr. Silberman has the opinion that Sarah Connor is loony and acts on that. And he's not ready to change that opinion, no matter what she says or does, at least not for another six months of her incarceration.

The fourth component that makes good character is *change*: Does the character change during the course of the screenplay? If so, how does he or she change, and what is the change? Can you trace this character arc from beginning to end?

In discussing *Terminator 2,* Sarah "does not change that much," Cameron said, "although she goes through a kind of epiphany after she experiences her character crisis [the moment when she cannot kill Miles Dyson]. But her crisis happens relatively early in the story."

But what if your character is a robot? If you consider the prospect of an emotional change occurring within a robot, you find there's an immediate contradiction. A robot cannot change unless it has been reprogrammed by someone or something outside itself. (As we shall see, a scene had been written where the Terminator is reprogrammed, but it was omitted from the final cut.) In this case, as Cameron has mentioned, there will be a major change within the Terminator. At the beginning of the screenplay, Schwarzenegger's dramatic need is simple: to protect and save John Connor. That is the first directive of the warrior machine, to preserve itself so it can function.

During the story there is a change in the Terminator's "character," and his dramatic need changes to fit the moral beliefs of John Connor. And we know the Terminator cannot change his need, he "cannot self-terminate"; he needs John Connor to do that for him. This means that the Terminator has to disobey his own built-in program.

To do that, Cameron said, "he must make a command decision, and it is the only true act of free will that he has in the entire film."

Wait a minute. A robot with free will? Even though that's a contradiction, it's the basic issue that concerned Cameron in approaching the sequel. If you look at the two films you'll see there's a thematic continuity that runs between them, because both deal with the conflict between destiny versus free will.

If these films are about anything, Cameron maintained, it's an exploration of the eternal conflict between destiny and free will. How do you get that to work? I asked him.

Cameron took another sip of coffee, put down the cup, and asked, "At what point is everything we do in life preordained in some way?" In other words, if we can go forward in time and look back on it, if we can jump around in time, then isn't everything we do in our life already part of a movie that's already been shot? Or is there a way you can change it? Can you get it to a certain point on the decision tree and then go the other way?

He paused for a moment, thinking. "Basically, what I did in *Terminator 2* is say that everything is meant to be a certain way. At least to that point in time where they're sending somebody back from that future. But can you grab that line of history like it's a rope stretched between two points, and pull it out of the way? If you can pull it just a little bit before it rebounds, and cut it exactly at that moment, then you can change it and go in a different direction. Like catastrophe theory. If you do that you get a future that no longer exists at all, except in the memories of the people that are here now. They have a memory of a future that will never happen, which is curious, because it defies our Newtonian view of the world. But it is possible.

"That became my point of departure," he said, smiling slightly. "It's like the Terminator's been born from the forehead of Zeus but he's an anomaly in our time because he's the only one who has memories of a time that will never exist. He becomes an integral part of the ongoing fabric of the world, and it's his existence here that prevents that particular future from ever popping into existence. In a spiritual sense, it would be like a manifestation of God changing the path."

I took a sip of coffee, and as I put down the cup I casually mentioned that there seemed to be a spiritual awareness creeping into the American screenplay. As we study the forces of destruction to our environment; sense the wanton violence raging throughout the land; experience the decay of the cities, the dissatisfaction with politics and politicians, the failure of the American Dream, the helplessness of the homeless, it seems we're becoming more and more aware that a spiritual aspect is missing from our lives. There's a longing to incorporate into our lives some kind of spiritual perspective about the moral order of the universe.

Cameron agreed, then continued, "There's a million ways to

look at all these different paradoxes and ellipses. As a matter of fact, in the first script I wrote a scene where Sarah is driving along, talking to herself on the tape machine, and she says, 'But if you had done this then this would have happened, and if you did that then that would have happened and then you wouldn't have even existed, and I could go crazy thinking about it. I just have to deal with what's in front of me.'

"Ultimately, it gets back to morality," Cameron concluded. "Because if the universe can't be explained, if everything can't be known, then we'll never know what's right or what's wrong. We can only know what we feel is right and wrong, which is why I like the idea of the kid spontaneously creating a sense of what's right and what's wrong. It's the same way in *River's Edge* (Neal Jimenez) when the little kid is about to shoot his brother, and he suddenly realizes he can't, you don't do something like that. Even if nobody's ever told him, he knows it.

"As I got ready to write the screenplay," Cameron said, "I kept asking myself, What's the real goal of this movie? Are we going to blow people away and get them all excited? Is that it? Or is there a way we can get them to really feel something? I thought it would be a real coup if we could get people to cry for a machine. If we could get people to cry for Arnold Schwarzenegger playing a robot, that would be terrific.

"That was the fun of the whole thing. It wasn't all the chases and special effects and all that stuff, though I get off on that on a day-to-day basis. I love sitting at the KEM [the editing machine] and making cuts and getting the action working, but when I look back I feel the real thrill was being able to contour a response that was totally opposite from what we got the first time. And to just have fun with that. To play against the expectations. You've got to do that in a sequel."

And that's where we begin.

10

Liquid Metal:

Writing the Screenplay

After the tremendous success of *The Terminator* in 1984 (the film grossed $84 million), the rights for a film sequel were tied up in a legal morass of complicated details and egos. A number of people claimed they owned the rights to the sequel, and no one would agree on a solution that would make everyone happy. Jim Cameron could not even begin to think about a sequel until all the legalities were straightened out. Finally, in 1990, Mario Kassar, the head of Carolco Pictures, who had known Cameron since *Rambo: First Blood,* worked out a solution and solved the problem. There was going to be a sequel.

But there was a hitch. Carolco insisted that the sequel be released in the summer. From a financial point of view it made a lot of sense because summer attracts the largest audiences of the year, but from a logistical point of view it was going to be a nightmare. Carolco wanted the film to be released on July 4, 1991, and that's the announcement they made at the Cannes Film Festival. That meant Cameron had only thirteen months to write the screenplay and make the movie. Though he had speculated on various story lines through the intervening years, nothing had been set. More importantly, many of the special effects he was thinking about, so vital to the film's success, had not even been invented.

So began the experience of writing the screenplay "in the pit," an expression writers use when they're under the gun and are forced to meet an unrealistic deadline. To collaborate on the script with him, Cameron called in William Wisher. Cameron had known Bill Wisher from high school in Orange County; they had hung out together for a while, went their own ways, finally reconnected. Wisher was an actor who became interested in writing, so he "designed a one-year writing course for myself." He read a couple of screenwriting books, *Screenplay* and *The Art of Dramatic Writing,* saw lots of movies, and read any scripts he could get his hands on. He got a feel for the medium and started writing. He got the usual response: "Someone would say, 'We think you're a good writer,'" Wisher told me one sunny afternoon, " 'but we don't want to buy *this* story; but I will hire you for a dollar and a cup of coffee to rewrite this low-budget thing I'm doing, without credit.' So I did that for two years and pretty soon I was getting two dollars and a cup of coffee."

When Cameron was writing *The Terminator,* he called Wisher and asked if he would help write some scenes for him. "I said sure, and we sat down and talked about it. He had a treatment [a fifty-page narrative synopsis of the story], and after many discussions I went off and wrote those scenes he told me to write, and he went off and wrote all the other stuff. Then we went over the whole thing together."

In the six years between the two scripts, Cameron and Wisher would occasionally get together and fantasize about the sequel: "What if it was this kind of a story? What if it was that kind of a story? Would Sarah be alive? Would she be dead?" They were questions that remained speculations, unanswered.

Then Cameron called and told him the news: "I have good news and bad news," Wisher remembered. *Terminator 2* was a go project, the good news, but they had only eight weeks to write the screenplay, the bad news. They were already behind schedule.

They worked in Cameron's little office at his house and started thinking out loud: "Where would Sarah be ten years down the road? She knows what the future will be, and she's the only one in the world who does. She had become a fighter at the end of the first film, so she'd be taking on the defense system and trying to find out who was going to build Skynet.

"What would happen if you went around telling people that the end of the world was coming? We finally agreed that she probably trained herself to survive the blast, knowing what her role would be. It was a strong possibility that she would be in an insane asylum, so we began to work the story out from there.

"In the last shot of the first film," says Wisher, "Sarah is speaking into a little tape recorder; she's starting the journal that she's going to give to John when he's old enough to understand all this. So we assume that she would continue to do that.

"Knowing what John has to do in the future, Sarah would begin telling him this stuff as soon as he could talk. John was going to become the leader of the world," says Wisher, "so he's going to have to shoulder the responsibility of the entire human race. John grew up on a diet of knowing what he had to become. And he resented the hell out of it.

"By the time he was ten years old he had spent his years of childhood thinking and knowing what his future was going to be. He knows, from future experience, that killing is bad for you. Because the Terminator was sent from the future by John, the leader, to protect John, the child, the boy's character has to be woven with a strong moral fiber. So the fact that the Terminator cannot kill people becomes a major point of the story.

"We liked the idea of the kid, but we didn't know what to do about the Terminator. For a while we thought about having a double Terminator—you know, a double Arnold—but it might have gotten too complicated, so we discounted it. Then we had one of those 'no-brainer' ideas one day where the Terminator was reprogrammed to play a good Terminator; we could have some fun with that. We wanted him to change, and we wanted Sarah to change; she starts out one way, becomes fixated on that, ends up becoming more of a machine than he does. We wanted the two of them to change characters as the film went on: She becomes the Terminator while he becomes a human being. And it's partly through the Terminator's transformation that she understands what humanity really is."

So "we kicked it around a bit, then sat down and wrote. We

paced around, talked it out, then hit the keyboard. In the first act we knew we had to have the players on the board and identified. So who was going to be first? Should we introduce Sarah first, or go with John first? We knew in very thick blocks what we had to do. So we sat down and asked, How do we start? Where do we enter the sequence?

"We started tossing around ideas: What's the idea for this scene? For that scene? And any time one of us had an idea we would talk about it, then one of us would sit down and write. When we got tired, we'd trade places and continue typing. We gave every scene a separate file; we had a file for the nuclear blast scene, for Sarah's escape from the hospital, for the kid robbing the ATM machine, and so on."

"We kept the hammer down," added Cameron, "forcing ourselves to produce. 'Let's just make scenes,' I said, 'just keep it flowing. If it's shit, we'll throw it out later.' And as the deadline loomed, the nights got longer.

"The last twenty-five pages of the script were written nonstop, and when I finally gave the computer the print command to spit out the entire script," recalled Cameron, "the limo was waiting in the driveway to take me to the airport so we could announce the film at Cannes. We had been up for thirty-six hours straight."

Life in the screenwriter's fast lane. Believe it or not, many scripts getting ready for production go through this process. Because Cameron and Wisher had prepared the key elements of the story line into a solid dramatic structure, with ending, beginning, Plot Point I, Plot Point II, and Mid-Point, the script fell together with a minimum of creative obstacles.

When you look at the structure of *Terminator 2,* you see that it's structured into six major sequences, these "block" sequences thread the entire film together as if they were a strand of pearls.

That's the strength of structure: it holds everything together.

After the introduction of the Terminator, T-1000, John, and Sarah, the first key element in the story is the chase sequence in which Terminator rescues young John from the T-1000; that's Plot Point I. Pinch I is when John and the Terminator break Sarah out of the state hospital. The Mid-Point is the rest stop at Enrique's, where they load up on guns and ammunition. It is here that Sarah has her nightmare vision and goes after Dyson. Pinch II is the sequence that begins at Dyson's house, where Sarah cannot bring herself to kill him, and ends when they all get to the Cyberdyne factory. Plot Point II is the big escape-from-Cyberdyne sequence. Act III is all action as they elude the T-1000 chasing them in the helicopter, and the final action sequence takes place inside the steel factory.

"If you go back to the first film," Wisher continues, "the Terminator is just a force. The ultimate killing machine. He's not really a character; he's the embodiment of the ultimate tidal wave, or earthquake, or lightning bolt, or heart attack, the thing you cannot stop. Originally, the Terminator was of average height and stature; he was supposed to look very unimposing. A sort of nobody who would blend into the background. So having a six-foot-three Arnold, an imposing figure like that as an infiltration unit was a little unrealistic."

If the T-1000 were not an imposing figure, it dramatically makes his threat all the more horrifying. But it's one thing to write this kind of liquid metal robot, it's another to create it.

However, it took some of the most sophisticated computer-generated imagery ever seen to produce the spectacular special effects of *Terminator 2*. Audiences have never seen a character flow through a barred entrance of a prison, or rise out of a tessellated linoleum floor, or watch hundreds of shattered fragments melt and flow together to form a liquid metal robot who could change into another character.

But if you dig into the body of James Cameron's work, you can see that the origins of the T-1000 had its computer graphics roots in *The Abyss*. As mentioned in Chapter Eight, one of the things Jim Cameron wanted to do was create a shape-changing bad guy, someone or something who could be anything or anybody. When directing *The Abyss*, Cameron wanted to create an alien that was an intelligent stream of water flowing across the floor. "The water tentacle was not the alien itself," he says, "but a tool the aliens create to look around and communicate in the humans' environment. A sort of probe. . . ." What ultimately happened was the creation of the "Water Weenie," as the computer graphics guys affectionately called it.

"It evolved into a kind of water tentacle," says Cameron, "a pseudopod. But how was it going to communicate? So I thought, What better way to communicate than to imitate what it sees? Because that's what we do. Somebody says a word, we imitate the word. It's a soundless, nonverbal, nonacoustic device, so it would have to be done with imagery. So it imitates what it sees, and it starts to communicate that way. The obvious thing to imitate is the person in front of it. And then I got this image of a face that was a water version of the person. I had no idea how to do it, so I went to the computer graphics guys and asked them, and they said they'd give it a try and do some tests.

"We had sixteen shots in *The Abyss,* and they took about nine or ten months to do. In *Terminator 2* we had forty-two shots, and they took seven or eight months. What I learned is that you can't push technology. Once the demand is there, once the desire and the need is there, it really has to take its own time, unless there's some kind of breakthrough."

The Abyss became the effects breakthrough for the T-1000. A liquid metal robot. A shape-changer.

"By shape-changing," said Wisher, "the T-1000 could adapt itself into almost anything. And the more we thought about it, the more we could see it as an advanced prototype experimental Terminator that could think and have a personality, that could mimic other people's personalities, which the first Terminator could not do. And the idea of this guy, this little guy who could kick Arnold's ass, was fun to think about. But the real horrifying part of the T-1000 was that you couldn't kill him."

What could the T-1000 do that the Terminator couldn't do? What couldn't it do? "Could it turn into a Coca-Cola machine?" asked Wisher rhetorically. "No, because it can't change its mass. It certainly can't change its weight; weight and mass are two physical constants. But it can become things. It could not turn into a small dog because it was too big, there was too much mass, too much material. It could mimic weapons, but it couldn't mimic a weapon that would actually fire. A gun has moving parts, and there's gunpowder inside a brass shell, so it can't make itself into that.

"What it can do," he continued, "is make the outer surface of itself look exactly like the clothing of a uniform, and it could mimic the feel of flesh, to a very thin thickness.

"So we said, okay, it can't make itself into a gun, but it could certainly make itself into a knife. Or something flat, like linoleum. Knowing it could be a knife, we needed to show that once or twice because it would look cool, and we figured we could fit that into several different situations."

Wisher explained that "one of the reasons we settled on the shape changer, the T-1000, was that Jim knew there was the beginning of a technology to do that. We'd be writing a sequence, for example, like Sarah's escape from Pescadero, in which the T-1000 steps through the bars. But if he steps through them, it would be nice to let everyone know that he's really stepping through them; so we let the gun get caught up in the bars. He has to reach down and adjust it to get it through. So I asked Jim, 'Can you do that?' And Jim said, 'Yeah, I think I can figure out how to do that.' Jim either knew how to do it, or he was just guessing, based on what he knew about the process; if they didn't know how to do that now, they were close enough so they could figure out how to do it. And they did. The computer graphics guys were able to accomplish everything we asked them to do."

So how did they come up with all those computer graphics?

"To begin with," Cameron replied, "there's an area that the computer graphics guys have been working in for a long time called 'human motion animation.' It's been proven to be one of the hardest sciences, because the eye and the brain inherently know what is right or not right about human beings. There's nothing in the world we know more about than the human being. How they move, how they talk, how they smell, how they stand, all of that. We know that at some innate level you can't fool the human eye. So simulating human motion from scratch, mathematically, is very difficult. And years and years and years of work have pushed it to a certain level, and then that level had to be expanded, because it wasn't good enough anymore."

There were several different areas of special effects used for *Terminator 2:* Stan Winston created the Terminator makeup and animatronic puppetry. Dennis Muren, a six-time Oscar winner of Industrial Light & Magic, supervised the creation of the polyalloy

T-1000. Gene Warren of Fantasy II provided the future war in miniature and the truck crashes, and Robert and Dennis Skotak of 4-Ward Productions unleashed a nuclear holocaust on L.A.

"The stuff that was on the page had never been done before," said Larry Kasanoff, Cameron's former partner at Lightstorm Entertainment, "and it had to be done within a certain time. If the effects hadn't worked, the T-1000 wouldn't have been a threat and the movie wouldn't have worked. So the real risk for this movie was betting that the effects that had to be done could be pulled off within a certain period of time."

Computer-generated imagery has not really been around that long. Computer graphics had first been used in *Star Wars* for a few shots during Luke Skywalker's attack on the Death Star. Then came *Tron* (Steven Lisberger) for which twenty minutes of computer imaging were created for the Light Cycle race and the gossamer-winged Solar Sailer. But *Tron* failed because there was no real story line, and the effects were the main focus of the movie. There were more advanced effects in *Star Trek II* (Jack Sowards) and in *2010* (Peter Hyams) as well as in *Last Starfighter* (Jonathan Betuel), but they were not very sophisticated. Everyone knew the potential for really spectacular effects was there, but no one really knew how to tap into it.

Except Cameron. That's why the creation of the "Water Weenie" in *The Abyss* was the starting point for a whole new level of computer-generated imagery.

The transformation of the T-1000 involved a program called "morphing" (from metamorphosing). In computer graphics it is possible to transform one shape into another by letting the computer design the intermediate steps. That's accomplished by placing a series of grid control points on the object you want to transform so the computer can process each grid point.

"The start point in CGI," explained Cameron, "is always the final form. The software that averages two shapes together to create a new surface is called a 'body sock,' and they used it to take a number of forms and smooth them together, almost like there was a skin over it.

"I wanted the effect of the T-1000 to look like a spoon going into hot fudge; it dimples down, then flows up over and closes.

That's the look I wanted. You have to work with the viscosity in order to get that look just right. You have to figure out what the closure looks like. Does the color come back immediately, or is there a lag time between where the surface forms and then the color forms after that? We had to create a visual language for this guy. For example, when he forms up from his chrome shape, does he form up with the colors of his uniform and skin and all those things simultaneously? I finally chose to have him assume the absolute finished form in a kind of liquid chrome, and then have the color of his uniform be the last thing added. We emphasized the idea that the T-1000 was mimetic, that it was a camouflage technique in the way a chameleon would imitate a color it's sitting on, which is why we made up a name for him, a mimetic polyalloy; the ultimate chameleon."

Armed with this information, the crew at Industrial Light & Magic took actor Robert Patrick, dressed him in skullcap and briefs, and drew grid lines all over his body. Then they shot reference footage of him walking and running through the studio parking lot in San Rafael. It was essential to match the movements of the chrome version with the actor's as closely as possible, so when he walked or ran it was the computer imaging that made his movements so fluid and machinelike. There was only one drawback: The images created by the computer are clear and sharp, not like the blurry and fuzzy edges of reality, so the technicians had to blur and rough up the images to match the edges of their surroundings.

"The little details people don't ordinarily notice are incredibly helpful in creating the reality of the situation," explained Kasanoff. "For example, when the T-1000 rises out of the linoleum, two things make it look convincing. One is the reflections of the surroundings on the surface of the cyborg; the other is the tiny reflection his foot makes on the polished floor. Getting those kinds of things to look right and move right were incredibly difficult, but they make it seem real. When Jim saw the tests, he kept saying, 'Why does that foot look like it's not on the floor?' and the answer was because it needed a quarter of an inch of drop shadow around half of it—then it looked like it was on the floor."

All those images—the T-1000's head blowing apart, rising from the linoleum, moving through the bars, shape-changing into Sarah, or Janelle—would not have been possible without computer graphics imaging. It is truly the wave of the future.

But there are limitations to this fledgling science. For example, computer graphics cannot capture natural phenomena that move. "We can't do oceans," said Dennis Muren. "I mean, we can sort of do them and we can fudge them by mixing media, but it's not quite there yet. Somewhere down the line I know all that stuff is going to be done with the turn of a switch. The lighting, too, is a real weak point in this technology right now."

But computer graphics alone would not be enough to make *Terminator 2* the most popular film in the world. The story was the foundation, and the effects, no matter how brilliant, were only parts that served the whole.

Form and function, story and screenplay, were united into an incredible motion picture experience.

11

"Bad to the Bone":

Setting Up the Story

In the beginning, during the silent era, stories were told in pictures, so the great American filmmakers—Mack Sennett, D. W. Griffith, and Charlie Chaplin, among others—had to create a visually dynamic style. When sound was introduced in 1927, Hollywood had to import Broadway playwrights to write the dialogue.

What separates the novel, the play, and the screenplay? When you read a novel, the story usually is told through the point of view of the main character. We are inside his or her head and share the thoughts, feelings, memories, desires, and emotions that become part of that person's experience. The canvas of action takes place within the *mindscape* of dramatic action.

A play takes place onstage, with a proscenium arch, and the audience becomes the fourth wall, literally eavesdropping on the lives of the characters. The action onstage takes place in the *language* of dramatic action: Through the dialogue we hear the thoughts, memories, feelings, desires, and actions of the characters.

But the screenplay is different: It deals with externals, in little bits and pieces of action, shots and scenes, and it is those details, those visual impressions of dramatic action, that tell the story.

Look at the opening shots of *Terminator 2:*

EXT. CITY STREET—DAY

Downtown L.A. Noon on a hot summer day. The lunchtime crowd stacks up into a wall of humanity. In SLOW MOTION they move in herds among the glittering rows of cars jammed bumper to bumper. Heat ripples distort the torrent of faces. The image is surreal, dreamy . . . and like a dream it begins very slowly to:

DISSOLVE TO:

EXT. CITY RUINS—NIGHT

Same spot as the last shot, but now it is a landscape in Hell. The cars are stopped in rusted rows, still bumper to bumper. The skyline of buildings beyond has been shattered by some unimaginable force like a row of kicked-down sand castles. . . .

A TITLE CARD FADES IN:

LOS ANGELES, JULY 11, 2029

These details are the images that set the stage. After a series of shots of the desolation and fire-blackened bones, our gaze (the camera's eye) lingers on a tiny skull. Over these images we hear Sarah Connor's voice telling us what happened: "Three billion human lives ended on August 29, 1997. The survivors of the nuclear fire called the war Judgment Day. They lived only to face a new nightmare, the war against the machines. . . ." She stops talking, and we see a *metal foot* crushing the skull like china.

In these few pictures we have set up the time and place of action. The story starts at page one, word one. Because it's a sequel, the credibility of the story depends on giving the reader and the audience enough information to *see* what's going on.

What do we know from these first few images? Children are playing; then we see the same image in smoking ruins. In less than one page of screenplay we set up the entire story. We see the past, then cut to the future—one happy and carefree, the other blackened by the torch of some catastrophic event.

I call this technique the "contradiction of image" because the writer sets something up with one picture, than destroys it with another. In *Witness,* the opening shots lead us to believe that we are in the world of the nineteenth century; it is only when we see the title card, "Lancaster County, 1984," that we know we are in present time. One image destroys the other.

We set up the future so we can move into the past. And this is the future: a battle sequence involving death-hungry machines hunting the humans who are opposing them. We focus on the rebel leader, John Connor, "forty-five years old," the script says. "Features severe." The left side of his face is heavily scarred. A patch covers that eye. An impressive man, forged in the furnace of a lifetime of war. The name stitched on the band of his beret is CONNOR. We push in until his eyes fill frame, then . . .

Over this shot we hear the voice-over narration of Sarah giving us the necessary exposition to set up the story:

SARAH (VO)
Skynet, the computer which controlled the machines, sent two terminators back through time. Their mission: to destroy the leader of the human Resistance . . . John Connor. My son . . . The first terminator was programmed to strike at me, in the year 1984 . . . before John was born. It failed.

The second was set to strike at John himself, when he was still a child. As before, the Resistance was able to send a lone warrior. A protector for John. It was just a question of which one of them would reach him first. . . .

In just two pages of screenplay we know everything we need to know about the main characters: Sarah Connor; her son John; the Terminator, sent back to protect him; and the T-1000, sent back to kill him.

So we cut back to present time, and the story begins. We meet the Terminator. "Wild fingers of blue-white electric arcs dance in a steel canyon formed by two tractor trailers." His body, naked, his "physique, massive, perfect."

Then this naked figure strolls into a bikers' hangout, another contradiction of image, which adds an element of humor. We see "a digitized electronic scan of the room, overlaid with alphanumeric readouts which change faster than the human eye can follow." He walks up to a tough-looking biker and tells him, "I need your clothes, your boots, and your motorcycle." In answer, the biker stubs out his cigar on the Terminator's chest.

This is an action film. And we know it immediately because a fight follows, and bodies are tossed around like popcorn popping. The biker is thrown into the kitchen, where "we hear a sound like sizzling bacon." That's all it takes for the biker to give the man what he wants: his clothes, his boots, and his motorcycle.

Outside the bar, the Terminator looks like what he is: one tough dude. Lloyd, an old, fat biker, holds a shotgun on him and tells him, "I can't let you take the man's bike, son. Now get off or I'll put you down!" In reply, the Terminator yanks the "10-gauge Winchester lever-action shotgun" away from him, reaches into the biker's pocket, pulls out some dark glasses, and puts them on as we hear the song, "Bad to the Bone." He kicks the bike over, and he roars off in a shower of gravel.

"Terminator never threatens," read the stage directions; "he just takes."

It's a very good opening. Not only do we know what's happening, we also have a good visual introduction to the Terminator because we *see* him in action. Already "the audience knows what he is," says Jim Cameron. "When he walks out of the bar with all that stuff on and puts on those sunglasses, we know that you know this guy is one badass killer.

"The first time I saw the film with an audience," Cameron continues, "that moment got the biggest reaction. And I thought, Why are they reacting so strongly here? Because there's nothing more I have to do to make this guy the baddest-ass killer in the world. If they get that within the first three minutes, then all the killing and mayhem and feats of indestructibleness I put after that aren't going to get me any more of a reaction than the moment I've already created. So at that point I became convinced the movie would work: We know that you know, so now we can do anything.

"At first, when we laid the 'Bad to the Bone' music over, the editors didn't like it; it wasn't serious enough. But I know there was some kind of self-approval, an interactive process going on with the audience here. They approve of the character just as he is. It's like, 'He's back, it's the guy we remember, and here we go again.' We don't have to spend half of the film getting to that point."

It is a totally opposite situation with the T-1000. We know he's a terminator, but we don't know whether he's the good guy or the bad guy. We meet him just like the Terminator. Blue-white electrical arcs are discovered by a solitary policeman, and then "a naked man glides from a shadowed doorway behind the cop," reads the script. "The flash of light and the fact that he is naked are pretty good clues that he has just arrived from the future. His features are handsome, bordering on severe. His eyes are gray ice. Penetrating. Intelligent."

The T-1000, now in the policeman's uniform, climbs into the squad car and punches in the focus of his mission (the dramatic premise); we see the name John Connor, followed by his police record onscreen: trespassing, shoplifting, disturbing the peace, vandalism. And he's only ten years old.

By using the visual printout of his background, we don't need *words* to explain who he is; we show who he his. Visually.

This sets up the cut that takes us to John Connor. The last line of dialogue, or image, in the current scene sets up the next scene. That's Cameron's writing style. So we cut to John working on his little Honda 125 dirt bike. The woman Janelle is yelling at him to clean up his room, but he simply revs up his bike to drown out her words. "Your foster parents are kinda dicks, huh?" says his friend Tim. With only one line of dialogue we know he's in a foster home.

When Todd, his foster father, yells at him, "Do what your mother says and clean up your room," John replies, "She's *not* my mother, Todd!" And he peels rubber.

In one scene we see that John is a rebel fighting authority. When his friend asks John if his real mother "is dead or something," John replies, "She might as well be."

Every scene sets up the next, like links in a chain of dramatic action. This last line of John's leads us directly to his mother, Sarah Connor, who is at Pescadero State Hospital for the criminally insane.

This is how she's introduced:

Tendons knot and release as SOMEONE does pull-ups. A mane of tangled hair hides the face that comes INTO FRAME, dips, comes back. . . . A WOMAN in a tank top and hospital pants is hanging from the top leg of the vertical bedframe. The inmate, face hidden, pulls up, dips, pulls up. Like a machine. No change in rhythm.

In the corridor outside, a group of hospital interns led by the "smug criminal psychologist," Silberman, tells us about her. "The next patient," he says, "is a twenty-nine-year-old female diagnosed as acute schizoaffective disorder. The usual indicators . . . depression, anxiety, violent acting out, delusions of persecution." They reach the room, and Silberman flicks on the intercom. "Morning, Sarah."

She turns slowly into CLOSE-UP. SARAH CONNOR is not the same woman we remember from last time. Her eyes peer out through a wild tangle of hair like those of a cornered animal. Defiant and intense, but skittering around looking for escape at the same time. Fight or flight.

We learn about Sarah's background from Silberman's point of view (remember James's theory of illumination): "The delusional architecture is interesting. She believes a machine called a 'terminator,' which looks human, of course, was sent back through time to kill her. And also that the father of her child was a soldier sent to protect her. . . . He was from the future, too . . . the year 2029, if I remember correctly."

This exposition has been conveyed to us within the first ten pages of the screenplay; the characters have been set up and introduced, the dramatic premise stated (two terminators have been sent back—one to kill John, the other to protect him), and the dramatic situation presented (the cataclysmic event has happened and the machines have taken over).

Now we expand the characters and see what kind of a kid John Connor is: He's at a bank, where he "slips a stolen ATM card into the machine's slot. The audience knows it's something he's rigged up because, trailing from the card, is a ribbon wire that goes to some kind of black-box electronics unit he's got in his ever-present knapsack." Film is behavior; action is character; what a person does is who he is. John is smart, he's a leader; he's unconcerned with the law; he takes what he needs.

They rip off a cool three hundred bucks, and when John's friend asks him how he learned all this stuff, John replies, "From my mom. My real mom, I mean." John shows him a Polaroid of Sarah —"pregnant, in a jeep near the Mexican border," read the stage directions. "John doesn't know it now, but he will carry that photo with him for over thirty years, and give it to a young man named Kyle Reese, who will travel back in time to become his father. Yes. *That* photo."

John tells his friend that his mother's "a complete psycho. That's why she's up at Pescadero. She tried to blow up a computer factory, but she got shot and arrested. . . . She's a total loser," he observes, but the stage directions indicate that "John has tried to sound macho casual, but we see in his eyes that it really hurts."

By page twelve we are ready to move the story forward, and the dramatic hook, or inciting incident, is played out at John's house. The officer (the T-1000 we'll find out later) asks Todd and Janelle if he can speak to John. When they tell "the cop" that John's not home, "the cop" asks them for a picture. He thanks them and then leaves, but not before we learn that "another guy was here this morning asking about him, too. A big guy, on a bike." Now we know both of them are hunting John—one to kill him, the other to protect him—and we don't know which is which.

The screenplay now includes a dream sequence in which Sarah sees "Kyle Reese, sitting on the edge of her bed, looking exactly the same as we last saw him in 1984. Scruffy blond hair and a long raincoat." They both acknowledge that this is a dream, but when he asks about John, she becomes frightened, and buries her face in his shoulder. "They took him away from me," she says. Reese replies, "It's John who's the target now. You have to protect him. He's wide open. . . . Don't quit, Sarah. Our son needs you." She struggles not to cry, like a vulnerable little girl, and explains, "I'm not as strong as I'm supposed to be. I can't do it. I'm screwing up the mission." Reese tells her that she must "remember the message . . . the future is not set. There is no fate but what we make for ourselves."

This is the first time we hear that message, which is the theme of the film. The scene was shot, but omitted from the final film. Sarah then relives her recurring nightmare we saw in the opening: children playing, a blast, and the world bursts into flame.

The illustrated version of the screenplay published (Applause Press) explains Sarah's first nuclear nightmare was cut because of scheduling conflicts and the desire to simplify the amount of puppetwork needed to shoot the dream imagery. The dream scene involving Kyle Reese was filmed, then cut because of time. The nightmare was repeated three times in the original script—twice in Sarah's nightmares and once verbally. In the script's first draft Silberman and the attendants are also terminators, which is revealed as Sarah struggles with them, exposing metal endoskeletons under their flesh.

Then she wakes up . . . in her cell, shackled to the bed. Sunlight hurts her eyes. She looks desperate and defeated. She knows the war is coming. It visits her every time she closes her eyes. Lost and alone, Sarah feels all hope recede for herself and for humanity.

We know, of course, that her recurring nightmare is real. So in the next scene we see Sarah on video as she was when she first arrived, and then witness her in the present; the whole point of the scene is to establish her need to see John. When Silberman ignores her request he abruptly changes the subject and asks if she still believes "that the company covered it up." She shakes her head, no.

But that reference to the "company" provides the verbal transition that actually takes us to the company, Cyberdyne; we meet Miles Dyson, the "star of the Special Project's division. He's brilliant, aggressive, driven . . . a man with much to do," a man who becomes a major force in shaping the future as we have seen it.

The scene sets up the "small artifact in a sealed container. . . . Dyson removes it and handles it like the Turin Shroud. Next to the cabinet is a larger object . . . an intricate metal hand and forearm . . . all that remains of the terminator Sarah destroyed." The scene is placed here to show that Sarah has been telling the truth about the company's cover-up.

We cut back to Sarah in the interview room at Pescadero; Silberman denies her request to see John: "You see, Sarah," he says, "I know how smart you are and I think you're just telling me what I want to hear. I don't think you really believe what you've been telling me today."

"We go tight on Sarah's reaction," read the stage directions. "And we see Silberman is right. She was playing him and it didn't work. And she knows she's fucked."

She blows it. She "leaps across the table at him," attacking him until she's finally subdued. A "model citizen," Silberman quips into the camera.

By page twenty we're ready to set up Plot Point I, the moment when the Terminator rescues John from the T-1000. For this to happen, both terminators have to find John Connor.

They do it at the galleria. John is playing video games when the two terminators start hunting the ten-year-old. When John sees the "cop" coming after him, he bolts, the T-1000 after him. We cross-cut to the Terminator "walking through the crowd in slow motion. Scanning. He moves with methodical purpose, knowing the target is close. We see that he is carrying a box of LONG-STEM ROSES. Like some hopeful guy with a hot date."

So begins the exciting chase sequence that establishes the structural foundation for the entire film. In a small corridor, John is directly in the line of fire as the Terminator pulls the shotgun from the box of roses. John looks for a place to run, a place to hide, but finds none. The T-1000 turns the corner, confronts the Terminator, and the two behemoths engage in combat. "Get down," the Terminator says to John.

The machines blast away at each other, and we see the first of the forty-two special effects that were designed for this movie. The

Terminator protects John as the T-1000 is literally ripped apart by shotgun blasts, but his insides are chrome; there is no blood, no messed-up flesh. The T-1000 falls to the floor, lies still for a moment, and as John and the Terminator watch, "the cop sits up unharmed and gets to its feet. The 'cop,' who not only isn't a cop, he clearly isn't even human, pulls the trigger so fast it almost seems like a machine pistol."

"Blam Blam Blam Blam!" The bullets tear into the two combatants. Then they go at it hand to hand, slamming into walls and through windows until the Terminator is hurled through a plate glass window. "A Japanese tourist cautiously steps forward and takes pictures of the body." (That was changed on the set; the man taking the pictures is William Wisher, the cowriter.)

John races to his bike but has trouble starting it, which, of course heightens the action as the T-1000 races after him. The bike finally catches and he slams it into gear.

The young boy shoots into busy traffic as the T-1000 races after him. Seeing a big-rig tow truck, he runs over, tosses the driver out like he's a bag of fruit, and jumps into the driver's seat.

Now we can intercut among the three parties to generate a strong rhythm of tension and suspense: John trying to escape on his little Honda, the T-1000 driving the huge Kenworth rig, and the Terminator searching for John.

Writing an action sequence is a highly specialized skill; the movement has to be dynamic and fast, the high-risk stunts larger than life. Jim Cameron is a master at creating wonderful action sequences. There's an old Hollywood expression, If it ain't on the page, it ain't on the stage. Here's Plot Point I. Look at how a good action sequence is written.

EXT. FLOOD CONTROL CHANNEL

John slides his bike down the service ramp faster than he's ever done it before. He races along the bottom of the canal, turning into a narrower tributary, which has vertical sides.

He looks back. No sign of pursuit. Suddenly he sees the sun blocked out by a great shadow. The Kenworth tow truck, big as a house, all chrome and roaring diesel engine, crashes through the fence and launches itself right into the center of the canal.

It crashes down, fifteen feet to the ground going about sixty, hits at an angle, and tears into the concrete wall with a hideous grinding of metal. It ricochets back and forth between the walls; then, bellowing like a gutshot stegosaurus, it just keeps on plowing forward, gathering speed.

John looks back and sees this wall of metal almost filling the narrow concrete canal and he milks every last bit of throttle the little bike has. The Kenworth is all muscle, tearing along the canal like a train in a tunnel. Its big tires send up huge sheets of muddy spray, backlit in the setting sun. It looks like some kind of demon. And it's gaining.

ABOVE THEM, on the service road running parallel, Terminator is fighting to overtake them. It looks down and sees John with the two truck from Hell catching up to him. It is only about twenty feet behind him and still gaining.

ANGLE IN THE CANAL, looking back past a desperate John, at the wall of the metal filling frame behind him.

ABOVE, Terminator cuts the bike suddenly hard to the left, leaving the road. Hitting an earth embankment just right, it jumps the bike into the air like Steve McQueen in The Great Escape *and vaults the fence bordering the canal. It slams down at the edge of the canal and tears along, inches from the drop-off on a dirt path, accelerating past the truck in the channel below.*

John hits some water and slows momentarily, losing speed. The massive push-plate on the front of the truck slams his back fender. Panicked, he pulls a little ahead. All this is happening at about sixty miles an hour. Top speed for the little dirt bike.

SLOW MOTION as Terminator jumps the bike again. This time the seven-hundred-pound Harley sails out into space and drops into the canal. It arcs down between the truck and John, hitting on its wheels. It bottoms out, an explosion of sparks from under the frame. Only the ultrafast reflexes of a machine could keep the bike upright. Terminator fights for control.

[This particular effect was done hooking guide wires on Schwarzenegger and the bike. Then the effects people wrote a computer program that erased the guide wires, frame by frame. In future films, says Cameron, this program will revolutionize action films.]

It guns the throttle and the powerful bike roars up beside John's tiny Honda. Terminator sweeps the kid off his machine with one arm and swings him onto the Harley, in front of him. John's Honda weaves and falls, smashed instantly under thundering tires.

[The "convertible" tow-truck scene where the top is sheared off was filmed on location when Cameron discovered the big rig wouldn't fit under the overpass; it's one of the standout moments in the chase.]

The Harley roars ahead. It hits eighty. Ahead is an overpass, and supporting it is an abutment which bisects the canal into two channels. The Harley thunders into one channel, which is essentially a short tunnel.

The truck can't fit on either side. Neither can it stop, at that speed. Tires locked, it slides on the muddy concrete and piles into the concreted abutment at seventy.

Terminator and John emerge from the tunnel, looking back to see a fireball blasting through behind them as the truck's side tanks explode.

Terminator stops the Harley. John peers around its body to see the destruction. A burning wheel wobbles out of the tunnel and flops into the mud. Terminator revs the bike and they roar away, down the canal, disappearing around a bend.

ANGLE ON THE FIRE, as a column of black smoke rises from the overpass. Smoke boils from the tunnel as well, and inside it is a solid wall of flame. A figure appears in the fire. Just an outline. Walking slowly . . . calmly. The figure emerges from the flames.

It is human-shaped but far from human. A smooth chrome man. Not a servomechanism like Terminator is underneath, with its complex hydraulics and cables . . . this thing is a featureless, liquid chrome surface, bending seamlessly at knees and elbows as it walks. It reminds us of mercury. A mercury man. Its face is simple, unformed. Unruffled by the thousand-degree heat, it walks toward us.

With each step detail returns. First the shapes and lines of its clothing emerge from the liquid chrome surface, then finer details . . . buttons, facial features, ears.

But it's still all chrome. With its last step, the color returns to everything. It is the cop again . . . handsome young face, blond hair, mustache. Icy eyes. It stops and looks around.

It is a perfect chameleon. A liquid metal robot. A killing machine with the ultimate skills of mimicry for infiltration of human society.

We see who he is. What he is.
The rest we'll find out later.

12

Escape from Pescadero:

The First Half of Act II

John sits perched in front of the Terminator as the Harley roars down the street; he is unable to shake off the experience of what just happened. "Stop the bike!" he finally yells to the cyborg. What's going on here?

As we've seen, Act I is almost all action interspersed with some necessary exposition. But the characters still don't know what's going on. John knows the Terminator has saved him from the cop. But who is the cop? And why does he want to kill John?

Good screenwriting allows the main character to discover what's going on at the same time as the audience discovers what's going on. Character and audience are connected by the community of emotion.

The Harley stops, and John turns to the Terminator. "Now, don't take this the wrong way," he says, "but you are a *terminator,* right?"

"Yes, Cyberdyne Systems, Model 101."

"Holy shit," John exclaims. "You're really real. You're . . . uh . . . like a machine underneath, but sort of alive outside."

"I'm a cybernetic organism. Living tissue over a metal endoskeleton." The character learns as the audience learns. Now we can set up the conflict effectively.

When the screenwriter stares into that sixty-page unit of dramatic action that makes up Act II, it's important to remain focused on the dramatic need of the character. It establishes the foundation of the conflict that pushes the action forward through Act II and will provide a context for the Confrontation.

Now John Connor has to find out who saved him, and why. He's heard about the Terminator all his life, and now suddenly his life has been saved by it. Why?

> JOHN
> You're not here to kill me. . . . I figured out that part for myself. So, what's the deal?

> TERMINATOR
> My mission is to protect you.

> JOHN
> Yeah? Who sent you?

> TERMINATOR
> You did. Thirty-five years from now you reprogrammed me to be your protector here, in this time.

John gives him an amazed look.

> JOHN
> This is *deep*.

For sure it's deep. What's so important about this scene is that it sets up the dramatic premise of the screenplay. The Plot Point at the end of Act I is always the *true* beginning of your screenplay. Act I sets up the story components. Then the screenwriter has to establish the dramatic need and create obstacles to that need; the story becomes the main character overcoming obstacle after obstacle to achieve his or her dramatic need.

If the Terminator is sent to protect John, who's the cop, the T-1000? The Terminator explains it's "an advanced prototype, a mimetic polyalloy." Liquid metal. Then John learns the truth: "You are targeted for termination," the Terminator says. "The

T-1000 will not stop until it completes its mission. Ever." The dramatic premise. John's dramatic need is simple: to escape and save his life, to survive.

The Terminator tells John they must leave the city immediately. When John asks if he can go home, the answer is "negative. The T-1000 will definitely try to reacquire you there."

Even though John doesn't much care for his foster parents, he feels he's "gotta warn Todd and Janelle." But it's too late. Sometimes a screenwriter creates tension in a scene by showing a person, or a scene, or a situation that looks normal, but at the end we know it's not normal at all. Hitchcock used to do this all the time. What seems the most normal can actually become the scariest.

John calls home; Janelle answers, and everything seems perfectly normal. But the stage directions indicate something else is going on: "In the backyard John's German shepherd is going bonkers, barking at something." John immediately knows something's wrong: "She's never this nice," he explains.

Todd enters the kitchen complaining about the barking dog, and Janelle turns, stares hard at him, then extends her arm toward him: "THUNK! Her free hand seems to do something out of frame. There is a gurgling, and the sound of liquid dribbling onto the floor. (Don't go away. We'll find out what happened in a moment)" is a little humor added for the readers. Yet her expression doesn't change.

"The dog's really barking. . . . What should I do?" John asks the Terminator. "What's the dog's name?" "Max." Terminator takes the receiver, and in perfect mimicry, copies John's voice: "What's wrong with Wolfy?" he asks. "Wolfy's fine, honey," Janelle replies. "Where are you?"

Terminator hangs up the receiver and tells John, "Your foster parents are dead. Let's go." And he walks away, leaving John staring after him.

Now we *see* what the screenwriters meant in their little aside. We discover some of the properties of liquid metal:

INT. VOIGHT HOUSE—KITCHEN

Janelle hangs up the phone. Her expression is neutral. Calm.

PAN OVER along her arm, which is stretched out straight from the shoulder. Partway along its length her arm has turned smoothly into something else—a metal cylinder which tapers into a swordlike spike. Now we see Todd Voight PINNED TO A KITCHEN CABINET by the spike, which has punched through his milk carton, through his mouth, and exits the back of his head into the cabinet door. His eyes are glassy and lifeless. . . .

The spike is withdrawn—SWIISHHITT! . . . Janelle doesn't bat an eye as the spike smoothly changes shape and color, transforming back into a hand, and then . . .

JANELLE CHANGES rapidly into the COP we know now as the T-1000. The change has a liquid quality.

This little scene is very important to the rest of the screenplay: We see how dangerous the T-1000 really is; we see it, then explain it; a story told with pictures. "You're telling me it can imitate anything it touches?" John asks incredulously. "Like, it could disguise itself as anything . . . a pack of cigarettes?" No, "it can't form complex machines," Terminator explains, like a gun or explosives. "They have chemicals, moving parts. It doesn't work that way. But it can form solid metal shapes."

Discovering what the T-1000 can do is one of the thrills of the movie. We learn more about the T-1000 as the characters learn about it. Character and audience are joined in the lack of discovery.

The next few scenes set us up for Pinch I: breaking Sarah out of the hospital. We've seen Sarah in her present state, and now we learn how she ended up at Pescadero. John explains: "We spent a lot of time in Nicaragua . . . and for a while she was with this crazy ex-Green Beret guy, running guns. She'd shack up with anybody she could learn from. So she could teach me how to be this great military leader. Then she gets busted and it's like . . . sorry, kid, your mom's a psycho."

We sense the anger and sadness in his remark. When he learns that the T-1000 will "terminate" Sarah, he tells the Terminator they must go there directly. Not only is this the next story point, it also is the moment when Cameron introduces the basic morality of John's character that he spoke about in Chapter Nine.

Writing an action film is different from writing other kinds of films. The characters are almost always in the arena of action. *Terminator 2* is not about the intricacies of character revelation; it's about a relationship placed within the context of action. Action sequences reveal character.

When the Terminator tells John that his mother is "not a priority," John gets pissed and walks away. But he takes only a few steps before the Terminator grabs him and pulls him back to the motorcycle. John yells for help. Two jock types working on a car nearby come over to help him as John tells the Terminator to "let go of me." The Terminator complies, dropping him on his ass. When John asks why he did that, the Terminator replies, "because you told me to." John looks at him in amazement. "You have to do what I say?" That "is one of the mission parameters," the Terminator explains.

When the two guys appear to help John, the boy changes his mind, telling them to go "take a hike." The two guys get pissed, and John orders the Terminator to get rid of them. The Terminator tosses the two guys around, then whips out his .45 and points it directly at the head of one of them. John knocks his arm away and deflects the bullet. He screams at the Terminator to put the gun down and suddenly understands that "you were gonna kill that guy."

"Of course," he replies. "I'm a Terminator." "You just can't go around killing people!" John proclaims. When Terminator asks "Why?" John replies, "You just can't. Okay? Trust me on this."

This little scene, deceptively humorous, states the moral tone of the script and sets the stage for the Terminator's transformation of character. It establishes the idea that killing people is wrong, no matter what the situation. It is the first step in the Terminator's learning process.

The last line of the scene sets up the following scene, which will lead us to Pinch I: John tells the Terminator, "I'm gonna go get my mom. You wanna come along, that's fine with me."

And we cut directly to the interview room at Pescadero State Hospital. An apparently drugged-out, nonreactive, distant Sarah is vacantly listening to two cops describe the gunfight in the mall. They show her pictures of the Terminator and tell her that John's foster parents have been killed. "Don't you care?" they plead. But she doesn't react; no one's home. Then we see her slip a paper clip off the photos and hide it between her fingers. That night, after the night orderly straps her into the restraints and licks her face like a dog before he leaves, Sarah snaps awake. She spits out the clip, and after a few suspenseful moments (it's important to create tension whenever you can) she slips off the restraint lock. Free at last.

Just in time. At the front gate a police black-and-white pulls into the hospital grounds. It is the T-1000.

The action builds step by step toward breaking Sarah out of the hospital. The screenwriter must choreograph three elements in the forthcoming sequence. One is Sarah, who knows the Terminator is back. She breaks out of her cell at the same time the second element, the T-1000, enters the hospital grounds. While the T-1000 is stalking Sarah, the third element, John and the Terminator, are racing toward the hospital. Each element works against the other, generating tension, leading us directly into the dynamic action sequence.

Sarah is the lead-in to everything else, so we follow her escape attempt first. As the night attendant notices a broken mop handle, Sarah lunges and viciously subdues him. She moves down the hall like a cat on the hunt, holding "the baton like a pro, laid back along her forearm police-style. She looks *dangerous*."

Cut to the T-1000 at the nurses' station as the cops who were questioning Sarah leave.

Step by step, detail by detail, image by image, they build the sequence. The security guard makes his rounds, stops for a cup of coffee. Suddenly the very ground he walks on ripples into life, and a shape emerges out of the linoleum: It is the security guard's double image.

One of the things that makes the sequence so effective is that Cameron cast identical twins to play the security cop. As the guard walks down the corridor we experience an eerie feeling, heightened by the music.

ANGLE ON FLOOR *as the guard's feet pass through* FRAME. *An instant later* the floor starts to move. *It shivers and bulges upward like a liquid mass, still retaining the two-tone of the tile. It hunches up silently into a quivering shadow in the darkness behind the guard.*

Up ahead we hear typing. The night nurse has her back to us, working. The guard stops at the drinking fountain. Bends to take a sip. Behind him the fluid mass has reached six feet of height and begins to resolve rapidly into a human figure. It loses the color and texture of the tile and becomes . . . THE GUARD.

The T-1000's mass has been spread out a quarter of an inch thick over several square yards of floor. The guard walked over the T-1000, and his structure was sampled in that instant. Now we see it drawing in and pulling up to form the figure of the guard.

The T-1000/guard's feet are the last to form, the last of the "liquid floor" pulling in to form shiny black guard shoes. The shoes detach with a faint sucking sound from the real floor as the T-1000/guard takes its first step.

The real guard spins at the sound of footsteps to see . . . himself. *He has one deeply disturbing moment to consider the ramifications of that. Then he sees his double calmly raise its hand and, inexplicably, point its right index finger directly at the real guard's face, about a foot away. In a split second, the finger spears out, elongating into a thin steel rod, which snaps out like a stiletto, slamming into the guard's eye. It punches into the corner of the eye, past the eyeball like a transorbital lobotomy tool, and emerges from the back of the guard's skull.*

*Life quietly empties from the guard's face. He is dead weight now, hanging from the rod/finger, which suddenly retracts—*SSNICK. *As the guard slumps, the T-1000 takes his weight easily with one hand and walks him, like it's carrying a suit on a hanger, back toward the night desk. The wounds are so tiny, no blood drips onto the floor.*

When the nurse asks what the guard has, he replies, "Just some trash."

Tension builds further as Sarah moves toward the nurses' station. Inside, Silberman is with an orderly; the T-1000 passes the window. Sarah slams the police baton into Silberman, breaking his arm. She takes him hostage, loads a huge syringe with Liquid-Plumr, and jabs it against his neck, "so don't fuck with me." They start moving toward the outside.

As John and the Terminator approach the guard gate, John reminds him, "You're not gonna kill anyone," and makes the cyborg swear on it. With that, the Terminator pulls his .45 and shoots the guard in the knee. "He'll live," says the Terminator.

Cross-cut to Sarah forcing her way through the lockout corridor. The escape sequence has now been set up with all the elements: Sarah trying to get out of the maze of locked corridors; the T-1000 hunting her; and John and the Terminator attempting to rescue her. The sequence itself is seven-plus pages of nonstop action—more than seven minutes of screen time.

As Sarah races toward freedom, her worst fear comes true: The Terminator steps out of the elevator to confront her. "Sarah reacts, stricken by the image from her worst nightmares. Her eyes go wide as momentum carries her forward. Her bare feet slip on the slick tile. She slams to the floor, staring up at the leather-clad figure with the shotgun. She loses all semblance of courage and some of her sanity. . . . In slowed-down dream time, Sarah scrambles back along the floor like a crab, spinning and clawing her way to her feet along the wall. She runs like the wind, like in her nightmare."

When John steps out and sees his mother freak out, he immediately knows what happened. He races after her, but before he can reach her she's caught by the orderlies as the Terminator comes up from behind. *It is exactly her nightmare,* the stage directions state emphatically. The Terminator handles the orderlies as if they had "stepped on a land mine," then goes after Silberman struggling with Sarah. The doctor "is grabbed by a roll of skin at the back of his neck and lifted like a cat. The doctor feels his feet pedaling above the ground. He looks into the expressionless face. And it hits him. Sarah was right: This guy *isn't* human. He feels the fabric of his reality crumbling."

The Terminator extends a hand to help her up and says, "Come with me if you want to live."

As she gets up, the last element of the escape sequence comes into play: The T-1000 strides down the corridor, heading straight for the lockout bars. But something strange happens; he

reaches the bars. It doesn't stop. Its body divides like Jell-O around the bars. As it squeezes itself through like metal Play-Doh, its surface reforms perfectly on our side. We see it deform and squeeze through like a viscous paste forced past an obstacle. . . . There is a CLINK and we see that the guard's gun has caught against the bars . . . the only solid object. The T-1000 turns its wrist and tries again, slipping the gun endwise through the gap.

It's important to remember that the special effects in the script were written before they were created. They are woven directly into the story line and integrated right into the action. They become part of the story, not an adjunct to it, as the effects in *Tron* or *The Last Starfighter* were.

"Go!" yells the Terminator. "Run!" Sarah doesn't need to be told twice. The T-1000 walks toward them, opening fire with the Browning Hi-Power. Once again, the battle rages between the Terminator sent to protect John, and the T-1000, sent to kill him.

Pinch I is the escape from Pescadero State Hospital; once outside the unit, Sarah, John, and the Terminator are relentlessly pursued by the T-1000. The T-1000 chases them into the elevator, even though his "head is blown apart into two doughy masses lying on the shoulders, but re-forms quickly."

We see more of his shape-changing abilities as his arms become knives and prybars slicing through the reinforced steel of the elevator as if it were Jell-O. They race into the garage, and Sarah forcefully commandeers a hospital security car; they jump inside, and they're outta there. But the T-1000 doesn't quit.

Terminator cuts the wheel hard. The car slows into a reverse 180, swapping ends with a screech. T-1000 is almost on them. Terminator punches it. The car accelerates forward. T-1000 leaps. Lands on the trunk. Its hand is a metal crowbar slammed down through the trunk lid. Feet dragging on the pavement, it slams its other hand down, punching another metal hook into the trunk lid, pulling itself up. Terminator turns to Sarah.

TERMINATOR

> Drive.

Terminator heaves himself half out of the driver's window. Sarah slaps her foot down on the throttle and steers from the passenger side.

T-1000, fully on the car now, holds on with one hook hand while it slams the other into the back window, sweeping away the glass and missing John by inches as he ducks. It draws back for another swing, lunging forward as—

Terminator whips the shotgun down over the roof of the car. Fires point-blank. Hits the T-1000's arm just above the "hand" which anchors it to the car. The 12-gauge blows the arm apart, severing the hook hand.

T-1000 tumbles backward off the accelerating car. John looks out the back window, his eyes wide. He sees the T-1000 roll to his feet and continue running. But he's dropping way behind now. Sarah has the car floored and the liquid-metal killer won't catch them on foot.

John watches, in awe, as the "crowbar hand," stuck into the trunk right in front of him, reverts to the neutral polyalloy, a kind of thick mercury. The gray metal slides off the trunk of the car and falls onto the road to lie there in a quivering blob.

The car speeds off into the night. REVERSE on the T-1000, walking now, coming right up into close-up, watching the taillights recede. It looks down.

ANGLE ON BLACKTOP, tight on the liquid metal blob. Next to it is the T-1000's shiny cop shoe. The mercury blob crawls and rejoins the main mass, disappearing into the "shoe."

The car zooms down the interstate, lights out. They are free at last, at least for now. There is room to breathe, and some time for mother and son who have been separated for so long to catch up with each other.

Sarah is angry that John went to the hospital to rescue her. "You can't risk yourself, *not even for me, do you understand?* You're too important!" The stage directions read, "We see his chin quiver. He's a tough kid, but all he really wants is for her to love him."

He starts to cry, but Sarah has no pity, no mercy. "*You* can't cry, John. Other kids can afford to cry. *You can't.*" At this point the Terminator "sees the water leaking from his eyes. It doesn't make any sense to him." "What's wrong with your eyes?" he asks.

So much for reunions.

They pull into a deserted gas station to assess the damage. Terminator sews up Sarah as John looks in wonder at the Terminator's leather jacket riddled with bullet holes.

At this point there is a scene written that was filmed but later omitted. John asks the Terminator if he "can learn." He replies, "My CPU is a neural-net processor . . . a learning computer. But Skynet presets the switch to 'read only' when we are sent out alone." Sarah cynically comments that it "doesn't want you thinking too much, huh?" But John asks if we can "reset the switch."

There follows a scene where Sarah and John operate on the Terminator to remove the pin switch that governs the cyborg's learning capabilities. They change the mode from "read" to "write," thus enabling the Terminator to learn from experience, one of the major themes of the movie. After they remove it, Sarah goes to smash the little ceramic rectangle brain, but John stops her. "Don't kill him," he tells his mother, "it's the only proof we have of the future . . . about the war and all that." "We may never have this opportunity again," she says. John looks at her and says, "Mom, if I'm supposed to ever be this great leader, you should start listening to my leadership ideas once in a while. 'Cause if you won't, nobody else will."

"Smart kid. He's got her. She nods, reluctantly," read the stage directions. They implant the pin in the "write" mode, and the Terminator springs back to life. "Was there a problem?" he asks.

Mother and son look at each other. "No problem. None whatsoever," he replies.

They omitted this scene from the final film because it was felt it was unnecessary to the plot, so it was cut for time. Instead, Cameron dropped in a voice-over line of the Terminator: "The more contact I have with humans, the more I learn," he says, and condenses the information of a three-page scene into one line. Such is the magic of film.

The next morning they steal a station wagon and head south. And, as they drive, a banter begins between the Terminator and this ten-year-old kid, who wants to teach the Terminator to be "cool." It is the first lesson in the cyborg's "humanness."

"If someone comes off to you with an attitude, you say, 'Eat me.' If you wanna shine them on, it's '*Hasta la vista,* baby' . . . or 'Later, dickwad.' Or if someone gets upset you say, 'Chill out.' Like that. Or you can do combinations."

"Chill out, dickwad," intones the Terminator. "Great," says John. "You're getting it."

"*No problemo,*" he replies.

This takes us up to the Mid-Point.

13

Things to Come:

The Mid-Point and Beyond

A good action film lets the audience breathe. The story should move forward in a series of peaks and valleys. In B action movies the action starts on a high note and continues in a straight line throughout the entire film. There is no explanation of character or premise; it is just nonstop action. After a while you just get bored, as you do when you watch a porno film. A good action film will have situations and characters that are interesting and keep the story moving forward; but there are moments that are quiet and contemplative, rest points between the strong action scenes. Peaks and valleys; breathing space.

In *Terminator 2* the Mid-Point is a rest point, the place where these strange comrades in arms recuperate from their wounds, establish a connection with each other, and make a plan of attack. All three know it's only a matter of time before the T-1000 tracks them down.

They stop for some cheeseburgers at a roadside truck stand and watch a couple of kids play with their water pistols. "Bang, bang, you're dead!" goes the familiar refrain. Obvious, yes, a little too direct, yes, but it sets up a throwaway line made up on the set and spoken by the kid's mother: "Break it up before I wring both your necks." John watches this little drama and turns to the Terminator:

"We're not gonna make it, are we? People, I mean." To which the Terminator replies, "It is in your nature to destroy yourselves."

It is this spiritual tone that elevates *Terminator 2* so far above the normal Hollywood action film. More about that later.

In most films there's no time to spend a moment on a scene like this, but in the context of a nonstop action piece it is this very *contradiction of image* that makes it stand out in such bold relief.

During this exchange, Sarah is quiet, but after a moment she turns to the Terminator and tells him she wants to know about Skynet, which is responsible for what's going to happen on August 29, 1997. Terminator explains that Miles Dyson will create a "revolutionary type of microprocessor. In three years Cyberdyne will become the largest supplier of military computer systems. All stealth bombers are upgraded with Cyberdyne computers, becoming fully unmanned." And the politicians in Washington figure they can "let a computer run the whole show," Sarah says. The whole thing is run by machines. Terminator continues to outline the near future: "Human decisions are removed from strategic defense. Skynet begins to learn at a geometric rate. It becomes self-aware at 2:14 A.M. Eastern Time, August 29. In a panic, they try to pull the plug."

And so, the big bang. Our worst nightmare.

Sarah wants to know everything about Miles Dyson: "What he looks like. Where he lives. Everything." She knows there's only one course of action she can pursue: If she can eliminate Dyson, eliminate the microprocessor he has yet to create, she can prevent this particular future from happening.

This takes us to the Mid-Point, when they pull into a deserted desert compound near the Mexican border. Sarah approaches an old, dilapidated trailer and confronts Enrique, who is pointing a 12-gauge pump at her. As they rekindle their friendship, the Terminator and John are uncovering an arsenal of buried weapons; rifles, pistols, a rocket launcher, mortars, hand grenades, radio gear.

Sarah emerges from the trailer dressed in boots, fatigue pants, black T-shirt. Shades. "She looks hard," the script reads.

Inside the compound, John and the Terminator are growing closer. The ten-year-old explains, "I grew up in places like this, so I just thought it was how people lived . . . riding around in helicopters. Learning how to blow shit up."

"The Terminator pulls back a canvas tarp, revealing a squat, heavy weapon with six barrels clustered in a blunt cylinder. Chain ammo is fed from a canister sitting next to it. A GE minigun—the most fearsome antipersonnel weapon of the Vietnam era. The Terminator hefts it, then looks at John as if to say, 'Can I? Please?' "

"It's definitely you," John tells him.

As the Terminator fixes the water pump on the old pickup, John lays down a steady stream of dialogue, telling us more about his childhood: "I wish I coulda met my real dad," he says wistfully. "Mom and him were only together for one night, but she still loves him, I guess. I see her crying sometimes. She denies it totally, of course. Like she says she got something in her eye."

"Why do you cry?" the Terminator asks. John doesn't know why. "We just cry. When it hurts." Does "pain cause it?" the cyborg asks. "No, it's different. . . . It's when there's nothing wrong with you but you hurt anyway. You get it?" the kid says.

No, he doesn't get it. Yet. But the character arc of the Terminator is now beginning to shift. He is learning about human behavior, learning about emotions and feelings, all the things he is not programmed for.

And as the Terminator and the kid bond together, Sarah makes an observation about them:

SARAH'S POV . . . we don't hear what John and the Terminator are saying. It is a soundless pantomime as John is trying to show some other gestures to the cyborg. Trying to get him to walk more casually. John walks, then the Terminator tries it, then John gestures wildly, talking very fast . . . explaining the fundamental principles of cool. They try it again. Continued ad lib as we hear:

SARAH (VO)
Watching John with the machine, it was suddenly so clear. The Terminator would never stop, it would never leave him . . . it would always be there. And it would never hurt him, never shout at him or get drunk

> SARAH (VO cont'd.)
> and hit him, or say it couldn't spend time
> with him because it was too busy. And it
> would die to protect him. Of all the would-
> be fathers who came and went over the
> years, this thing, this machine, was the only
> one who measured up. In an insane world, it
> was the sanest choice.

This scene foreshadows the end sequence, especially the line, "It would die to protect him." It is every son's fantasy of his father figure.

As the sun fades and long shadows stretch across the desert compound, Sarah sits at a picnic table. "She hasn't slept in twenty-four hours and she seems to have the weight of the whole world on her shoulders. She idly starts to carve something on the tabletop. . . . Her head droops. She closes her eyes."

Sarah's nightmare begins, and we are part of it. Children play as a younger Sarah leads her little two-year-old through the playground. She sees a woman on the other side of the fence, and when she looks closer she is surprised to see herself, in present time. She looks at herself behind the fence yelling, screaming, pleading to the mother and child, but no sound comes out.

SUDDENLY THE SKY EXPLODES.

And, we're into the nightmare. It is horrifying. She watches her dream self explode into flame and burn to skeleton; and where life once occupied the face of the earth, there is nothing but scorched bone and ash.

The future. This galvanizing force propels her into action. Sarah wakes up, startled, "looks down at the words she has carved on the table . . . they are 'NO FATE.' Sarah struggles to breathe, running her hand through her hair, which is soaked with sweat. She can escape from the hospital, but she can't escape from the madness which haunts her. . . . Then something changes in her eyes. She slams her knife down in the tabletop, embedding it deeply in the words."

And we shock cut directly to her striding purposefully across the compound. She "carries a small nylon pack and a CAR-15 assault rifle. Her face is an impassive mask. She has become a terminator." She throws the gun into the pickup and slams it into gear. John runs after her, but it's no use. She doesn't stop. She's on a mission —to set the future straight.

It's interesting to note the changes in Sarah and the Terminator that have begun to evolve at this point in the screenplay. This is merely the first stage, the first fluttering of wings. Sarah is becoming more like a machine as she seeks to fulfill her dramatic need, to make the future safe for humankind, and the Terminator is beginning to learn about the human species. There's also a larger subtext here, and that should be mentioned: As technology becomes more advanced, human beings seem to become more dehumanized. Sarah becomes a machine so she can kill Dyson; Dyson is also like a machine, obsessed with finding the secret of the little microprocessor, and forgoing his family obligations.

"The future is not set. There is no fate but what we make," John says regarding Sarah's message carved into the top of the picnic table. "She intends to change the future somehow," the Terminator replies. Of course; she's going to kill Miles Dyson and thus prevent the future from happening. "There is no fate but what we make."

When the Terminator responds, "Killing Dyson might actually prevent the war," John gets pissed and states, "Haven't you learned *anything*?! Haven't you figured out why you can't kill people?"

The Terminator looks at him blankly, unable to comprehend the concept.

Again, the last line of dialogue from one scene leads us directly into the next—and Miles Dyson.

We met Dyson earlier, in Act I, but didn't find out too much about him. Now, of course, we know that he's the man directly responsible for creating the microprocessor that will change the fate of the world. But Cameron and Wisher know they cannot present him as a heavy, or "bad guy"; Dyson's character must be presented sympathetically. It would be easy to point the finger and say he's the bad guy. That's the logical thing. But then, life is never logical, is it?

We see Dyson in a totally unexpected context: We see he's a nice guy with a beautiful family, a man with the same problems all of us have (his wife wants him to spend more time with her and their children). In short, we can identify with him and feel sympathy for him. In this way Cameron and Wisher play against the grain of the scene, which makes good screenwriting.

Miles Dyson's house is "high-tech and luxurious. Lots of glass," the script reads. "Dyson's study is lit bluish with the glow from his computer monitors. He is at the terminal, working. Where else? We see him clearly in a long shot from an embankment behind the house."

Outside, Sarah moves into position, raises the CAR-15 rifle, and screws the long, heavy cylinder of a sound suppressor onto the end of the barrel.

As we watch Dyson's home life, we see through his actions that he's obsessed with cracking the secret that eludes him. As we follow his child's radio-controlled truck through the halls (in a shot that's reminiscent of a famous shot in Kubrick's *The Shining*), we see a red dot appear on the back of Dyson's head. Van Ling, in the illustrated screenplay of *Terminator 2,* writes that "the shock of seeing the red dot of Sarah's laser designator appear on the back of Dyson's head plays better than any cross-cutting suspense sequence might . . . and drives home the coldness of Sarah as a terminator —the first time we see her as an assassin."

We hold on the red dot on the back of Dyson's head until, suddenly, *thump*! His son's toy truck slams into his foot, breaking his concentration. Dyson jerks, startled, and looks down to see what happened when POP! His monitor screen is blown out, spraying him with glass.

Sarah pumps round after round into the house, shattering everything. Dyson lunges to the floor as his wife screams hysterically. The house is literally blown apart as Sarah totally loses it, locked in the frenzy of her fury. Sarah moves into the plush living room and confronts the terrified family.

"It's all your fault!" Sarah screams as Dyson tries to understand what's going on. "We see her psyching herself to pull the trigger . . . needing now to hate this man she doesn't know," read the stage directions. "She's bathed in sweat, and it runs into her eyes. Blinking, she wipes it fast with one hand, then gets it back on the gun. The .45 is trembling. TIGHT ON SARAH as we see the forces at war behind her eyes. She looks into the faces of Dyson, Tarissa [his wife], and Danny, the little boy. Sarah takes a sharp breath and all the muscles in her arms contract as she tenses to fire. But her finger won't do it. She lowers the gun very slowly. It drops to her side in one hand. All the breath and energy seem to go out of her. . . . She backs away, slumps against a wall, slides to her knees. The gun hangs limply from her fingers. She rests her cheek against the wall."

At that moment the front door is kicked in by John and the Terminator. John immediately sees what's happening and rushes to his mother's side. She "reaches out and takes his shoulders, drawing him to her. She hugs him and a great sob wells up from deep inside her, from a spring she had thought long dry. She hugs him fiercely as the sobs rack her. John clutches her shoulders. It is all he ever wanted."

When Dyson asks, "Who are you people?" it's time to show and tell. John tells the Terminator to show him the future. The Terminator takes a knife and cuts his arm just below the elbow, then strips away the skin, revealing a "skeleton made of bright metal and laced with hydraulic actuators."

It is the same hand that is locked away in the lab at Cyberdyne. Dyson recognizes it immediately. "Now listen very carefully," the Terminator says to the scientist.

We don't have to hear what is said. We know the story. So all we need is Sarah's brief voice-over explanation of the things to come: "Dyson listened while the Terminator laid it all down. Skynet. Judgment Day . . . the history of things to come. It's not every day you find out you're responsible for three billion deaths. He took it pretty well, considering. . . ."

This, of course, sets us up for what happens next. If Dyson is successful in creating the final piece in the puzzle that creates the probable future, the only way they can change the future is to annihilate everything relating to that future: All the research, files, equipment, and disks at the Cyberdyne factory must be destroyed. "Now?" Dyson asks.

We cut to the Cyberdyne factory. Another good example of "enter late and get out early."

Over this we hear Sarah's turmoil: "The future," Sarah says in voice-over narration, "always so clear to me, had become like a black highway at night. We were in uncharted territory now—making up history as we went along."

We enter the Cyberdyne factory, Pinch II, and we're ready to strap ourselves in for what we know will be a tremendous action sequence.

They make their way inside, manage to "convince" the guard to let them into the security area, and make their way upstairs. Dyson explains the vault "needs two keys to open, mine and one from the security station." But security guard number two finds guard number one locked in the bathroom and switches on the silent alarm. Dyson tries to access the lock on the vault, but it doesn't work. "We should abort the mission," he says. But Sarah won't have it: "We're going all the way," she states emphatically.

When the security guard calls the cops, we have all the elements we need to create a highly charged, tension-filled, cross-cutting action sequence. All the pieces are in place, save one—the T-1000, and that will come in later.

Through multiple explosions, fire, deadly halon gas, and general all-around mayhem, they force their way into the heart of the computer complex. Fittingly, John gets them inside; he breaks into the lab the same way he broke into the ATM machine—using his makeshift keyboard. The Terminator moves through all the physical obstacles without effort, always making sure his "wards" are safe. These actions are what make him seem heroic, a figure larger than life, willing to sacrifice his life, if necessary, for the future.

Dyson indicates which things to destroy, and they waste no time doing it. "I've worked for years on this thing," Dyson says, then wields an ax and demolishes it.

Police and SWAT teams surround the building and move into position. The Terminator tells the others that he'll take care of the police, and John reminds him of his promise that he's not going to kill anyone. "Trust me," he responds in a line now famous, and moves to the large floor-to-ceiling windows.

He stands there in the glare of police searchlights and opens fire. The police chopper swings in close as we intercut John and Dyson breaking into the vault area. The SWAT team makes its way up the stairs as the Terminator keeps the police at bay. True to his word, there are no casualties.

But Dyson has been fatally hit. In the moral order of things it is appropriate that the man whose fate it is to create the probable future should be the very man who destroys it. The technology that destroys mankind is now playing a part in saving it; the death of the man brings the death of his work, and the future is saved. At least for now.

John, Sarah, and the Terminator make their way out of the building, while in the vault, "Dyson is lying amid the ruins of his dream," the script reads. "Sprawled on the floor, he has his back propped up against the desk. He is bathed in his own blood, which runs out in long fingers across the tiles. His breathing is shallow and raspy. He holds the book, trembling, above the switch. CUT TO THE PUPIL OF HIS EYE at the moment of death, the instant the light fades from his eyes and he is gone. His arm drops and he falls forward . . . as the face of the building EXPLODES in an eruption of glass and fire."

Amid the fire, smoke, and debris we see a lone LAPD cop moving through the wreckage on his motorcycle. It is the T-1000 come to haunt them.

The escape from Cyberdyne is the Plot Point at the end of Act II. We follow John, Sarah, and the Terminator as they reach the lobby of the building and suddenly confront the SWAT team. Tear gas is tossed into the elevator. The Terminator tells them to put on their gas masks and stay put, and he strides forward defiantly, directly into the fire of the SWAT team. "The corridor is filled with CRACKING THUNDER. The rounds tear into the Terminator's chest. Stomach. Face. Thighs. His leather jacket leaps and jerks as the rounds hit him. . . . The Terminator draws his .45 smoothly. Unhurried. He shoots the nearest man in the left thigh. As he screams and drops, the Terminator shoots him in the right thigh," then rips a tear-gas launcher away from a fallen cop.

"He fires three gas grenades into the lobby. It fills rapidly with the white gas, cutting visibility to a few feet. It is total pandemonium. . . ." The Terminator climbs into the police van, and after a few moments we see THE SWAT VAN CRASHING INTO THE LOBBY in an explosion of glass and debris. The cops scatter as the van screeches across the lobby floor, turns in a smoking one-eighty, then slides to a stop in front of the bank of elevators. The Terminator backs up until he seals the corridor with the back of the van.

"Sarah and John stumble along the corridor, coughing. They leap into the back of the van, and the Terminator hits the throttle. The van roars across the lobby and exits through blown-out windows."

On the second floor, the T-1000, astride his Kawasaki, sees the trio escaping. "It knows. It looks around, sees the helicopter hovering outside the building, and does not hesitate. It twists full throttle and BLASTS OUT THROUGH THE GLASS, airborne on the motorcycle. It rockets across the gap to the hovering chopper and slams into the canopy. . . . Nightmarishly, the pilot watches as the T-1000 smashes its head through the Plexiglas canopy and rapidly POURS ITSELF through the jagged hole. It re-forms instantly." The T-1000 tells the pilot to "get out." The man nods, opens the door, and leaps out.

It's a funny bit.

The chase is on—taking us to Act III and the Resolution. From here on it is full-blown, nonstop action.

14

The Perfect Sacrifice:

The Tin Man Gets a Heart

OKAY, BUCKLE YOUR SEAT BELTS, HERE IT COMES. . . .

That's the way the screenplay reads at the beginning of Act III. The entire act is an action sequence. From page one, word one, everything in the story has been leading to this moment. All good action films—whether it be a *Star Wars, Aliens, Dances With Wolves,* or even *Witness, The Silence of the Lambs,* or *The Terminator*—have carefully structured and set up their story lines in Act I, expanded them through character and conflict in Act II, just to reach that point in Act III where the story can carry itself. Resolution, remember, means solution—the solution to your story, and this is the moment when we can pay everything off, when the story literally resolves itself.

If you look at a schlocky exploitation action film, you'll find that action replaces character. Instead of building and defining the characters in Act I or Act II, they simply replace any needed character scenes with action sequences, so the action continues non-stop. There's no breathing space for the audience to get to know and understand the characters. The result is usually a slick, non-stop action piece sacrificing character to action.

But if you set up the characters and situation in Act I, you're ready to roll when you hit Act III. In *Terminator 2,* Act III hits on the run—John, Sarah, and the Terminator explode out of the Cyberdyne factory in a torrent of glass and flame, with the T-1000 hot on their trail.

The three of them drive down the highway in the commandeered SWAT van that "is a rolling armory. There are rifles, ballistic vests, all manner of equipment." As they race away, the police helicopter with the T-1000 at the controls stays right on their tail. Sarah takes the initiative. She yanks down an M-16 and starts blasting away at the helicopter. As the van spins and speeds down the freeway, the T-1000 is simultaneously flying and shooting. If you look closely during this part of the chase sequence you'll see a few cuts of the T-1000 using *four hands:* two to shoot and reload its weapon, and two to fly the helicopter.

Sarah takes a bullet in the thigh and is slammed hard against the floor. As she writhes in pain, the helicopter gets closer and closer, then SLAMS into the back of the van. The force of the impact cripples the helicopter and it "hits the pavement, flips sideways, and cartwheels . . . smashing itself into a shapeless mass of twisted metal." It's a nice action piece.

At this point it might be interesting to note that one of the basic screenwriting principles James Cameron has used from the beginning of his career now comes into play. When the audience thinks the film is over is when "they should be suddenly thrust into a new territory that heightens the emotional experience," Cameron says. "If you, as a screenwriter, can create certain ground rules and get the audience into your rhythm," Cameron continues, "you can get them right out to the end of the dock, then give them a big kick in the ass and they're going to suddenly find themselves in a new place where they never thought the journey was going to take them."

Just look at Cameron's films and you can see what he's talking about. In *Aliens,* the entire film is a journey into new territory, but the final confrontation takes place not in an alien environment but on the familiar ground of Ripley's spaceship. When Ripley breathes a sigh of relief thinking she's safe, that it's all over, that's when she suddenly realizes the nightmare has followed her back "home." But the tool she finds to save herself has been there the entire time. It "makes the twist something of a surprise," Cameron confides.

In *The Abyss,* the final Confrontation takes place on the bottom of the ocean, another world. The first time I saw the film, I was totally riveted with Ed Harris's free fall, the wall dive sequence that is the Plot Point at the end of Act II. I never thought he would hit bottom. Down and down and down and down and down he falls, and when he finally does land on the bottom of the ocean, he is literally in another world. No matter what you may think about the special effects, and whether the computer graphic images of the "Water Weenie" worked or didn't work, it is effective.

In all of Cameron's films, it is this drive to explore new territory that inspires him. "When I start a deep dive over a coral reef wall," he observes, "and the wall continues down for two thousand or three thousand feet, you're filled with this incredible desire to go deeper and deeper to find out what's there. My marine biology training teaches me that you run out of interesting stuff about two hundred feet down and it doesn't start getting interesting again until you're down about a thousand feet, but somewhere in there you're dead."

This screenwriting technique is something that Cameron began using in *The Terminator.* After Kyle Reese (Michael Biehn) blows up the tanker truck and the Terminator is seemingly blown to pieces, Sarah rushes to him. Then suddenly out of the fire steps the Terminator, and the audience collectively goes, "Oh, no, it's not over," and we brace ourselves for another round. Sarah helps the injured Reese into the factory [Cameron likes factories and machines because of their visual element], where he takes a pipe bomb and basically sacrifices himself when he shoves it into the Terminator and blows it to pieces. But it ain't dead yet, and it is Sarah (as it dramatically should be) who finally manages to crush it in a compression unit. Only now does the light in the eyes of the seemingly indestructible Terminator go out.

These two sequences were the two "kickers" in *The Terminator.* It seems like these little sequences are a James Cameron signature, like Hitchcock's shot of himself in his movies that was his little "signature."

OKAY, BUCKLE YOUR SEAT BELTS, HERE IT COMES. . . .

The SWAT van loses a tire, and screams to a stop, flipping over on its side. For the chase sequence to continue we need a vehicle change. So as the T-1000 emerges from the shattered helicopter, a tanker truck carrying a load of liquid nitrogen brakes hard to avoid the helicopter wreckage. Before the driver can ask the T-1000 if it's all right, a blade slices through the driver, and the cyborg climbs into the cab and floors it. The liquid nitrogen is a wonderful touch, and it's set up here so it can be paid off later.

"We need your truck," says the Terminator to the man driving a makeshift pickup. The trio climb inside, and the Terminator steps on the accelerator, but not much happens. The tanker bears down on them, and barrels into the old pickup, bashing it across the road. The Terminator slides to the passenger side and tells John to take over the wheel. The Terminator smashes the windshield, then fires the M-79 one-handed. It explodes against the tanker, blowing a hole in the cargo, and liquid nitrogen spills through the opening, leaving a vapor tail behind it like a comet streaking through the night sky.

"John cuts across the highway and takes an off-ramp," read the stage directions, getting us ready for the "kicker." The tanker screams forward, pushing the little pickup toward the steel mill, and there's nothing John can do about it.

"The semi rams the back of the pickup again. Spewing smoke and vapor like some demon locomotive, the tractor-trailer pounds into the back of the pickup, driving it right through the intersection at the bottom of the ramp, and straight toward the steel mill." The Terminator pulls himself on the roof of the pickup, leaps across to the truck, and fires his grenade directly into the face of the T-1000. "The EXPLOSION blows out all the glass and fills the cab with smoke and fire. The Terminator grabs onto the air horn as the truck starts to SHUDDER AND SCREAM. IT IS JACKKNIF-ING.

"Almost dream-slow the cab begins to swing sideways, until its tires are shrieking over the pavement. The tractor is smashed back at right angles to the tanker-trailer, which begins to slide broad-side.

"The juggernaut bucks and shudders as the tires are smoking sideways across the pavement. It begins to topple. The Terminator holds on as the side of the cab becomes the top. With an unholy scream, like the unoiled hubs of Hell, the whole rig slides on its side at 60 miles per hour toward the steel mill. A sheet of sparks sixty feet wide trails behind it on the pavement."

Pickup and tanker explode through the entrance of the mill, and there is a thunderous carnage of twisted steel. The tanker splits wide open, and a river of liquid nitrogen pours out at −230 degrees.

How ingenious to use liquid nitrogen; how inventive. "The T-1000 staggers, moving slowly, painfully," read the stage directions. "It has finally been affected by something. Its feet are freezing to the ground as it walks. . . .

"Clink! One of its feet breaks off at a glassy ankle. It stumbles forward, and its other foot snaps off. As it catches its balance on the stump of its other ankle, the whole lower leg shatters at the impact. It topples forward to its knees. Catches itself on one hand. Liquid nitrogen flows around the hand.

"Now the hand is stuck to the pavement. The T-1000 pulls and Clink! the hand snaps off at the wrist. It looks stupidly at the glassy stump of a wrist. For the first time we see an expression on its face we know to be a true one. The expression is pain. Agony. Its mouth opens in a soundless scream as the hoarfrost races up its legs, across its body. And that's the position it freezes in. It has become a statue, kneeling in the frozen vapor, that surprised look of agony frozen on its face. The liquid nitrogen stops flowing and begins to evaporate. The Terminator, just beyond the boundary of the cold, can see the T-1000 clearly. 'Hasta la vista, baby,' he says, and fires his weapon, blowing the T-1000 into a million pieces."

It looks like the end.

But this is a Cameron movie. Here comes "the kicker." We see the T-1000 shards melting, liquefying, the droplets creeping together. Plip. Plop. Merging together into a sliding, slithering blob of mercury. Oh, Jesus!

Sarah, John, and the Terminator fight their way through the intense heat and go deeper into the bowels of the machinery, the air vibrating with a pounding roar. Sarah is hurt, her leg is bleeding badly, and it takes all of John's efforts to drag her forward.

We watch as the T-1000 comes together and rises into frame, fully formed. Sarah and John move deeper into the maze of the steel mill. With perfect devotion the Terminator stays behind to confront the T-1000 and save the young boy's life. The two behemoths dance in battle as Sarah lowers John onto a conveyor belt in a last-ditch effort to escape. The T-1000 slams the Terminator into a large machine, pinning his arm to the moving parts. We can hear the servos whining with overload.

The T-1000 turns and goes after Sarah. As he does, we see the Terminator straining to reach a steel bar. It is an effort of sheer will, as his dramatic need to protect his young ward remains unshakable.

Sarah, weak and struggling, fires a riot gun into the T-1000, but it quickly re-forms. Before she can get another shell into the magazine, a steel needle slams through her shoulder. Another needle is pointed at her eye, and the T-1000 says, "Call to John. Now."

Before she can respond, a heavy steel bar slashes him in two. The Terminator is back! The two cyborgs go at it, blow for blow, servos straining, until the T-1000 slams a heavy steel bar through the back of the Terminator, pinning him to the steel catwalk like a harpooned fish. Slowly we watch as the light goes out of his eyes.

When John crawls out of the shadows he sees two Sarahs, and one of them is pointing a shotgun directly at him. For a moment he doesn't know which is which, until the one with the gun tells him to "get out of the way." He ducks. The other Sarah spins, turning into the T-1000 as the real Sarah fires the shotgun, blowing him apart. She fires again. And again. And again. Each time the T-1000 is hit it staggers backward to the edge of the molten steel, until she's out of ammunition. The T-1000 is mangled, twisted, deformed—but still "breathing."

We intercut back to the Terminator as the light in its eyes suddenly springs into life. He struggles to reach the M-79 that lies just within reach, picks it up, staggers to his feet, and goes after the T-1000. At this point it is interesting to note that the Terminator, with his face blown half apart, is both man and machine; the machine part cannot be killed, and his human awareness has taught him something about loyalty in his dedication to John. The unstoppable killer has become the unstoppable savior.

With his one good hand the Terminator hoists the M-79 and fires at the T-1000, the grenade exploding inside its body. "A huge hole is blown clean through it, and it is ripped open and peeled back, half inside-out," the script reads, the force of the explosion throwing it backward into the molten steel vat.

"The T-1000's head and upper body reappear above the molten steel. It is screaming. A terrifying, inhuman siren of a scream." We watch it in its death throes, changing and morphing and transforming its form into many of its different incarnations. Then it turns inside out, the screams of life finally dissolving into molten steel.

From dust to dust. Ashes to ashes, steel to steel . . . this time it's really the end of the machine. At least until *Terminator 3*—but that's not going to happen for many years.

The three tattered warriors pick themselves up wearily. "I need a vacation," quips the Terminator.

They walk to the edge of the pit. The Terminator looks down. "Is it dead?" John asks. "Terminated," replies the Terminator. John takes out the hand of the first terminator, throws it into the molten steel, and it vanishes. "And the chip," adds the Terminator. John tosses it into the smelter.

"Thank God it's finally over," Sarah says. The Terminator looks at her steadily and says, "No. There is another chip. And it must be destroyed also." He touches his metal finger to the side of his head. It takes John a moment to understand what he's talking about. "No!" he cries out. "Stay with us!" he begs the Terminator, who has become father, brother, friend, and protector to him. It is the closest he has ever come to having a real father, real friendship. We recall Sarah's words, "Of all the would-be fathers who came and went over the years, this thing, this machine, was the only one who measured up."

"I have to go away, John," says the Terminator. "Don't do it. *Please* . . . don't go . . ." John pleads as tears stream down his face.

"It must end here . . . *or I am the future*," says the Terminator, in a line that was later cut; he puts his hand on John's shoulder. He moves slightly, and the human side of his face comes into the light. He reaches toward John's face. His metal finger touches the tear trickling down his cheek. "I know now why you cry. But it is something I can never do," he says softly, gently. He understands what the young boy must be going through, but he also knows there is a larger purpose to his action. It is his human side talking; the Terminator's heroic transformation is complete.

"Are you afraid?" asks Sarah in a line that was omitted. "Yes," replies the Terminator. They lock eyes. "Warriors. Comrades," read the script. The Terminator and John embrace, then "he turns and steps off the edge. Slowly they watch him sink into the lava. He disappears . . . the metal hand sinking last . . . at the last second it forms into a fist with the thumb extended . . . *a final thumbs-up.* Then it is gone."

The emotional impact is tremendous—it leaves us in a state of stunned awe as we ponder the significance of his action.

We hold on this image of molten steel for a long moment, then dissolve into a little tag scene. We are racing down a dark highway at night as we hear Sarah's final voice-over: "The unknown future rolls toward us. I face it for the first time with a sense of hope, because if a machine, a terminator, can learn the value of human life, maybe we can, too."

Words to think about, to ponder and contemplate. Words to live by. When I first saw the film, the memory of James Joyce's last lines in *A Portrait of the Artist as a Young Man* kept echoing in my head: "I go for the millionth time to encounter reality, and to forge in the smithy of my soul the uncreated conscience of my race. O Father, O artificer, stand me now and ever in good stead." That was the feeling I had. It was like I had a peek into the window of the future, had just glimpsed the future of film. It was an ending that haunted me for days.

When I read the script I was surprised to find that the little tag scene had been conceived in the editing room after the film had been completed. As written, the last scene in the script was totally different from what was on the screen. It was what is called a "book end." (A "book end" is where the first and last scenes are continuations of each other—for example, opening with a scene, then going into flashback to tell the story, finally ending with the conclusion of the first scene. Joyce does this with the opening and closing sentence in *Finnegan's Wake*.) When I asked Jim Cameron's assistant about it, he told me the last scene had been shot, but after the previews it became obvious it didn't work, so Cameron dropped it.

Here it is, in its entirety. From the Terminator's sacrifice, we go to:

THE SUN, PURE IN A CLOUDLESS SKY. Tilting down reveals that we are in a park, very green. People are casually dressed, having fun. Cycling, reading . . . children are playing in a playground.

Beyond the line of trees we see the skyline of Washington, D.C., with the Capitol Building and the Washington Monument. The skyline is subtly changed, with a lot of new buildings, advanced high-rises.
A CARD APPEARS.

July 11, 2029

WE MOVE THROUGH THE PLAYGROUND. [Just like the opening] Children swinging on swings. Sliding down slides. Timeless things that four decades of technical advancement will not change. Over this we hear:

SARAH (VO)
August 29, 1997, came and went. Nothing
much happened. Michael Jackson turned
forty. There was no Judgment Day. People
went to work as they always do, laughed,
complained, watched TV, made love.

We pass a jungle gym, neither melted nor burned, but full of kids swinging and yelling raucously. Past it we drop down to see a boy pumping the pedals of a tricycle.

> SARAH (VO cont'd.)
> I wanted to run down the street yelling . . .
> to grab them all and say, "Every day from
> this day on is a gift. Use it well!" Instead I
> got drunk.

We come to rest on an elderly woman seated on a bench. It is Sarah, now sixty-four years old. The world has aged her, but she seems at peace in this moment. She speaks into a microcassette recorder.

> SARAH (VO cont'd.)
> That was more than thirty years ago. But the
> dark future which never came still exists for
> me, and it always will, like the traces of a
> dream lingering in the morning light. And
> the war against the machines goes on. Or, to
> be more precise, the war against those who
> build the wrong machines.

There is a man in his forties playing with two small children nearby. He turns. It is John Connor. Though he has the same stern features in adulthood, there is no eye patch, no scarring. He is far from the haggard man of grim destiny we saw in the world that might have been. But there is still penetrating intelligence, even wisdom, in his eyes.

> SARAH (VO cont'd.)
> John fights the war differently than it was
> foretold. Here, on the battlefield of the Sen-
> ate, the weapons are common sense . . .
> and hope.

A FOUR-YEAR-OLD GIRL runs to her to have her shoelace tied.

> GIRL
> Tie me, Grandma.

Grandma Sarah smiles. It is the only time we have seen her smile so far. She bends as the little girl puts her foot up on the bench. She ties as we hear:

SARAH (VO cont'd.)
The luxury of hope was given to me by the Terminator. Because if a machine can learn the value of human life . . . maybe we can, too.

Sarah ruffles the kid's hair as she runs off to play with her dad.

FADE OUT.

It's easy to see why the preview audience didn't respond. It seems out of place in the film. First of all, it takes place in the light, in sunshine, whereas most of the film seems to be dark and brooding, haunting. Also, it would be difficult to see Sarah this way after we've seen her as a warrior. It was a pretty clear-cut decision, so Cameron wisely dropped the scene.

As I was pondering the ending of the film, I realized it was the Terminator's action that affected me so deeply, his absolute willingness to sacrifice his life for the good of humankind. It is a noble action, a heroic action. It was his devotion to John that made his action so moving, so inspiring.

If you look at the template of the "hero" in classical myth and literature, you begin to sense the importance of the Terminator's actions. A hero is someone who gives up his or her life to something bigger, something larger than oneself. "Life consists in action," Aristotle declares, "and its end is a mode of action not a quality." Just look at Oedipus, at King Lear; it is their *actions* that make them tragic figures, and that's exactly what the Terminator does: He sacrifices his life, his microprocessor chip, for the future of humankind and the good of humanity. His action makes him heroic. It becomes, in the words of the Scriptures "the perfect sacrifice."

The Terminator's action becomes the perfect segue into Sarah's last line: ". . . if a machine, a terminator, can learn the value of human life, maybe we can, too." It is an echo of time past, a portent of things to come. Out of the sacrifice of a given life comes new life, a new way of being, a new way of becoming. It teaches us the value of life, leading to a transformation of consciousness.

It's quite possible the Terminator might be considered a kind of role model for the future American hero; God knows, we need it. Even though he's a machine, a cyborg, we see by his *actions* that he is someone who believes in a higher nature, a higher power, that he is someone willing to sacrifice his life for a cause, for a belief higher than his own.

There is a text from an ancient Hindu scripture that sums it up very well:

> A river doesn't drink its own water,
> A tree doesn't eat its own fruit,
> A man who gives his life for another
> is God
> Walking this earth.

The Silence
of the Lambs

15

Apples and Oranges:

The Silence of the Lambs

Recently I was talking with a prominent studio executive, and during the course of the conversation he began telling me his theory about what a film audience wants to see. He mentioned something called the "community of emotion," and when I asked him to explain, he said that when an audience watches a movie they almost become one entity. They are "swept" along on this tide of emotion, joined in this "community of emotion." Whatever their differences, whether man or woman, whether they're named Seth, Bill, Barbara, or Rebecca, whether they're white or black, Asian or Mexican, they are joined together in the fabric of a movie experience he called the "community of emotion."

All differences disappear. The audience becomes one.

I was struck by the truth of his observation, thought it accurate and astute.

Seeing *The Silence of the Lambs* reminded me of this "community of emotion." The audience I saw it with became so totally absorbed in the drama and tension that all of us reacted as one being, carried away on the same waves of emotion. The film is excellent, maybe even extraordinary, but what amazed me the most about it was that the material was a great screenplay adaptation of a great book.

Yes, Jonathan Demme's direction was wonderful; yes, all the performances were unique, outstanding; yes, it was skillfully edited and photographed; yes, yes, yes. But what made this film so extraordinary was that the script was a great adaptation of a great novel.

That doesn't happen very often. Usually when I see a movie adapted from a successful book, such as *Prince of Tides* (adapted by Patrick Conroy from his novel), I'm disappointed. Adapting a book into a screenplay is a very difficult and complicated process. What makes it so difficult is that the novel and the screenplay are different *forms,* as similar and as different as an apple and an orange.

Adaptation is a singular art. Adapting an existing work, whether it be a novel, play, magazine article, newspaper story, or biography, to a medium such as the screenplay, is difficult indeed. Not many can do it well. Each form is so different from the other that a screenplay adaptation should be considered an original screenplay.

In a novel the dramatic action of the story, the narrative line, is usually told inside the head of the main character; the reader knows his thoughts, feelings, memories, hopes, and fears. There may be chapters written from other characters' points of view, but the dramatic action always occurs *inside* the main character's head, within the *mindscape* of dramatic action.

If you look at a play, it, too, is different. There is the proscenium arch, of course, and the audience becomes the "fourth wall," and we eavesdrop on the characters and their situation. But the real action of the play occurs in the *words* the characters speak, through the *language* of dramatic action.

The screenplay, of course, is different; it is a story told in pictures, in dialogue and description, and placed within the context of dramatic structure.

Words and pictures; apples and oranges.

Very rarely does a great book turn into a great movie.

When the movie *The Silence of the Lambs* first came out in 1991, the word spread immediately that it was a very good film, a film that should not be missed. Because I was scheduled to conduct a European workshop, I didn't have time to see it before I left.

But things work out the way they're supposed to work out. While I was waiting at the airport for the flight to leave, I happened to be browsing through the bookstore when I saw a copy of the Thomas Harris novel. I bought it, and as the plane took off, I started reading.

It was an extraordinary reading experience. I couldn't put it down. I was literally hooked by everything: the style of writing, the complexity of character, the horror of it all. Before I knew it, the plane touched down in Frankfurt; I had read almost the entire flight. It was a real "page-turner."

When I returned to L.A., the film had been in general release for several weeks and had been very well received, both critically and commercially. Everybody, it seemed, was talking about "Hannibal the Cannibal."

Because the novel was so good, I had some trepidation about seeing the movie. I didn't want the experience of reading the novel influenced by the film, be it good or bad. My curiosity won out, and I went to see it. It was a weeknight in Westwood, yet the theater was crowded because the word of mouth was strong. When the lights went down and the curtains parted, and we saw those first shots of Jodie Foster climbing up the rope, hauling herself over the incline, I was totally hooked. So was everyone else.

There are not many films I can say that about. Jonathan Demme had done an excellent job of telling a story with pictures, and Ted Tally's script captured the essence and riveting terror of the novel. Form and content seemed to be beautifully matched.

I thought about the film over the next several days and felt it to be a landmark film, a film that reached a new level of horror. It wasn't the "normal" horror story, like Nightmare Freddie coming back for another *Friday the 13th,* or Jason in *Halloween.* No, it was something else, something more than that. To think that my next-door neighbor could be Hannibal Lecter, or the person at the next table could be Jame Gumb, was a horrifying thought, so abhorrent I could hardly deal with it.

It was a real human horror story.

A few years ago I attended a film festival in Rio de Janeiro with Jonathan Demme, and I knew he was a very good, original filmmaker. From the sprightly *Something Wild* with Melanie Griffith to the very underrated *Married to the Mob* and *Swimming to Cambodia,* I had always admired his work.

I did not know Ted Tally, the screenwriter who received the Academy Award for *Silence of the Lambs,* though I knew his name, having seen his credit on *White Palace* (adapted from the novel by Glenn Savan). I found out later that Tally's *White Palace* script had been rewritten by Alvin Sargent. *White Palace* is a well-crafted little film (except for the ending, which doesn't work) starring Susan Sarandon and James Spader, and directed by Luis Mandoki, the young, gifted Mexican director.

I wanted to talk to Ted Tally about writing the *Silence of the Lambs* screenplay, and tracked him down through his agent at ICM in New York, Arlene Donovan. "He lives in Bucks County, Pennsylvania," she told me, and "rarely comes to L.A."

After a few phone calls we arranged a time to talk, and I interviewed him by phone.

After we exchanged our hellos, he told me he was just finishing a difficult adaptation of Rosellen Brown's novel *Before and After.* He was having a hard time, he explained, not only with the script but also because his wife was not feeling well, having to be confined to bed for the last two months of her pregnancy.

A screenwriter has to learn the *craft* of writing in pictures. Ted Tally is a writer who comes from theater, a graduate of the prestigious and highly acclaimed Yale School of Drama, one of the finest graduate theater programs in the country. Over the next few years he wrote many pieces for the stage, many for small houses off-Broadway. How difficult was it for him to make the transformation from stage to screen?

"In the beginning, I spent years worrying about the various technical details, like camera angles," he began. "Everybody kept telling me I should 'think of a screenplay as a play where you can change locations as much as you want.' It really wasn't as bad as I thought it was going to be, because the image is very important in the theater, too, it's just a bit more cumbersome."

He paused for a moment, then continued. "As far as I'm concerned, I'm still learning about writing for film; it's really an evolutionary process. I've picked up a few tricks of the craft, but I still don't feel like I know how to write a screenplay."

I asked how he began his journey into screenwriting, and he replied, "One day, I received a call from Lindsay Anderson [the dynamic English documentary and feature film director of *This Sporting Life* and *If,* among others]; he told me he had seen a play of mine called *Terra Nova,* and was looking for a writer for an epic film that was set in India, and asked if I would be interested in doing it.

"I was taken back because I had never written a screenplay before, never even seen a screenplay. So over the next year, off and on, I worked with Lindsay, and he took me through the process. The script was called *Empire,* a huge, humongous thing that would have cost a fortune to make. But it was wonderful being thrown in and told to swim. I'd been writing plays for these little fifty-seat theaters, and suddenly there I was writing dialogue and Hindu slang and cavalry charges."

Empire never got made, but after this experience he wrote several unproduced screenplays and television pieces. "I tried to write the screenplays in between theater projects, but after a while I began to feel frustrated because I wasn't fully committed to either medium. So I started rethinking my priorities. Soon after, another of my plays had a disappointing reception, and I realized I had a choice to make in my life. What was I going to do? Write for the theater, or write for the screen? I was thirty-five years old.

"So after careful consideration, I decided to concentrate on screenwriting; I wanted to see if I could make something happen. And then about a year later I got the assignment to adapt *White Palace.*"

I asked how he felt about writing for film. In film, the screenwriter's words are not always respected, and everybody, from the director and producer to the studio executive and actor, changes lines and scenes almost at will. The changes are not always in the best interests of the screenplay; often they are more a function of ego, than of necessity. It's different in the theater because the Dramatists' Guild states that no one can change a line in a play unless it's approved by the author.

Tally thought for a moment, then replied, "I think the differences between the writer in the theater and the writer for the screen have been exaggerated."

It was an answer I hadn't expected, so I asked him why.

He answered, "They're both collaborative. Even the Dramatists' Guild Agreement doesn't help when tensions fray in the rehearsal hall and everything is going badly, when something clearly doesn't 'play' and you have to work it out.

"At that point you have to rely on tact, diplomacy, on compromise, just to survive. In a way you're just as much at the mercy of the director and the actors in theater as you are in the movies. You've got this strange kind of art form that can't come to life without a tremendous number of people helping you. I think if you're a writer, you're either drawn to this kind of collaborative work or you're not.

"You either like the collaborative process and are excited by its possibilities, or you're not," he emphasized. "Every time the director or actors or designers do something you're not thrilled with, there's probably one or two other times they make you look better than you really are. Everyone makes everyone else look better; that's what a true collaboration is."

Interesting. I asked how he got the assignment of adapting *Silence of the Lambs.*

He told me, "I pursued this like a real job. It was something I really wanted to do. I met the author, Thomas Harris, at an art gallery a while ago, and had dinner with him a couple of times. He knew I was a big fan of his, so he sent me a critic's copy of *Silence of the Lambs* before it was published.

"As soon as I read it I knew it would make a great film. I assumed that somebody like Bo Goldman [*One Flew over the Cuckoo's Nest, Scent of a Woman*] was already writing the screenplay, but I asked my agent to pursue it anyway. [In the novel, Jack Crawford tells Starling never to "assume" anything because "you make an *ass* out of *u* and *me*."] She found out that Orion Pictures was actively involved in getting the rights to the book, but as yet no one had been assigned to write the screenplay. So I went after it.

"At that time," Tally said, "Gene Hackman was going to star and direct it, so I met with him and got him to agree to let me do the screenplay.

"But when I was halfway through the first draft, Hackman backed out of the project, and it became very difficult completing it. I was literally dangling in the wind. I didn't know what was going to happen, whether Orion was going to continue it or abandon it. But just before I finished the script, Mike Medavoy [at the time, head of Orion Pictures, and recently the head of TriStar] hired Jonathan Demme to direct it.

"I really think Jonathan signed on just by reading the novel; I'm pretty sure he didn't want to read the script. We talked on the phone and agreed to meet over lunch. I was really nervous, and also a bit possessive; I was the only one on the ship at that point, and had been ever since Hackman backed out of the project.

"But we hit it off right away, and I told him it was hard for me to believe this movie was really going to be made. All my fears came up, years of Hollywood frustration. And he was really great. He said, 'I promise you this movie's going to get made. And you are the only writer who will ever work on this movie. I am the director, I don't pretend to know how to do what you do. But I promise you I will never make you live with anything in this movie that you're not happy with. Now let's go to work.' "

The screenwriter's dream.

"You can imagine what it was like," Tally continued. "I felt like a drowning man being thrown a life jacket. And Jonathan was as good as his word. I spent weeks on the set. He said, 'I don't understand why more directors don't do this. You're a vital resource. Why should people think your expertise stops at writing words on a page?' "

It's easy to see why Jonathan Demme brings out the best in people.

Both Jonathan Demme and the studio liked Tally's first draft, so they gave the project a "green light" (in studio jargon the picture is put into the production schedule as a "go" project and given a production start date), "and we were off and running. It happened so fast I was literally in shock," Tally added. "I had never worked with Hollywood like that before. I met Jonathan in April or May and we were shooting by November. It was incredible."

I wondered whether Thomas Harris had read the screenplay. "No," he replied. "Tom pretty much keeps his distance from Hollywood. Since he was already working on another book, he didn't want our vision of this thing rattling around in his head. He was extremely supportive and very sweet; he even volunteered to open up his files for me, but I preferred to do it just on my own. And I think he was very happy with that."

What did he think of the film? "I don't think he's seen the movie to this day," Tally replied. "He watched the clips that were shown during the Oscars, but that's about it. He's been very, very cautious that *his* vision of Hannibal Lecter was not affected by our vision. He told me once that he read about John Le Carré seeing Alec Guinness in one of the George Smiley movies and Le Carré felt that the character he had created was lost forever, because Guinness could do the character better than he could. He could only see that face for his character.

"I think Tom took that lesson to heart," Tally went on. "He thought we would be much better off if we did our own thing. He even told me, 'Ted, the novel and the movie each have their own agenda. They're not the same thing.'

"What he was really saying, of course, was that we should do what we had to do, and not worry about his feelings."

Apples and oranges.

Every screenwriter approaches the adaptation of a book differently. After all, the word "adapt" means to "make something fit or suitable by changing or adjusting; or to alter or modify an already existing condition." In other words, to change "this" into "that." Alvin Sargent (*Julia, Ordinary People, Straight Time,* and *White Palace,* to name just a few) reads the novel, the source material, until he "makes it his own," as many times as that takes. Then he writes individual scenes in a random fashion, then puts them all together on the floor and shapes a story line out of those individual scenes.

I wanted to find out how Tally approached the adaptation. "I broke down the book," he began, "scene by scene. It's the way I approach every screenplay adaptation. I try to establish the line of events; this event happens, then this event, then this and this happens. What's important from the book is what sticks in your mind. So I put those scenes on cards, one by one, just getting the story down, concentrating on the main needs of the adaptation."

Which are what? I asked.

He thought about that for a few seconds, then said, "I knew this had to be Clarice's story. Even though the book goes inside Lecter's mind, inside Crawford's mind, inside Jame Gumb's mind, the book basically follows her. I knew this has to be Clarice's movie. Anything she's not in has to be cut, if possible. If it's not cut, then it has to be kept to an absolute minimum. This story is her journey. Approaching it this way meant automatically reducing the book.

"One of the risks I had to take," he continued, "was that we wouldn't know very much about Gumb; we wouldn't have any background on him. He's a cipher to her. If *she* finds out more about him, then we find out more about him. When she has to guess, we must guess, too. But a determined focus on Clarice meant losing some wonderful things that were in the book—Jack Crawford's dying wife, for example. I bitterly tried to hang on to that in the first couple of drafts, but by the third draft I realized it wouldn't work; it had to go. I had to be ruthless in terms of what I kept and what I didn't. Some things I managed to hold on to until the third and fourth drafts.

"For example, there was a sequence in the book where Clarice gets in trouble. She has a confrontation with Senator Martin, the mother of the kidnapped girl [played by Diane Baker]. It's a very strong scene and I wanted to hang on to it, but Jonathan simply said, 'We don't have time for this confrontation. The dramatic focus has to be on Clarice and Lecter, then on Lecter's escape.' And he was right. It was a matter of paring down the action and shifting the scene order. Adaptation forces you to think in a logical way about telling the story."

I asked him to elaborate on that. "The first thing you have to do," he began, "is a massive amount of editing. *The Silence of the Lambs* is a 350-page novel which had to be reduced to a 120-page screenplay. It's like a third of the novel.

"When you're reducing a book that dramatically, the author's arrangement of the story will not necessarily hold up anymore. You may have to shift several scenes in order to follow the main story line.

"The last thing you're concerned with," Tally said, "is invention for its own sake. If it ain't broke, don't fix it. But because you're deliberately breaking the book apart in order to make it into a screenplay, you're going to have to invent new scenes. It might be inventing a way to meld two or three scenes from the novel into one scene in the screenplay. And that means you're going to have to invent transitions to keep the action moving forward. And then you're going to have to invent dialogue for those transitions because you've lost so much information it's probably confusing."

Then he added as an afterthought: "You don't want to be a slave to the book. You want it in your head but you don't want it oppressing you. After a while you reference your own story outline more than you do the novel. And once you complete the first draft, you virtually have no reference to the published novel at all. It becomes about itself only. It starts to develop its own logic and meaning in writing."

In other words, it's a case of apples and oranges.

16

Three Fathers:

From Book to Film

"*Behavioral Science, the FBI section that deals with serial murder, is on the bottom floor of the Academy building at Quantico, half-buried in the earth. Clarice Starling reached it flushed after a fast walk from Hogan's Alley on the firing range. She had grass in her hair and grass stains on her FBI Academy windbreaker from diving to the ground under fire in an arrest problem on the range.*"

Those are the first words of the Thomas Harris novel. Words, not pictures. If you're adapting a novel into a screenplay, you don't simply open your script with a scene or sequence that mirrors the opening of the book. You have to go beyond that and find the metaphorical image that *captures the essence* of the book.

The Silence of the Lambs is really a story of transformation. Joseph Campbell points out that the ancient rites of initiation—boyhood to manhood, girl to woman—are woven into the fabric of our lives. Bar mitzvahs, confirmations, and other such rituals are our contemporary "rites of passage" ceremonies. Campbell says, "In childhood we are in a condition of dependency under someone's protection and supervision for some fourteen to twenty-one years. You are in no way a self-responsible, free agent, but an obedient dependent, expecting and receiving punishments and rewards. To evolve out of this position of psychological immaturity to the courage of self-responsibility and assurance requires a death and a resurrection. That's the basic motif of the universal hero's journey—leaving one condition and finding the source of life to bring you forth into a richer or mature condition."

To grow and evolve into this new level of awareness, of consciousness, one has to confront certain hardships or obstacles, tests that measure one's skills, aptitudes, desires, and intentions. The dragon was St. George's test. Buffalo Bill is Clarice Starling's test. Clarice Starling undergoes a terrifying rite of passage that becomes her personal journey of transformation. When her ordeal is finally over, she's undergone a transformation of character, reached a new level of consciousness and enlightenment. And in the process she has gone from student to professional.

This theme of transformation plays a major part in the book, but trying to capture it in a screenplay adaptation is very difficult; it's easier for most screenwriters to bury a theme like this, focusing on formula action sequences or melodramatic situations instead.

How did Ted Tally and Jonathan Demme deal with this undercurrent of transformation? Were they going to deal with it, or skillfully ignore it? "At one point," Tally recalled, "we talked a lot about what the opening credit sequence should be; 'arty' shots, moths fluttering around and being born with lots of abstract close-ups. But after Jonathan returned from a visit to Quantico [where the FBI Academy is], he said it's an incredible location, with woods, jogging paths, cliffs. It was too good not to use. So he thought that should be the credit sequence, just showing Jodie jogging around the grounds. In all my drafts I had opened with Clarice walking into Crawford's office, but I knew this would be better. It would 'open up' the material, make it more dynamic, more visual. So Jonathan filmed her on the obstacle course and used it for the credit sequence.

"I found it interesting that I didn't foresee the ambiguity it would convey—the sense of isolation in the woods: Is she chasing something, or is she being pursued by something? She looks nervous and strained, and it almost feels like she's being chased.

"One of the film critics who reviewed the film said the film begins with a woman climbing toward you, which is the perfect metaphor for what she's about to go through, physically and mentally—like climbing out of the chrysalis. And the movie ends with a man walking away from you into a crowd. There's a closure there, a symmetry between the opening moment and the final moment."

Even though the sequence wasn't planned (Jonathan Demme and Jodie Foster worked it out on the set), it was one of those "lucky accidents" that happens to work perfectly. Because it underscores the theme of transformation that runs through the book, it works on a much deeper level than one might find in those ordinary kinds of thrillers we see every weekend at the movie theater.

On another level, it's a story about an orphaned girl and her relationship with three fathers. "There's her real father," Tally observed, "a kind of ghost figure. Then there's Jack Crawford, who's loving but very stern and distant; emotionally he doesn't give her anything. Then there's Lecter, who's fascinating, brilliant, but horrible."

The "father quest" is a major theme of literature. In mythological terms the quest is an adventure, much like finding your career or job in life (finding "what I'm supposed to be doing with my life" is the way Callie Khouri phrased it). A person's character, many psychologists say, is inherited from the father, and searching for the father is really searching for your own true nature. Character is destiny. As *The Silence of the Lambs* unfolds, each of the these "fathers" has something to teach her in her journey from student to professional.

"School's out, Starling," is the way Crawford puts it.

In explaining Buffalo Bill and the significance of the cocoon found in the throats of the victims (the visual metaphor of "Billy"), Hannibal Lecter states, "The significance of the chrysalis is change. Worm into butterfly, or moth. Billy thinks he wants to change. He's making himself a girl suit out of real girls. Hence the large victims—he has to have things that fit."

Change is the only constant in the universe. Most of us avoid it like the plague or confront it with fear and trembling. That's not in the character of Clarice Starling; it's not her nature. But all change ensures that some pain must be endured. To be the hero of this story, to make this transformation, Clarice will have to complete those incomplete memories of her father, something she's run away from and buried long ago. In other words, she has to die to be reborn, so she can move into the future. It's no accident that Lecter calls her "Agent Starling."

The script opens as "Clarice Starling approaches us briskly down a long corridor. Trim, very pretty, mid-20's. She wears a gray 'FBI Academy' sweatshirt, an ID badge, a navy ball cap. There are grass stains on the knees of her khakis, grass and sweat stains on her shirt. She reaches a closed door, stops, a bit flushed."

The nameplate reads BEHAVIORAL SCIENCE/Special Agent Crawford.

From "her POV we see a cramped and obsessively cluttered room. Case file materials—police and lab reports, manila folders, photos—are stacked mountainously high on the desk, the floor, the chairs. On the walls: maps, charts, and screaming newspaper headlines (BUFFALO BILL CLAIMS 5TH VICTIM, FBI: STILL NO LEADS ON BUFFALO BILL). Most prominent of all is a row of five enlarged black-and-white photos—the faces of young women, taken from life.

"Clarice steps further into the room, staring at A BLACKBOARD filled with feverishly scrawled notes: 'Big women only . . . Skinning=Hunter? Trapper? . . . Lunar cycle? *No.*'"

Within a few swift shots there's been a lot of *visual* information revealed. The script is set up immediately from page one, word one and establishes the necessary information to set up the dramatic premise of the movie: how to capture Buffalo Bill.

When Crawford enters the room, he's described as being "haggard, haunted; his face is a road map of places we could not bear to visit." (As Tally mentioned, Crawford's relationship with his dying wife, which is such a strong undercurrent of the novel, had to be deleted from the screenplay. The focus will always be on Clarice; it is her story.)

Crawford fills us in on who she is and why she's here. We learn she's in the top quarter of her class, majored in "psych and criminology, graduated *magna cum laude.* Summer internships at the Reitzinger Clinic. Now you're in training for the FBI. It says here you want to come work for me in Behavioral Science."

This is the kind of scene screenwriters hate. It is pure expository dialogue, which reveals information the reader and audience must know to move the story forward. Most of the time these scenes are very hard to write because they're so direct.

Crawford tells her he's got "a little errand" for her to do. "Why me?" Clarice asks. Crawford tells her they're in the process of interviewing all the serial killers currently in custody . . . "but the one we want the most refuses to cooperate. So I want you," he says to Starling, "to go after him again today, in the asylum." When she asks who the killer is, he replies, "The psychiatrist—Dr. Hannibal Lecter."

"Hannibal the Cannibal?"

Crawford nods, then continues. "Lecter," we learn, "was a brilliant psychiatrist. . . . If he won't cooperate, then I just want straight reporting. How's he look? How's his cell look? What's he writing?"

He cautions her to be very careful with him. "You tell him nothing personal, Starling. Believe me, you don't want Hannibal Lecter inside your head. Just do your job but never forget what he is."

"And what is that?" Clarice asks.

We cut to the next scene, where we HEAR the answer. Most screenwriters would have Crawford answer the question of just who Hannibal Lecter is. But instead of Crawford answering the question, we hold on Clarice but HEAR the voice-over words of Dr. Chilton answering it. "Oh, he's a monster," he says. "A pure psychopath . . ." After the line is spoken we cut directly into the next scene, at the State Hospital, between Clarice and Dr. Frederick Chilton.

It's a wonderful film transition that takes us from Crawford's office directly into the next scene. Transitions are a way to bridge time and move the action forward quickly, visually. Even though this screenplay is an adaptation, the script is filled with great visual transitions, pieces of film or dialogue that bridge one scene with the next. You may say that the director or the film editor is responsible for creating these visual transitions, and that's true *some* of the time. Most of the time screenwriters don't know how to write good visual transitions, so their scripts seem to be episodic and disjointed. They leave the transitions to the director and just hope for the best. Remember: Never "assume" anything because it "makes an *ass* out of *u* and *me.*"

As far as I'm concerned, it is the screenwriter's responsibility to write the transition scenes that move the story forward. The style and sophistication with which Ted Tally creates these visual transitions, as well as the visual clarity of Jonathan Demme's filmmaking, make *Silence of the Lambs* a wonderful moviegoing experience. You can't ask for more than that.

There are many ways to create visual transitions: picture to picture, sound to sound, image to image, word to word, fades and dissolves, and so on. Generally Tally plays the last line of the current scene over the first line of the next scene. End one scene with a question, for example, then answer it in the next scene.

This kind of overlapping transition scene has been done many times before, of course, most notably in *Julia,* Alvin Sargent's Academy Award-winning screenplay adapted from Lillian Hellman's *Pentimento.* But Tally's transitions push the art of connecting one scene with another just a little bit farther. What is so nice is that we're really not aware of these transitions. If you're watching a movie and become aware of the visual transitions, or feel the "arty" influence of the director in each scene, the chances are that it's not a very good film.

Tally keeps Clarice as the main focus, the focal point of the action, so we know only as much as she knows. In that way the main character and the audience are linked together in a "community of emotion."

So far everything in these first few pages of screenplay has been meticulously designed to lead us to the dramatic hook or inciting incident that occurs at about page ten. In *The Silence of the Lambs* the dramatic hook is the introduction of Hannibal Lecter.

So far the information we've been given leads us to believe he's some kind of monster (remember Henry James's theory of illumination). Since the relationship between Clarice and Lecter is the engine that drives the story forward, the screenwriter has been very careful to set up our expectations; we expect Lecter to be some kind of crass monster.

As Chilton leads Clarice through the menacing maze that makes up the state institution, we learn more about Lecter. "On the afternoon of July 8, 1981," Chilton begins, "he complained of chest pains and was taken to the dispensary. His mouthpiece and restraints were removed for an EKG. When the nurse bent over him, he did this to her" . . . and he shows her a small, dog-eared photo. "The doctors managed to re-set her jaw, more or less, and save one of her eyes." He pauses, then says, "His pulse never got over eighty-five, even when he ate her tongue."

He did what?

As we move with Clarice down the long corridor we really don't know what to expect.

MOVING SHOT—

with Clarice, as her footsteps ECHO. High to her right, surveillance cameras. On her left, cells. Shadowy occupants pacing, muttering. . . . Suddenly a dark figure in the next-to-last cell hurtles toward her, his face mashing grotesquely against his bars as he hisses.

DARK FIGURE
I can sssmell your cunt!

Clarice flinches momentarily but then walks on.

DR. LECTER'S CELL

is coming slowly INTO VIEW. . . . Behind its barred front wall is a second barrier of stout nylon net. . . . Sparse, bolted-down furniture, many softcover books and papers. On the walls, extraordinarily detailed, skillful drawings, mostly European cityscapes, in charcoal or crayon.

CLARICE

stops at a polite distance from his bars, clears her throat.

CLARICE
Dr. Lecter . . . my name is Clarice Starling.
May I talk to you?

DR. HANNIBAL LECTER

is lounging on his bunk, in white pajamas, reading an Italian Vogue. *He turns, considers her. . . . A face so long out of the sun, it seems almost leached—except for the glittering eyes and the wet, red mouth. He rises smoothly, crossing to stand before her: the gracious host. His voice is cultured, soft.* [*Notice how brief, yet accurate, the description is.*]

DR. LECTER
Good morning.

This is not what we expected at all. It's a good example of playing against the grain of the scene. Lecter's politeness takes us by surprise and contradicts the image of him that's been painted for us.

In the movie Lecter's visual introduction was made stronger, more dramatic; instead of lounging on his bunk when she arrives, he is standing, waiting for Clarice to come to his cell. We see Lecter through her eyes, as *she* sees him, so *we* see him.

He seems cultured, mannered, not at all the kind of person who would eat someone's liver with "a nice bottle of Chianti."

Like a snake exploring a bird's nest, Lecter, the psychiatrist, takes the initiative: "May I see your credentials?" he asks. When he learns Jack Crawford sent a "trainee" to him, she manages to sidestep his thrust and parries with one of her own: "We're talking about psychology, Doctor, not the FBI. Can you decide for yourself whether or not I'm qualified?"

"Mmmm," Lecter replies: "That's rather slippery of you, Agent Starling," and like the gentleman he appears to be, says to her, "Sit. Please."

He tests her immediately. "What did Miggs say to you?" he asks. Clarice doesn't hesitate; she's right up front with him, open and honest. "He said, 'I can smell your cunt.' "

Lecter is impressed with her candor, her self-assurance and willingness to speak freely. We learn that Lecter has extraordinary powers: His skills of observation, his intelligence and perception, his sense of smell are all amazing. He tells her she uses "Evyan skin cream, and sometimes you wear L'Air du Temps . . . and you've brought your best bag . . . much better than your shoes." The psychopath is also a mad genius. It's what makes him so frightening.

When I asked Tally how he approached this encounter between Clarice and Lecter, he told me, "A lot of the dialogue is straight out of the book. If you're adapting a book and the author writes brilliant dialogue," he says, "that's a gift from heaven. When you get so close to the novel, your ear becomes tuned to the author's voice, and you're inspired to mimic. It's not always easy to mimic a character like Lecter, but if you listen to what you've been given, you can do it."

Tally's job in this scene was to take a powerful ten-page chapter filled with detail and descriptions and build it into a not-too-long dialogue scene. The dialogue between the two had to be cut, trimmed, and accented, and then new dialogue put in to make the transitions as seamless as possible. As it turned out, the scene runs almost six pages, almost six minutes of screen time. That's quite a long scene. Most scenes this long never seem to work; they sag and drag and go on forever.

As we've seen in *Thelma and Louise* and in *Terminator 2,* a good scene between two characters in a screenplay doesn't need to run more than one or two pages, maybe three, max. Tally's playwriting ability allowed him to construct this scene and make it as dramatically effective as it is. Of course, the performances are wonderful, but even so, the scene always keeps our interest. More important, it sets up the core of the relationship between Starling and Lecter.

We learn more about Lecter as we *see* the drawings on the wall. One of them is the Duomo, the great Italian church "in Florence, as seen from the Belvedere." When Clarice asks if he drew it from memory (the key question in the scene), he replies, "Memory, Agent Starling, is what I have instead of a view."

That simple statement declares Hannibal Lecter's *dramatic need*

—what your main character wants to win, gain, get, or achieve during the course of the screenplay. Hannibal Lecter wants a view: He wants to see trees, the sky, smell the air, see a leaf falling on the wind. All the way through the script he alludes to having a view: It is what he wants, what he strives to get, his *dramatic need*. He has information about Buffalo Bill that Jack Crawford needs, and he wants to exchange that information for a view. Maybe they can make a deal. Lecter is the type of character who must always be in control of a situation, so he will be the one to decide if and when he will share information.

When Clarice changes the subject to the questionnaire Crawford has given her, Lecter, always the psychiatrist, the teacher, chides her by saying, "No, no, no. You were doing fine. You'd been courteous and receptive to courtesy, you'd established trust with the embarrassing truth about Miggs, and now this ham-handed segue into your questionnaire. It won't do. It's stupid and boring."

Here Lecter makes his first reference to "Buffalo Bill." "Do you know why he's called Buffalo Bill?" he asks. "Tell me. The newspapers won't say."

"I'll tell you if you'll look at this form," she replies. He thinks about it, nods his agreement. "It started as a bad joke in Kansas City Homicide," she says. "They said . . . this one likes to skin his humps."

Lecter thinks that's "witless and misleading. Why do you think he removes their skins, Agent Starling? Thrill me with your acumen."

She says it excites him. "Most serial killers like to keep some sort of—trophies." "I didn't," he says. "No," she replies. "You ate yours."

Touché. He smiles to himself, tells her to send through the questionnaire. He glances through a few pages and is deeply insulted; his personality changes as quickly as a shadow across the sun. "Oh, Agent Starling," he says, "do you think you can dissect me with this blunt little tool?" and he slams the sliding food tray back through. "His voice remains a pleasant purr," say the stage directions.

LECTER
You're sooo ambitious, aren't you? You
know what you look like to me, with your
good bag and your cheap shoes? You look
like a rube. A well-scrubbed, hustling rube
with a little taste. . . . Good nutrition has
given you some length of bone, but you're
not more than one generation from poor
white trash, are you—Agent Starling . . . ?
That accent you've tried so desperately
to shed—pure West Virginia. What is your
father, dear? Is he a coal miner? Does he
stink of the lamp? And oh, how quickly the
boys found *you*. All those sticky fumblings
in the backseats of cars, while you could
only dream of getting out. Getting anywhere, yes? Getting all the way to the
F . . . B . . . I.

Every word he says hits her like a "small, precise dart." Visibly
shaken, she takes a moment to compose herself, then comes back
swinging like the fighter she is: "Are you strong enough to point
that high-powered perception at yourself?" she retorts. "Look at
yourself and write down the truth. [She slams the tray back at
him.] Or maybe you're afraid to."

"You're a tough one, aren't you?" he replies. And he turns his
back on her. When she persists about the questionnaire, he replies,
"A census taker once tried to test me. I ate his liver with some fava
beans and a nice Chianti. . . ."

He steps backward and returns to his cot, "becoming as still and
remote as a statue." He's checked out, gone.

Frustrated yet resigned, Clarice picks up her bag and turns to
go. As she passes Miggs's cell, he hisses something and flings his
palm toward her. Clarice is "splattered on the face and neck—not
with blood, but with pale droplets of semen." She gives a little cry,
touching her fingers to the wetness. Stunned, near tears, she forces
herself to walk on, fumbling for a tissue.

Lecter is calling her, agitated, demanding. She returns to his cell and he tells her, in another revealing insight, "I would not have had that happen to you. Discourtesy is—unspeakably ugly to me."

"Then do this test for me," she urges. "No," he replies, "but I will make you happy. I'll give you a chance for what you love most, Clarice Starling." "And what is that?" she asks.

"Advancement, of course."

Perceptive. The desire to get ahead has motivated her most of her life; it is the foundation of her character. In the novel, Thomas Harris describes her as being *"an isolated member of a fierce tribe with no formal genealogy but the honors list and the penal register. . . . None of the Starlings had been very smart, as far as Starling could tell, except for a great-aunt who wrote wonderfully in her diary until she got 'brain fever. . . .'*

"School was the thing in America, and the Starlings caught on to that. One of Starling's uncles had his junior college degree cut on his tombstone.

"Starling had lived by schools, her weapon the competitive exam, for all the years when there was no place else for her to go."

Turning this novelistic perception into dynamic behavior is the art of adaptation. The novel is *source* material; the film is behavior.

Lecter's made a decision: It's time to show and tell. So he's going to test her, give her what she wants the most, and this is the narrative thread that takes us farther into the story. Lecter is going to give her the chance to advance her career and possibly get himself a view. Lecter tells her to "go to Split City. See Miss Mofet, an old patient of mine. . . ."

"School's out, Starling."

17

Partners in Crime:

Plot Point and Beyond

In the seminars and workshops I conduct around the world, I always stress the visual element in screenwriting, telling a story with pictures. The language of film, its grammar, is made up of shots, scenes, and sequences. They are the elements of the screenwriting language. Since the screenplay is a story told with pictures, we always have to focus on what the camera sees.

The shot is what the camera sees. A scene can be made up of one shot, or many shots. A scene is the cell, or unit of dramatic action, defined by two things: *place* and *time*. Each scene takes place in a definite place at a definite time. If you change either place or time, you must change the scene. If, for example, your scene takes place inside an office, and the character walks into the reception area outside the office, you must change the scene; you have changed the place. If you change the time, say, and have someone in the same place only a few hours later, you have to change the scene because you've changed the time.

The scene is made up of a shot or shots in a specific place at a specific time, so each scene becomes identified by INT. STORAGE AREA—NIGHT. In other words, the scene takes place inside, in the storage area, at night; the specific time does not make too much difference unless it is essential to the story.

A *sequence* is a series of scenes connected by one single idea, with a beginning, middle, and end; a wedding, a funeral, a dance, a sporting event, a chase, a seduction could all be sequences. You build, or construct, a sequence the same way you structure and build the unit of dramatic action that makes up Acts I, II, or III, only on a smaller scale.

As Clarice walks out to her car, shaken and disturbed from her encounter with Lecter, the image begins to "blur, almost dizzily," and we're into the first of two flashback sequences that deal with Clarice's relationship with her father.

EXT. THE HOSPITAL—PARKING LOT—DAY

The grim Gothic pile of the asylum looms overhead as Clarice rushes out the front doors. She is badly shaken, almost stumbling, as she rubs at her face. She looks around and finally, with some relief, spots

HER CAR

an old Pinto, parked nearby. This image begins to BLUR . . .

CLOSE ON

her face, fighting tears, as we begin to WHIRL AROUND *her, almost dizzily. She is seeing, in her mind's eye—*

IN FLASHBACK

A screen door banging open, on a wooden porch, and a ten-year-old girl—the young Clarice—rushing outside, down the front steps, and running joyfully across her front yard to—

MOVING ANGLE—THE GIRL'S POV—

A car—late '60s vintage—parked in the dirt road. A MAN, Clarice's father, is just climbing out. He's tall, handsome, and has a marshal's badge pinned on his dark suit. He grins, seeing her, and spreads his arms wide as

THE YOUNG CLARICE

rushes into them, and he sweeps her up in a hug, spinning her around, the CAMERA SPINNING with them, and capturing both their laughing faces, before we abruptly return to—

THE ADULT CLARICE

alone in the parking lot, sagging against her car. Her face is buried in her arms, her shoulders shaking. We HEAR the steady, rapid series of GUNSHOTS as we

CUT TO:

And we're into the next scene as the sound of gunshots leads us into the FBI firing range, where Clarice is practicing her shooting. It's another example of a very good film transition that bridges both time and place.

Flashbacks are a tool the screenwriter uses to provide the reader with information he or she cannot get in any other way. It is a tool, or device, that is, more often than not, abused and overused in the contemporary screenplay, especially by aspiring screenwriters who think the flashback is an easy way to reveal character information crucial to the plot. It's not true. There are other, more effective ways to reveal information than using flashbacks.

You have to be careful writing flashbacks. When they are done well, as in *The Silence of the Lambs,* and used sparingly, they work beautifully; when not done well, a flashback draws attention to itself and interrupts the flow of film narrative. The screenwriter must always serve the needs of the story, and many times a flashback simply gets in the way; it reveals information we can get some other way—for example, through dialogue or a newspaper headline. The screenwriter should never put anything in a flashback that's redundant, that repeats something we can see or hear otherwise. If there's any rule about writing flashbacks, it should be that a flashback gives you information about the character or story that you cannot get in any other way. It usually reveals *emotional* rather than physical information, and it's got to move the story forward. Don't show it if you can say it, might be a good rule to follow.

When I asked Ted Tally about this particular flashback, he replied, "It was a legitimate flashback because we would have no idea what she was thinking as she walked to the car unless we saw it."

At this point in the screenplay, remember, we are still setting up the relationship among her "three fathers," Lecter, Crawford, and her biological father. To sharpen and dramatize the father theme, we need to develop the relationship with her biological father and see how it affects her.

It is through this relationship that those long-forgotten and painful memories of childhood bubble to the surface: the death of her biological father and the slaughtering of the spring lambs.

Hannibal Lecter has given Starling information that might be very important to the FBI in their search for Buffalo Bill. But Clarice is still a student, an FBI trainee, and needs to be guided in her rite of passage.

Up to this point we've seen her only once at the Academy—the opening sequence with Crawford—and we still don't know what she does, or what her training is all about. The screenwriter must expand our information about the main character, so we need to follow her, see her, in a "day in the life" situation.

In this second ten-page section of the script, the story line must stay focused on the main character. The main character needs to be in almost every scene, as the various elements in the story line are established to follow and expand the narrative line.

What does Clarice do at the Academy? What kind of training does she go through, and what does it consist of? In other words, *how does it look?* We need to *see* her in school, acting on the information given to her by Hannibal Lecter.

The transition that leads us into this second unit of dramatic action is the sound of gunshots that ended the last scene, the flashback. In the screenplay we see Clarice on the Academy firing range, emptying shot after shot into a moving target. When she's finished (and they cut this from the final film) she "puts a final, emphatic shot right through the figure's forehead, from point-blank range. The instructor looks at her, surprised," the screenplay reads.

At this point the sequence of events differs between the script and the movie. In the script we next see Clarice looking at microfilm in the Academy library, rolling through page after page, devouring the "horrors" Hannibal Lecter has committed. Newspaper headlines or stories are a good way to reveal more visual information—just as long as it's not overdone.

As she's scanning the headlines, her roommate, Ardelia, comes and tells her that Crawford's on the phone and wants to talk to her. Then Ardelia leans close and whispers, "Where were you all afternoon?"

"Pleading with a crazy man, with come all over my face," Clarice replies. And they both laugh. Ardelia replies (in my favorite line), "Ummmmm . . . wish *I* had time for a social life." Even though this little exchange was cut from the final film, it shows us something very special about their relationship in a very short scene. Some screenwriters might take as much as three or four pages to show the same thing effectively.

The next scene in this little sequence shows Clarice on the phone with Crawford. He asks her about "Miss Mofet." She tells him, "Lecter altered or destroyed most of his patient histories prior to capture. No record of anyone named Mofet. But 'Split City' [this was changed to 'Your-Self' in the film] sounded like it might have something to do with divorce. I tracked it down in the library's catalog of national Yellow Pages. It's a ministorage facility outside Baltimore, where Lecter had his practice."

That's when Crawford tells her, "Miggs is dead." Shocked, Clarice asks how it happened, and Crawford tells her the orderly heard "Lecter whispering to him all afternoon, and Miggs crying. They found him at bed check. He'd swallowed his own tongue."

That says a lot about Hannibal Lecter.

"Lecter did it to amuse himself," Crawford continues. "Why not? What can we do? Take away his books for a while, and no Jell-O. . . ." Then he softens: "I know it got ugly today, but this is your report, Starling—take it just as far as you can. On your *own* time, outside of class, now carry on."

She slams down the receiver and then we cut to Starling and Ardelia studying together while jogging. This little scene is a very good example of keeping a scene visually active while revealing more about character. The location, the jogging path, is outside, so it opens up the story visually, taking us away from the closed interiors of Lecter's hospital, or Crawford's office. It's important to open up your screenplay like this, to let dialogue scenes take place outside while something else is going on; it adds to the dimension of character. It also gives the director and the cinematographer a chance to open up the story visually.

> ARDELIA
> Title 18—3232?

> CLARICE
> Murder or manslaughter. 3281?

> ARDELIA
> Venue in capital cases. 3281?

> CLARICE
> No limitation on capital offenses. 3282?

> ARDELIA
> Indictment period. Non capital cases. 3109?

> CLARICE
> Breaking doors or windows for entry or exit.
> Rule 404?

> ARDELIA
> Rule 404? Character evidence not admissible to prove conduct. 3107?

> CLARICE
> Service of warrants or seizures by the FBI.
> 3052?

> ARDELIA
> Powers of the FBI.

Then we cut to Clarice barging into a room, her gun drawn.

In every scene so far, the focus has been on Clarice, showing us her skills, setting up her ability to respond to stress in a hazardous situation. In other words, we, the reader and audience, must feel confident that when she goes into "the field" she will be able to take care of herself. Like the bird she's named after, she must have wings to fly when she leaves the nest. If she has no chance against Buffalo Bill, there's no real suspense at the end. The screenwriter already knows that the end of this film is going to be a madman hunting her in the basement. So we have to see that she's smart, ambitious, and can take care of herself; she works very hard to achieve success, no matter what the task is. She is a person who is in the top quarter of her class. That's why she was chosen to run this "little errand" for Jack Crawford and interview Hannibal Lecter in the first place.

That's what the art of screenwriting is all about: revealing character.

And that's just what the next little scene in this sequence does. Clarice and a trainee break into a room, guns drawn. But the instructor steps out from behind the door and goes, "Bang, bang, you're dead, Starling. Where's your danger area?" "In the corner," she replies. "Did you check the corners?" he asks. "No, sir." "That's why you're dead. Let's go out and do it again."

The sequence ends with a couple of shots of her studying, and then we cut to the "YOUR-SELF MINI STORAGE—DUSK (RAINING)."

That's the sequence as written. It begins with the microfilm and telephone call with Crawford and ends with the storage facility, leading us to the Plot Point at the end of Act I.

But that's not the way Demme structured it in the film. They rearranged these scenes, cutting out some entirely, condensing one, and building this unit of action into a smooth and natural transition to the Plot Point at the end of Act I.

In the film, Demme opens with Clarice on the firing range pumping bullet after bullet into the targets, then cuts directly into Clarice breaking into the room, then to Clarice jogging and studying with Ardelia, using only the last question and answer between them, and then ends with Clarice viewing the microfilm. When she speaks to Crawford on the phone, the scene opens with him telling her, "Miggs is dead," in the middle of the scene, originally as written. After her response to Miggs's death she tells Crawford she tracked down Lecter's "Miss Mofet" to "Your-Self Storage," and we cut directly to the beginning of the next sequence: "An orange neon sign, streaked with rain, looms over a hurricane fence, topped with barbed wire."

And over this, to lead us into this transition, we hear the voice of Mr. Lang explaining that Unit 31 was leased for ten years. Prepaid in full. The contract is in the name of a "Miss Hester Mofet."

Jackpot.

It's a much better visual transition, and it works better filmically than the screenplay would have. At this point we know a lot about Clarice Starling: We know she's intelligent, knows how to use fire-arms, is driven by "advancement," and seems to be able to take care of herself in a dangerous situation. In other words, she can handle it. Whatever Hannibal Lecter wants her to find, she will find; it is the Plot Point at the end of Act I.

"School's out, Starling."

Ted Tally begins the sequence at the Storage Facility after Clarice has arrived. Enter late and get out early. Clarice and Mr. Lang are standing in the rain in front of Unit 31. "So no one's been in here since 1980?" Clarice asks, establishing the obvious. She tries to lift open the door but can't—it's wedged tightly. Ever resourceful, she goes to her car, turns on the headlights, takes the bumper jack out of the trunk, puts it in place, and starts pumping up the handle. "The door SQUEALS slowly up, but sticks at about eighteen inches."

That's the beginning section of the sequence. The middle portion, the longest part, starts when she slips under the door and begins to explore the storage area. Since the place has changed, we're going from outside the door to inside the shed—in other words, from EXT. STORAGE SHED to INT. STORAGE SHED. It's a new scene.

Before she disappears inside, she wiggles out and tells Lang, "If this door should fall down—ha, ha—or anything else—would you be kind enough to call this number? It's our Baltimore field office.

They know you're here with me. . . . Do you understand?"
"Yes," he responds, and in a gesture of friendliness that is cut from
the film, he suggests that she tuck her pants inside her socks to
"prevent rodent intrusion."

We're with Clarice as she slides under the door; we see what she
sees, learn what she learns. She looks around, then spots the shape
of a large car underneath an American flag, a "1931 Packard.
Curtains close off the back passenger compartment." Clarice
shines her flashlight inside.

CLARICE POV

*as the thin flashlight beam picks out: an open album of lacy, old-
fashioned Valentines, a crumpled lap rug on the floor . . . and
then a pair of women's shiny, high-heeled pumps. Above these the
hem of a fancy satin evening gown—and a pair of stockinged legs.*

CLARICE [The subject of the shot]

recoils, alarmed, then steadies herself.

> CLARICE
> Mr. Lang? It looks like somebody is sitting
> in this car.

> MR. LANG (OS) [Out of Shot]
> Oh, my! Oh, my. . . . Maybe you better
> come out now, Miss Starling.

> CLARICE
> Not yet—just wait for me.

*She leans down with her camera, takes a FLASH through the gap,
then tries the door handle. Locked. So is the front door. She looks
around, aiming her light, and locates a tangle of coat hangers stick-
ing out of a carton of bric-a-brac. She takes out one of these,
straightens it quickly, bends the tip into a hook. [This was dropped
in the film; it's too much business, and there's not enough time.]*

CLARICE

opens the door—it hits stacked boxes and won't open far—then very cautiously leans inside, aiming her flashlight.

HER POV—MOVING LIGHT BEAM—

revealing more of the evening gown . . . a pair of hands, in white, elbow-length gloves—one rests on the lap, the other atop a large, beaded, drawstring evening bag . . . thick strands of costume pearls over the breasts . . . and finally the white neck stub of a female mannequin. No face or head.

CLARICE

sighs with relief. She takes a couple more FLASHES, then very carefully lifts out the Valentine album, holding it by the corners, sets it atop the car. Then she eases herself inside, onto the backseat, as the springs SQUEAK loudly.

ONE GLOVED HAND

slides off the lap, brushing Clarice's thigh.

CLARICE

starts a bit, then pokes at the gloved arm, hard. She peels back a bit of glove, revealing the white, synthetic elbow. She smiles, shaking her head at her own jumpiness, as she reaches over the manne-quin's lap to loosen the evening bag's drawstring.

A SEVERED HUMAN HEAD

stares back at her as the beaded material slides away.

CLARICE

lurches back, gasping loudly, and several long, heart-pounding moments pass before she can make herself look more closely.

THE HEAD

bobs gently in a pool of alcohol, in a laboratory specimen jar. It is a man's head, but grotesquely transformed by the addition of heavy makeup, earrings, and a sodden wig, into a woman's face. Over the years the makeup has smeared badly, and the pupils have gone almost milky white.

Then we CUT as a "loud CLAP of THUNDER" echoes across the sky, leading us into the scene, at the asylum.

That's the Plot Point at the end of Act I. So far everything in the screenplay has led us up to this moment; it is the discovery of Raspail's head that really begins the story. Lecter has given something to Clarice to entice Jack Crawford to make a deal with him; Hannibal Lecter wants his view.

It is the natural lead into Act II: Who killed him? Was it Lecter? Or Buffalo Bill? There is only one person who can really answer that: Hannibal Lecter. It is a tense, suspenseful moment that completes the action of Act I.

Act II begins at the asylum with an establishing shot of Clarice getting out of her car and rushing up the steps. Cut to Lecter's cell after she has arrived, another example of entering the scene late, at the last moment. "It's an anagram, isn't it, Doctor?" she states. "Hester Mofet . . . 'The rest of me. Miss the rest of me. . . .' meaning you rented that garage."

Everything inside the cell is in "shadows; we can't see him. Suddenly the food carrier slides out of the cell, making her jump."

"Dr. Lecter, who is he? Why keep him hidden all these years? And why reveal him now?"

"Why don't you ask me about 'Buffalo Bill?' " Lecter replies, avoiding the question. What he really wants is to see the case file on the serial killer. But Clarice persists about Miss Mofet: "You wanted me to find him."

Lecter pauses, sighs. "His real name is Benjamin Raspail," he begins. "A former patient of mine, whose romantic attachments ran to, shall we say, the exotic. . . . I didn't kill him, I assure you. Merely tucked him away. Very much as I found him, after he'd missed three appointments. . . . Best thing for him, really. His therapy was going nowhere."

In the novel, Raspail was a flutist for the Baltimore Philharmonic, and a patient in Lecter's psychiatric practice. Here's how it's written in the novel: *"On March 22, 1975, he failed to appear for a performance in Baltimore. On March 25 his body was discovered seated in a pew in a small rural church near Falls Church, Virginia, dressed only in a white tie and a tailcoat. Autopsy revealed that Raspail's heart was pierced and that he was short his thymus and pancreas. Clarice Starling,"* Thomas Harris writes, *"who from early life had known much more than she wished to know about meat processing, recognized the missing organs as the sweetbreads.*

"Baltimore Homicide believed that these items appeared on the menu of a dinner Lecter gave for the president and the conductor of the Baltimore Philharmonic on the evening following Raspail's disappearance."

There's not time to explain all that in the screenplay because the story always has to move forward, but we do learn more about Lecter. Clarice asks if Raspail was a transvestite, and Lecter says he was more or less a "garden variety manic-depressive, *very boring*. No, think of him as a kind of experiment. A fledgling killer's first effort at—transformation?"

Then Lecter makes an interesting segue, preparing us for the little game they're going to be playing: He wants to know how Clarice felt when she saw the dead man's head. "Scared, at first. Then—exhilarated," she answers. Ever the psychiatrist, he presses her further, wanting to know if she had any memories, or scenes from her early life that creep into her mind in moments like these.

"No," she replies. Lecter continues circling around the question of the murdered man, giving us more information about him and her. It is a little dance between them. He asks if Crawford wants her sexually. "That doesn't interest me, Doctor. Frankly, that's the sort of question Miggs would ask." "Not anymore," Lecter answers. (The following few lines were omitted from the film.)

> DR. LECTER
> Surely the odd confluence of events hasn't escaped you, Clarice. Jack dangles you in front of me. Then I give you a little something for your résumé. Do you think it's because I like to look at you, and imagine how good you would taste . . . ?

> CLARICE
> I don't know. Is it?

> DR. LECTER
> There's something Jack can give me, and I want to trade for it. But he hates me, so he won't deal directly. That's why you're here.

[Here's where the scene starts in the film.] Dr. Lecter slowly turns up the rheostat in his cell. As the lights rise, we see that the cell's been stripped bare. Gone are his books, drawings, mattress—even his toilet seat. She stands too, startled. They face each other.

> DR. LECTER (cont'd.)
> Punishment, you see. For Miggs. Just like that gospel program. When you leave, they'll turn the volume way up. Chilton does enjoy his petty torments.

> CLARICE
> What did you mean by "transformation," Dr. Lecter?

> DR. LECTER
> I've been in this room for eight years, Clarice. I know they will never, ever let me out while I'm alive. What I want is a view. I want a window where I can see a tree, or even water. I want to be in a federal institu-

> DR. LECTER (cont'd.)
> tion, away from Chilton. And I want a view.
> I'll give good value for it.

> CLARICE
> What did you mean by "fledgling" killer?
> Are you saying he's killed again?

> DR. LECTER
> I'm offering you a psychological profile of
> Buffalo Bill, based on the case evidence. I'll
> help you catch him, Clarice.

> CLARICE
> You know, don't you? Tell me who mur-
> dered your patient.

> DR. LECTER
> All good things to those who wait. *I've*
> waited, Clarice. But how long can you and
> Jack wait? Our Billy must already be search-
> ing for that next special lady.
> (a beat; then)
> Clarice . . . smile! We're going to be *part-*
> *ners*.

Clarice stares back at him, unsure how to respond. In the movie,
the line "We're going to be partners" was dropped because Lecter's
line about "Billy searching for that next special lady" becomes the
verbal transition leading us into the next scene—our first introduction to Buffalo Bill.

18

Quid Pro Quo:

Questions and Answers

In a screenplay, everything is related to everything else. Every scene, every line, every action, every reaction, all the pieces are related to each other. If you change this, you have to change that. A screenplay is organic.

This is a fact that studio executives, producers, and many directors do not respect or understand. If you add a few lines of dialogue, or introduce a new character, you inevitably alter the structure and narrative line.

Ted Tally observes this "law" carefully in the screenplay. Once the relationship with Lecter and Clarice has been established ("partners make strange bedfellows" goes the saying), the next level of the story—their relationship—is ready to expand. Who is "the next special lady" Buffalo Bill fancies? asks Lecter.

Again, a minor line becomes a major transition, because it leads us right into the abduction scene. We watch as a slow-moving car approaches us through an "eerie green tint." The young woman behind the wheel, singing along with Tom Petty, pulls into a parking space, yells a word of greeting to her cat perched in the window, then hesitates as she watches a man with a cast on his right arm struggling to hoist an armchair into the back of his truck.

When I first saw the film, I thought this was the Plot Point at the end of Act I. True, this scene spins off the rest of the action involving Clarice and her "three fathers," but it is the relationship with Clarice and Lecter that powers the story; it is the foundation that keeps things moving forward. The action of the abduction causes a reaction that will be the major story factor.

The kidnapping sequence always seemed a little out of place for me in the film. In the book, the progression of events is different; once Lecter decides to give information about Buffalo Bill to Clarice, a woman's body is found floating in a West Virginia river. It looks like a "Buffalo Bill-type situation." The action covers several chapters, and only after that does Bill kidnap his latest victim.

Ted Tally transposed this order of events in the screenplay and played the kidnapping first, *before* they find the body in West Virginia. In the script it is a dramatic necessity to introduce the kidnapping as early as possible. It is the engine that feeds the rest of the action.

The girl puts down her bag of groceries and offers to help the man, and together they lift the overstuffed chair into the rear of the truck. When she gets inside he asks a surprising question: "Are you about a size 14?"

I heard that line and a chill swept through me. And as I sat there, I realized the entire audience knew who this guy was; we were all caught in that groundswell of "community of emotion."

He hammers her with his forearm cast several times, then slits open the back of her blouse with a scissors, muttering "good" as he caresses the smooth skin of the victim's back. As the van pulls away we hear the cat in the window meow, the only witness to what happened.

Her name is Catherine Martin, and she is the daughter of a prominent U.S. senator.

The needs of the story dictate that we follow Clarice, the main character, as she discovers the trail leading to Buffalo Bill. That's why the kidnapping is not the Plot Point at the end of Act I. The severed head leads her to Lecter, the kidnapping to Buffalo Bill. Action, reaction.

"Starling!" bellows the instructor in the midst of attack training. "Pack your field gear. You're moving' out with Crawford.

. . . They found a girl's body in West Virginia . . . been in the water about a week. Looks like a Buffalo Bill-type situation."

We cut to the plane where Crawford is briefing Starling on Buffalo Bill. "He keeps them alive for three days," he begins. "Why, we don't yet know. There's no evidence of rape or physical abuse prior to death. . . . Then he shoots them, skins them, and dumps them, each body in a different river. The water leaves us no fingerprints, no fibers—no trace evidence at all." He shows her pictures, then comments on "Fredrica Bimmel, the first one . . . big girl, like all the rest. Her corpse was the only one he took the trouble to weight down, so actually, she was the third girl found. After her, he got lazy. . . ." That casual line is really the clue that ultimately leads to Buffalo Bill.

In two quick scenes they land at a small West Virginia airport, then are driving in a car. "Talk about him, Starling," Crawford says. "Tell me what you see." And like a student being quizzed, she clicks off her observations: "He's a white male. . . . Serial killers hunt within their own ethnic group. And he's not a drifter—he's got his own house somewhere. Not an apartment."

"Why?" Crawford asks. "What he does with them," she replies, "takes privacy, time, tools. . . . He's in his thirties or forties— he's got real physical strength, but combined with an older man's self-control. He's cautious, precise, never impulsive . . . and he'll never stop."

"Why not?" "He's got a real taste for it now," she observes. "And he's getting better at his work." Crawford is impressed and tells her so. But something bothers her; she wants to know if getting information on Buffalo Bill was part of a Crawford plan, and wishes she had been informed of it. Crawford's answer reveals just how smart he is: "If I'd sent you in there with an actual agenda, he would've known it instantly. He would've toyed with you, then turned to stone." He pauses, then remarks, "Lying and breathing are the same thing to him."

Pinch I begins as they pull into a funeral home and Crawford muses to himself (in a scene that was cut) about the process of hunting serial killers: "You think about Buffalo Bill long enough, you start to get a feel for him. Then, if you're lucky, out of all the stuff you know, one little part of it tugs at you, tries to get your attention. You let me know when that happens. Don't try to impose any patterns on this guy. Just stay open and let him show you."

In the script Tally inserts his second flashback sequence as Clarice and Crawford walk into the funeral home. But Demme changed that in the film, setting up the unspoken resentment between the local authorities and the FBI first, then inserting the flashback. Good structure holds everything together, yet remains flexible. Like the tree in the wind, it bends but doesn't break.

As Crawford and the police chief confer privately, Clarice is left to herself, surrounded by uniformed police. She's uncomfortable and doesn't know exactly what to do. We see what she is feeling, what she is experiencing, by now cutting to the flashback.

INT.—FUNERAL HOME

She stops, seeing—

COUNTRY PEOPLE

in their somber best, take their seats for the service. The music—"Shall We Gather at the River?"—is issuing from the open double doors. Several of the mourners glance over at her curiously.

ANGLE ON CLARICE

staring back at the mourners, hearing the music as a sense memory is triggered in her . . .

IN FLASHBACK—LOW ANGLE, MOVING—

as we approach, down the aisle of a country chapel, an open wooden coffin. Sad country faces turn, looking at us from the flanking pews. The b.g. [background] organ is "Shall We Gather . . ."

THE SAD, TEN-YEAR-OLD CLARICE

in her best dress, is reluctantly approaching the casket. Her hands are held by the plump hands of unseen matrons.

CHILD'S POV

on the looming coffin . . . closer and closer . . . until finally she can see, lying inside it . . . her dead father, arms folded, his marshal's badge still pinned to his lapel.

CRAWFORD (VO)

Starling? . . .

NEW ANGLE (PRESENT DAY)

as the grown-up Clarice turns toward the impatient Crawford. Like her, he carries a large case.

CRAWFORD (cont'd.)

We're back here.

What makes the flashback so effective is that we really don't know where we are. We started out in present time, then through the visual association of place we suddenly find ourselves in a past experience of the main character. What makes the flashback such an effective film technique is that we identify with it because our minds work the same way. Once again, we see the emotional significance of Clarice's long dead father and her need to complete the relationship with him; she must grow to change from a student into the professional.

They enter the embalming room to examine the floater. Here we see Starling come into her own. It's another good illustration of film as behavior: We see who she is by what she does. Action is character. It's described beautifully in the novel: "*Crawford saw that the atmosphere had changed here in the presence of the dead: that wherever this victim came from, whoever she was, the river had carried her into the country, and while she lay helpless in this room in the country, Clarice Starling had a special relationship to her. Crawford saw that in this place Starling was heir to the granny women, to the wise women, the herb healers, the stalwart country women who have always done the needful, who keep the watch and when the watch is over, wash and dress the country dead."*

Starling embodies this character born of her own genes, her own heritage: "Gentlemen," she says, "there's things I need to do for her. . . . Y'all brought her this far, and I know her folks would thank you if they could. Now, please—go on out and let me take care of her. . . . Go on, now." And as they file out of the room Crawford looks at her "with a new degree of respect," reads the script.

The focus of the scene now switches to the subject of the scene, the reason they're there, this dark green "body bag, tightly zipped, lying on a porcelain embalming table." Who is she? And what can she tell them? As the body bag is slowly zipped open, Clarice Starling braces herself for her first personal encounter with Buffalo Bill.

Clarice's back is to the camera, and as she swings around we see her change. We learn what she learns, see what she sees: "Star-shaped contact entrance wound over the sternum. Muzzle stamp visible at the top." The doctor pops in with a "wrongful death . . . she'll have to go to the state pathologist when you're done."

Crawford pushes Clarice: "What else do you see, Starling?" "Well . . . she's not local," she replies. "Her ears are pierced three times each, and she's wearing gold glitter nail polish. Looks like town to me. . . ."

In the book, the finding of the cocoon in the dead girl's throat is only a brief mention and nothing more. Only later does the cocoon become a major force of the story. But in the movie, when Clarice says "she's got something in her throat," the tension builds dramatically. The discovery of the cocoon is a nice little reminder about the difference between novels and films. Words and pictures. Apples and oranges.

The discovery of the cocoon is Pinch I, the sequence in the First Half of Act II that holds the story together, the clue that keeps us on the trail. Without the Pinch it would be hard for the story to move forward; instead, it would curl up within itself and go no-where.

In the rental car driving back, Crawford knows something is

bothering Clarice. Crawford says, "When I told that sheriff we shouldn't talk in front of a woman, that really burned you, didn't it?" (She is silent.) "That was just smoke, Starling, I had to get rid of him."

But it bothered her, and she tells him so: "It matters, Mr. Crawford. . . . Other cops know who you are. They look at you to see how to act. . . . It matters." It's a line that once again shows us the strength and independence of Clarice. It shows us who she is.

Cut to Clarice walking through the Museum of Natural History; darkened corridors lined with dinosaur bones, to an office where two entomologists play chess *with live beetles*. This is a very good illustration of "playing against the grain" of a scene. We expect to find the entomologists in an office or laboratory. Instead, they are doing something totally different and unexpected; it catches our interest.

The insect is identified as a partially developed adult moth, and when its wings are spread reveals "nature's perfect image of a ghostly human skull, something wonderful and terrible to see." The scientist observes, "Somebody grew this guy. Fed him honey and nightshade, kept him warm. . . . Somebody *loved* him."

Again, the perfect cut line, the perfect transition, that takes us directly to Buffalo Bill loving "his moth," Catherine Martin. She pleads with Jame Gumb (Buffalo Bill's real name) to let her go. Though we know he is a madman killer, a sick, vicious, sadistic psychopath, he has a little fat poodle, "Precious," whom he loves dearly. It is a wonderful element that adds dimension to the character; of course, such touches are what make Thomas Harris's novel so exceptional.

We cut directly to Clarice and Ardelia as they watch the news bulletin showing that Catherine Martin, the only daughter of Senator Ruth Martin, has been kidnapped by Buffalo Bill. From the news story we learn things about the victim, we see baby pictures and hear Senator Martin speak to Buffalo Bill: "You have the power to let Catherine go, unharmed. She's very gentle and kind— talk to her and you'll see. . . . You have the power. You are in charge." She mentions Catherine's name over and over again, and when Ardelia asks why, Clarice responds, "If he sees Catherine as a person, not just an object, it's harder to tear her up." "Please, release her unharmed," the senator continues. "Please, I beg you, release my little girl."

Crawford tells Clarice that they found a moth in Raspail's head, and the connection is established: The man who killed Benjamin Raspail is the same man who killed the floater. This means only one thing: Hannibal Lecter knows who Buffalo Bill is. If Lecter wants to deal, so does Crawford, and Clarice is the messenger.

We cut to Baltimore State Hospital, where an agitated Dr. Chilton accompanies Clarice down the corridor. "What you're doing, Miss Starling," Chilton complains, "is coming into my hospital to conduct an interview, and refusing to share information with me." She tells him that "this is the U.S. Attorney's number. Now, please—either discuss this with him, or let me do my job." And she leaves him.

We enter the scene with Lecter, the psychiatrist, ever the teacher, asking how she felt when she viewed "our Billy's latest effort. Or should I say, his 'next-to-latest.' " "By the book, he's a sadist," she answers. "Life's too slippery for books, Clarice. Typhoid and swans came from the same God. Tell me," he says, "Miss West Virginia—was she a large girl . . . big through the hips. Roomy."

"Yes," she replies, and tells him about the "insect deliberately inserted in her throat." Lecter asks if it was a butterfly. "A moth," she says, surprised. How did he know that?

"I'm waiting for your offer, Clarice. Enchant me."

It's interesting to note the two things going on in this scene: One is the story information we need to keep the action moving forward; the second is character information about Clarice. Tally weaves both of these elements together to paint a psychological portrait of Clarice with the narrative action. It gives the scene substance and dimension.

Quid pro quo. Clarice lays out Crawford's "offer" to Lecter: If he helps save Catherine Martin, he'll be "transferred to the VA hospital at Oneida Park, New York, with a view of the woods nearby. Maximum security still applies, but you'd have reasonable access to books. Best of all, one week a year you'd get to leave the hospital and go here." She points to her map. "Plum Island, where every afternoon of that week you can walk on the beach or swim in the ocean for up to one hour. Under SWAT team surveillance, of course. . . ."

Not a bad offer. But—and it's a very big "but"—if Catherine Martin should die, Lecter gets nothing.

> LECTER
>
> If I help you, Clarice, it will be . . . quid pro quo. I tell you things, you tell me things. Not about this case, though—about your-self. Yes or no?
> (She is silent.)
> Yes or no? Clarice. Catherine is waiting. Tick-tock, tick-tock . . .

She looks at him. A beat. They are standing uncomfortably close.

> CLARICE
>
> Go, Doctor.

> DR. LECTER
>
> What's your worst memory of childhood?
> (She hesitates.)
> Quicker than that. I'm not interested in your worst *invention*.

> CLARICE
>
> The death of my father.

> LECTER
>
> Tell me. Don't lie, or I'll know.

Clarice cannot bear the feverish excitement in his eyes. She looks past him, hesitating again.

> CLARICE
>
> He was a town marshal . . . one night he surprised two burglars, coming out the back of a drugstore. . . . They shot him.

DR. LECTER

Killed outright?

CLARICE

No. He was strong, he lasted almost a month. My mother—died when I was very young, so my father had become—the whole world to me. . . . After he left me, I had nobody. I was ten years old.

DR. LECTER

You're very frank, Clarice. I think it would be quite something to know you in private life.

[It is a great compliment he pays her. Tally also says, "It also implies a disturbing threat; to 'know' Hannibal Lecter is to risk being consumed by him."]

CLARICE

Quid pro quo, Doctor.

DR. LECTER

The significance of the moth is change. Caterpillar into pupa into beauty. . . . Billy wants to change, too, Clarice. But there's the problem of his size, you see. Even if he were a woman, he'd have to be such a big one. . . .

CLARICE

(puzzled)

Dr. Lecter, there's no correlation in the literature between transsexualism and violence. Transsexuals are very passive.

DR. LECTER

Clever girl. You're *so* close to the way you're going to catch him. Do you realize that?

CLARICE

No. Tell me why.

DR. LECTER

After your father's death, you were orphaned. What happened next?
   (Clarice drops her gaze.)
I don't imagine the answer's on those sec-
ond-rate shoes, Clarice.

CLARICE

I went to live with my mother's cousin and
her husband in Montana. They had a ranch.

DR. LECTER

A cattle ranch?

CLARICE

Horses—and sheep.

DR. LECTER

How long did you live there?

CLARICE

Two months.

DR. LECTER

Why so briefly?

CLARICE

I—ran away. . . .

DR. LECTER

Why, Clarice? Did the rancher fuck you?

CLARICE

No . . . ! Quid pro quo, Doctor?

DR. LECTER

Billy's not a real transsexual, but he thinks

DR. LECTER (cont'd.)
he is. He *tries* to be. He's tried to be a lot of things, I expect.

CLARICE
You said—I was very close to the way we'd catch him.

DR. LECTER
There are three major centers for transsexual surgery: Johns Hopkins, the University of Minnesota, and Columbus Medical Center. I wouldn't be surprised if Billy had applied for sex reassignment at one or all of them, and been rejected.

CLARICE
On what basis would they reject him?

DR. LECTER
The personality inventories would trip him up. Rorschach, Wechsler, House-Tree-Person. He wouldn't test like a real transsexual.

INT. DR. CHILTON'S OFFICE—DAY

Chilton, listening through a speaker, eavesdrops on the conversation.

CLARICE (VO)
How would he test?

DR. LECTER (VO)
Happy hunting. Oh, and Clarice—next time you *will* tell me why you ran away. Now listen carefully, because I won't repeat this. . . .

We cut to a close shot of a death's-head moth in Jame Gumb's cellar. Lecter's description of what to look for in discovering Buffalo Bill is played voice-over in the "eerie, dimly lit warren of a cellar" while we hear some rock music over the "rapid CLICKING of a sewing machine." We see Gumb the second time, hunched over his sewing machine, working on his "girl's suit," his little dog Precious sitting happily at his feet.

Precious moves into another area of the cellar: "At the end of this final corridor, the cellar widens into a low-ceilinged chamber, with two additional doorways, and in the center of this is the gaping circle of the oubliette. Precious sniffs her way over to the edge—excited, tail wagging—then BARKS happily as we hear a hoarse, ghostly moan from below."

"Pleeeeeeeeaasssse . . ." Catherine pleads, ending the scene.

Shocking and horrible, yes, but it leads us directly to the Mid-Point of Act II. Lecter is strapped to a rolling hand truck, completely engulfed in heavy restraints, ready to be transferred. Over his face is a hockey mask. Chilton has "bugged" Lecter's visit with Clarice, and tells the psychiatrist, "I called Senator Ruth Martin, and she never heard of any deal with you. They *scammed* you, Hannibal. . . ." He tells Lecter the "new deal" the senator offers. While he talks, Lecter's eyes travel to Chilton's pen lying half hidden under the sheets. The script reads, "We can almost hear his brain clicking."

Chilton demands Lecter tell him who Buffalo Bill is. "You'll answer me *now,* or by God, you'll never leave this cell. *Who is Buffalo Bill?*"

The screenplay carries a scene here showing a very impatient Crawford talking with the head doctor at Johns Hopkins, asking him to release vital information to the FBI. Finally, Crawford threatens to blackmail the institution unless the doctor cooperates. They wisely dropped this scene from the film. There's no time for it.

Instead, we cut from Chilton's question to Crawford learning that Lecter was transferred to Memphis at Senator Martin's request. (The FBI man talking to Crawford on the phone is Roger Corman, one of the most influential film makers and discoverer of film talent in the '60s.) It is a dynamic film transition taking us from the question ending one scene to its answer in the next scene.

The action in the First Half of Act II has been constructed step by step. For every question, there is an answer. Action, reaction. Lecter gives Clarice information about Buffalo Bill; Clarice gives Hannibal Lecter psychological information about herself.

Quid pro quo.

19

Teacher:

First Principles

Hannibal Lecter's transfer to Memphis is the Mid-Point of Act II. The scene opens with the plane landing, and the mad doctor is wheeled toward the two policemen who will be his armed guards. They've seen worse: "He's just an ol' broke-dick," one of them comments. "Won't be no trouble at all. . . ." Crawford's line in the previous scene about whether the cops in Memphis can handle him will be prophetic: "They'll use their best men. But they better be paying attention. . . ."

Two stretch limos pull up; Senator Martin and her aides step out and confront Lecter, who is still in his restraints. She tells him that she has brought an affidavit. "I won't waste your time and Catherine's time bargaining for petty privileges," Lecter begins. "Let me help you now, and I'll trust you when it's all over." The bargain is struck.

He tells them that "Buffalo Bill's real name is Louis Friend. I met him just once. He was referred to me in April or May 1980 by my patient Benjamin Raspail. They were lovers."

Then Lecter, in his quest to feast on "quid pro quo," asks the senator something personal; he is a psychiatrist, after all. "Did you nurse Catherine?" he asks her. "Breast-feed her?" Startled, unsure, she replies that she did. "Toughened your nipples, didn't it? Amputate a man's leg, and he can still feel it tickling. Tell me, Mom: When your little girl's on the slab, where will it tickle you?"

"Her eyes leap fire," the script reads. "Take this thing back to Baltimore," she commands, and turns her back on him. But as she walks away, Lecter yells the description: "Five-foot-ten, strongly built, about 180 pounds. Hair blond, eyes pale blue. He'd be about thirty-five now."

She turns, "trying to gauge the truth. His eyes are unblinking, guileless." She doesn't know whether it's true, but they have to go with it.

Lecter can't resist having the last word in this exchange. As the senator walks to the limo, he yells after her, "Oh, and Senator . . . *love* your suit!"

Cut to Clarice entering the Shelby County Courthouse, where Hannibal Lecter is temporarily housed. The place is swarming with police. We overhear Chilton telling the crowd of gathered media that his "name is Chilton. C-H-I-L—"

Clarice talks her way into seeing Lecter, checks her weapon, and rides up the elevator with the armed guard. "Is it true what they're sayin'?" he asks. "He's some kinda vampire?" "I don't have a name for what he is," Clarice replies.

We move with her as she makes the long walk into the large gymnasium, where Lecter, his back to us, is lounging in an iron cage, listening to Bach. "Good afternoon, Clarice," he says. She hands the doctor his drawings as a kind of "gift." He wants to know why she came, and she replies that she wanted to.

"People will say we're in love," he says playfully. "Pity for poor Catherine, though. Tick-tock." Thus begins the long scene that literally binds them together. They're connected in a profound way, like lost father and daughter, teacher and student. We know Lecter admires Clarice: "I think it would be quite something to know you in private life," he said in an earlier scene. More than that you're not going to get from Hannibal Lecter.

This "love scene" is the key scene in Act II. It cements their relationship. They confide in each other, and he gives her the vital information she needs to track Buffalo Bill. He is both a teacher and a father to her, guiding her into awareness and revelation. It is a remarkable scene.

FAVORING CLARICE

as she circles the cage, trying to keep his face in sight.

> CLARICE
> Your anagrams are showing, Doctor. "Louis Friend . . . ?" "Iron Sulfide." Better known as fool's gold.

> DR. LECTER
> Clarice . . . your problem is, you need to get more *fun* out of life.

> CLARICE
> You were telling me the truth back in Baltimore. Tell me the rest now.

> DR. LECTER
> I've studied the case file. Have you . . . ? Everything you need to find him is right in these pages. Whatever his name is.

> CLARICE
> Then tell me how.

> DR. LECTER
> First principles, Clarice. Simplicity. Read Marcus Aurelius. Of each particular thing, ask: What is it in itself, what is its nature . . . ? What does he *do*, this man you seek?

> CLARICE
> He kills w—

> DR. LECTER
> (sharply, as he stops)
> No! That's incidental.

CLOSER ANGLE

as he rises, pained by her ignorance, and crosses to the bars.

> DR. LECTER
> What is the first and principal thing he does, what *need* does he serve by killing?

> CLARICE
> Anger, social resentment, sexual frust—

> DR. LECTER
> No, he *covets*. That's his nature. And how do we begin to covet, Clarice? Do we *seek out* things to covet? Make an effort to answer.

> CLARICE
> No. We just—

> DR. LECTER
> No. Precisely. We begin by coveting *what we see every day*. Don't you feel eyes moving over your body, Clarice? I hardly see how you couldn't. And don't your eyes move over the things you want?

> CLARICE
> All right, then tell me how—

> DR. LECTER
> No. It's your turn to tell me, Clarice. You don't have any more vacations to sell. Why did you run away from that ranch?

> CLARICE
> Dr. Lecter, when there's time I'll—

> DR. LECTER
> We don't reckon time the same way, Clarice. This is all the time you'll ever have.

> CLARICE
> Later, listen, I'll—

> DR. LECTER
> I'll listen *now*. After your father's murder,
> you were orphaned. You were ten years old.
> You went to live with cousins, on a sheep
> and horse ranch in Montana. And . . . ?

She turns from him. He presses closer, gripping the bars.

> CLARICE
> And—one morning I just—ran away.

> DR. LECTER
> No "just," Clarice. What set you off? You
> started what time?

> CLARICE
> Early. Still dark.

> DR. LECTER
> Then something woke you. What? Did you
> dream? What was it?

When I started thinking about this scene, I found I really didn't understand the word "covet"—it means "to lust after," or "to desire." We all covet things in life, whether it's a new car, a new dress, or that new pair of skis you told yourself you were going to buy this season. Or, if you're not satisfied with who you are, you want to be someone different, like the person you saw last night. Whatever it is, we want it. All of us are filled with a stream of endless desires. Satisfy one, and another appears in its place. It never ends.

Buffalo Bill's desire, his dramatic need, is to get a new "girl's suit." Lecter's desire is to obtain a view, so he's teaching Clarice how to hunt a serial killer, and she's a very good student.

As they start trading information, Lecter's prompting leads Tally to insert a flashback at this point, expanding Clarice's memory of what happened at age ten. Though Tally wrote it, the flashback was never filmed. "The young Clarice is awakened at night," said Tally, "and hears these lambs being killed. She doesn't know what it is, so she sneaks out and we see the little girl. It was written to intercut with her talk to Lecter. Jonathan wasn't really sure about it. He said, 'I'm going to shoot it both ways, and I'll have it in the bank, but I just don't know if we can cut away from what's going on between her and Lecter. It's too powerful.'

"So what happened," Tally continued, "is that he was going to hold off on filming the Montana sequence, make it the last shot to be filmed. He had to wait for the spring lambing season in March, and the rest of the movie was going to be finished shooting by the end of February.

"So he shot the sequence between Jodie and Tony Hopkins, and told me the scene was so powerful as written that if he cut away from her into a flashback he'd be thrown out of the Directors' Guild.

"Since it was a complicated flashback, not shooting it saved a lot of money; I wasn't sorry to see it go. I told Jonathan that if I had known the scene wasn't going to be supported by the visual flashback, I probably would have written the dialogue between her and Lecter differently. But he said, 'You know what? You didn't need to, you got it in there anyway.' "

It certainly was the right decision. If this flashback had been inserted as written, it would not have served the story at all. This is the omitted scene, beautifully written, but unnecessary. It is their farewell scene.

"The dream," Lecter asks Clarice. "What was it?"

IN FLASHBACK—

The ten-year-old Clarice sits up abruptly in her bed, frightened. She is in a Montana ranch house; it is almost dawn. Strange, fearful shadows on her ceiling and walls . . . a window, partly fogged by the cold; eerie brightness outside.

CLARICE (VO)
I heard a strange sound. . . .

>   DR. LECTER (VO)
> What was it?

THE CHILD RISES—

crosses to the window in her nightgown, rubs the glass.

>   CLARICE (VO)
> I didn't know. I went to look. . . .

HIGH ANGLES (2nd STORY)—THE CHILD'S POV—

Shadowy men, ranch hands, are moving in and out of a nearby barn, carrying mysterious bundles. The men's breath is steaming. . . . A refrigerated truck idles nearby, its engine adding more steam. A strange, almost surrealistic scene. . . .

>   CLARICE (VO cont'd.)
> Screaming! Some kind of—screaming. Like a
> child's voice. . . .

THE LITTLE GIRL

is terrified; she covers her ears.

>   DR. LECTER (VO)
> What did you do?

>   CLARICE (VO)
> Got dressed without turning on the light. I
> went downstairs . . . outside.

THE LITTLE GIRL—

in her winter coat, slips noiselessly toward the open barn door. She ducks into the shadows to avoid a ranch hand, who passes her with a squirming bundle of some kind. He goes into the barn, and she edges after him reluctantly.

> CLARICE (VO cont'd.)
> I crept up to the barn. . . . I was so scared
> to look inside—but I had to. . . .

THE LITTLE GIRL'S POV—

as the open doorway LOOMS CLOSER. Bright lights inside,
straw bales, the edges of stalls, then moving figures. . . .

> DR. LECTER (VO)
> And what did you see, Clarice?

A SQUIRMING LAMB—

is held down on a table by two ranch hands.

> CLARICE (VO)
> *Lambs.* The lambs were screaming. . . .

A third cowboy stretches out the lamb's neck, raises a bloody
knife. Just as he's about to slice its throat—

BACK TO THE ADULT CLARICE—

staring into the distance, shaken, still trembling from the child's
shock. We see Dr. Lecter over her shoulder, studying her intently.

> DR. LECTER
> They were slaughtering the spring lambs?

> CLARICE
> Yes . . . ! They were *screaming.*

> DR. LECTER
> So you ran away. . . .

> CLARICE
> No. First I tried to free them. I opened the
> gate of their pen—but they wouldn't run.

CLARICE (cont'd.)
They just stood there, confused. They
wouldn't run. . . .

DR. LECTER
But you could. You did.

CLARICE
I took one lamb. And I ran away, as fast as I
could.

IN FLASHBACK

*a vast Montana plain, and crossing this, a tiny figure—the little
Clarice, holding a lamb in her arms.*

DR. LECTER (VO)
Where were you going?

CLARICE (VO)
I don't know. I had no food or water. It
was very cold. I thought—if I can even save
just *one* . . . but he got so heavy. So
heavy. . . .

*The tiny figure stops, and after a few moments sinks to the ground,
hunched over in despair.*

CLARICE (VO cont'd.)
I didn't get more than a few miles before the
sheriff's car found me. The rancher was so
angry he sent me to live at the Lutheran or-
phanage in Bozeman. I never saw the ranch
again.

DR. LECTER (VO)
But what became of your lamb?
(no response)
Clarice . . . ?

BACK TO SCENE—

as the adult Clarice turns, staring into his feverish eyes. She shakes her head, unwilling—or unable—to say more.

> DR. LECTER (cont'd.)
> You still wake up sometimes, don't you? Wake up in the dark, with the lambs screaming?

> CLARICE
> Yes.

> DR. LECTER
> Do you think if you saved Catherine, you could make them stop . . . ? Do you think, if Catherine lives, you won't wake up in the dark, ever again, to the screaming of the lambs? *Do* you . . . ?

> CLARICE
> Yes! I don't know . . . ! I don't know.

> DR. LECTER
> (a pause; then, oddly at peace)
> Thank you, Clarice.

> CLARICE
> (a whisper)
> Tell me his *name,* Dr. Lecter.

> DR. LECTER
> Dr. Chilton . . . I believe you know each other?

NEW ANGLE

as Clarice turns, startled, and the fuming Chilton seizes her elbow. Pembry and Boyle are beside him, looking grim.

CHILTON

Out. Let's go.

BOYLE

Sorry, ma'am—we've got orders to have you put on a plane.

Clarice struggles, pulling free of them for a moment.

DR. LECTER

Brave Clarice. Will you let me know if ever the lambs stop screaming?

CLARICE
(moving closer to the bars)
Yes. I'll tell you.

DR. LECTER

Promise . . . ?

DR. LECTER (cont'd.)
(She nods. He smiles.)
Then why not take your case file? I won't be needing it anymore.

He holds out the file, arm extended between the bars. She hesitates, then reaches to take it.

VERY CLOSE ANGLE—SLOW MOTION

as the exchange is made, his index finger touches her hand, and lingers there, just for a moment.

DR. LECTER'S EYES

widen, crackling at this touch, like sparks in a cave.

DR. LECTER (cont'd.)
Good-bye, Clarice.

CLARICE—

hugging the case file to her chest, stares back at him as the men crowd in on her, pushing her away.

HER POV—MOVING—

as Dr. Lecter, head cocked in a smile, slowly recedes. SOUND CUT TO—Glenn Gould playing Bach's Goldberg Variations. . . .

And we're out.

It's quite a scene. A strong scene, so strong that it would get in the way of the story; it would impede the action, not expand it. The dialogue's the same, there are no pictures with it. It keeps the visual focus on Lecter and Clarice and keeps the story moving forward.

Pinch II in *The Silence of the Lambs* is Lecter's escape. However, Lecter's removal from the action "leaves a very big hole in the movie," Tally observes, "because the psychological menace is gone. My problem was to keep the clock ticking, and keep the level of suspense as high as possible." The only way to do that is to make the ending so strong and powerful that we forget Lecter.

In the book, the escape is brilliantly executed by Tom Harris, and Ted Tally does a wonderful job capturing it in the script. It is a sequence that is lean, clean, tight, and scary, another of those unforgettable film moments. It opens with the guards complaining about having to bring Lecter his second meal. As Lecter prepares for the food tray, we see the flickering reflection from the silver pocket clip of Chilton's pen. Lecter takes the clip from his mouth, slips it between his fingers, and gets into position so his hands can be handcuffed to the bars. The guards enter.

Lecter works fast, and because the two policemen were not "paying attention," as Crawford had warned, they become Lecter's victims.

The killings are brutal and horrifying, accompanied with the lyrical refrains of the *Goldberg Variations*.

BOYLE

looks up, astonished, to find himself right in the grinning face of Dr. Lecter—who just as quickly rolls sideways, and snaps—

THE OTHER CUFF

around the bolted leg of the table. And suddenly all natural SOUND and MOTION are suspended as the MUSIC soars much louder, each separate note of it now echoing distinctly, and we see . . .

VARIOUS ANGLES—EACH BLURRING INTO STOP-ACTION—

Pembry starting into the cell, reaching for his riot baton . . .

Lecter smashing against the cell door, driving it into Pembry, pinning him across the chest, against the doorframe. . . .

Boyle, on one knee on the floor, digging desperately in his pants pocket for his handcuff key . . .

Pembry's eyes widening in horror as he stares at . . .

Lecter's bared teeth flashing toward him . . .

Boyle finding his key, but in his terror dropping it . . .

Lecter yanking the Mace can and riot baton from the dazed Pembry's belt, spraying him in his bloody face, then clubbing him to his knees . . .

Boyle, mouth open in a silent scream, finding his key again, unlocking the handcuff, but then, as he starts to rise, seeing . . .

Lecter standing over him, with the riot baton raised high; he swings it viciously down, again and again and again. . . . Then normal SOUND and MOTION are restored as we go to—

CLOSE ANGLE ON—

the cassette player, and the portrait of Clarice, both now flecked with blood. In addition to the Bach, we now hear soft PANTING, close by, and whimpering SOBS in the b.g.

ANGLE ON DR. LECTER

eyes closed, lost in a favorite passage of the music. His bloody fingers drift airily with the notes as his breathing slows to normal. He opens his eyes, sighs contentedly, looks down.

That's Pinch II. Now Lecter has to get out of the building. The screenwriter has a choice here—either show how he escapes, or cut to him after he's out of the building. In this case you can't really *not* show it. The way Lecter gets out is horrifyingly ingenious. The police hear gunshots, make their way up the stairs, and find the two bodies—one strung up like Christ, the other lying in a bloody mess. Of course, Lecter is where we least expect him. Pembry is alive, but when they attempt to give him an injection he conveniently has a "seizure," and they whisk him to the ambulance.

The suspense in the elevator is high, and we don't learn he has really escaped until we cut to the ambulance. Only when he pulls off "his face mask" and we see the smiling, bloody face of Hannibal Lecter, do we freak.

Then comes one of my favorite cuts of the movie. From Lecter's face we cut to the Academy, to Ardelia dropping the phone and racing down the corridor. In the script, Tally has the ambulance pulling into the Memphis airport; then he shows a brief flashback of Clarice as the rancher takes the lamb from her. It doesn't work at all, contrived and obvious, but when you're writing the screenplay, you really can't see anything except the page you're writing and the pages you've written. You have no overview. Of course, it's easy to see this in hindsight, but not so easy when you're in "the pit," grappling with the writing process.

"They found the ambulance," Ardelia gasps to Clarice, "in the parking garage at the Memphis airport. . . . The crew was dead.

He killed a tourist, too. Got his clothes, cash. By now he could be anywhere."

Clarice is convinced that Lecter won't come after her. "It's hard to explain," she says, "but he would consider that rude."

Then we're into the laundry room and the Plot Point at the end of Act II. Putting her in the laundry room is another way that Harris illuminates Clarice's character. In the novel he describes her emotional attraction to the laundry room like this: Ardelia *"found Starling in the warm laundry room, dozing against the slow rump-rump of a washing machine in the smell of bleach and soap and fabric softener. She knew that the washing machine's rhythm was like a great heartbeat and the rush of its waters was what the unborn hear—our last memory of peace."*

Clarice has the Buffalo Bill case file; it's only fitting that she try to figure out the puzzle (her final exam, Lecter might say) he has given her—a note scrawled across the Buffalo Bill case file. "Clarice," he has written, "doesn't this random scattering of sites seem a bit overdone to you? Doesn't it seem desperately random—like the elaborations of a bad liar? Ta . . . Hannibal Lecter."

"Desperately random." What does that mean? All the victims seemed to be random. "Except for the first girl, Fredrica Bimmel, from Belvedere, Ohio," Clarice says. "The first girl taken, but the third body found. . . . Why?"

"What did Lecter say about 'first principles'?" Clarice muses. "Simplicity . . . What does this guy do? He 'covets.' How do we first *start* to covet?

"We covet *'what we see every day.'* " They look at each other, and Clarice suddenly understands.

"Hot damn. He knew her."

20

Graduation Day:

Rendezvous

At the beginning of Act III, two elements are left unresolved: Will Clarice find Buffalo Bill before Catherine's killed? and How does she resolve the relationship with Hannibal Lecter? Those two story points have to be addressed during the third act.

Lecter's escape has left a gaping hole in the action. How did Tally compensate for this new situation? The only way he could make the story really work, he said, was to be certain the ending was as strong and powerful as it could be. "We knew the quality of suspense had changed, and had become more conventional in the third act. The last act is a very different quality from the psychological suspense set up in the first two acts.

"When I was writing the third act," he continued, "I was in New York borrowing an office from the writer/director Robert Benton (*Bonnie & Clyde, Kramer vs. Kramer, Places in the Heart*). He knew the book; we'd chatted about it, and he was always supportive and sympathetic. And I said to him, 'You know, at the hub of all this, when all is said and done, we have this brilliant character, Lecter, and this complicated, unusual investigation, but it's really a young woman in a basement being stalked by a madman, and we've seen that a million times. What am I going to do about that?'

"And he said, 'You know what? We need to see that. We want to see that. We've seen it a million times before, but we want to see it again, because you've promised us that we're going to see it. You've got one track with Buffalo Bill, and you've got another track with Clarice, and you have implied a promise that she's going to end up in that basement. Every time we see that basement throughout the movie you are implying a promise that she will have to go into it. Don't be concerned that it's been done many times before; we want to see it, we have to see it.'

"So," Tally went on, "if it was going to be a conventional suspense, the madman stalking the girl in the basement, then we'd better get a few original twists in there. It was a safety net waiting for me, because I knew that if I could just get her into that basement, I'm home free."

That meant most of the last act had to be a straightforward action sequence. Tally had to know the ending before he sat down to write one single word of screenplay. The scene in the basement is the focal point, the final destination, the end of the line that was set up from page one, word one. It is what Clarice's journey, her rite of initiation, has been all about; her final exam.

Plot Point II was the realization that Buffalo Bill must have known his first victim, Fredrica Bimmel from Belvedere, Ohio, "the first victim killed, the third one found." The only victim weighted down. "Desperately random," was not really so desperate, as Hannibal Lecter wisely observes in his note to Clarice. It was logical.

Clarice convinces Crawford to let her check it out—on her own time, of course. As a woman she might be able to see things about Fredrica that the original investigators may have missed. He gives her all the money he has with him, and sends her off with his blessing.

Here's where the script and the movie diverge. Tally wrote a lot of scenes that were filmed, but then during the editing process, Jonathan Demme restructured them to make Act III tighter, more suspenseful, highlighting the action of the madman stalking a woman in the basement.

Tally gets Clarice into the action immediately: One shot of the train heading into Ohio (each picture tells a story, and bridges time and place); then we see Clarice at the victim's house. The room is exactly as Fredrica left it. Clarice begins wandering, searching for anything Fredrica might be able to tell her. She meets her cat, finds pictures of an almost naked Fredrica, starts looking through her closet. That's when she sees the dress and notices the large triangular darts; they make the same pattern that was found on the "floater," at Pinch I.

Tally writes a larger scene than was used in the film. It was trimmed in the editing room. As Clarice goes through the photographs, we see:

THE FINAL SHOTS—

all of a naked Fredrica, seen from the side or back, as she peers coyly over her shoulder, or is frozen in helpless giggles. She has a very broad back; the photographer seems less interested in prurience than in her vast expanse of skin.

CLARICE

looks up, starting to tremble, as a taunting memory forms in her mind.

> DR. LECTER (VO)
> Billy wants to change, too, Clarice. But
> there's the problem of his size, you see. . . .

She turns, looking again at the sewing machine . . . then at the Polaroids in her hand . . . and then at the unfinished dress, hanging from the closet doorknob. Suddenly she stiffens, her attention riveted by something. . . .

ON THE PRINTED PATTERN—

at the lower back of the dress are two bold black triangles. We RUSH CLOSER to these shapes before jumping back to—

CLARICE

who stares at them, eyes widening.

> DR. LECTER (VO cont'd.)
> Even if he were a woman, he'd have to be
> such a big one. . . .

IN FLASHBACK—

those missing triangles of skin on the dead girl's back, in the funeral home in West Virginia.

CLOSE ON CLARICE

as she jumps to her feet, with a fierce joy.

> CLARICE
> *Sewing* darts. You *bastard.*

This portion of the scene was dropped probably because all the information is redundant. We've either seen or heard it before. Demme tightens up the action by having her discover the triangular darts, then cutting to her on a telephone telling Crawford, "He's making himself a 'woman suit' out of real women. . . ."

Crawford, speaking on a phone in a large turbojet, interrupts her: "Clarice . . . we know who he is! And *where* he is," and tells her they're already on the way. His real name is Jame Gumb, "a real beauty. Slaughtered both his grandparents when he was twelve, and did nine years in juvenile psychiatric. *Where,* Starling, he took vocational rehab, and learned a useful trade: sewing." Some of this was in the novel, some of it was made up. It doesn't matter; it was cut. But there was a new line added about Customs discovering that Jame Gumb had imported those rare death's-head moths illegally.

Crawford tells Clarice, "We wouldn't have found him without you, and nobody's ever going to forget that. Least of all me."

Great. But she'd rather be four hundred miles away, with Crawford, ready to pounce on the serial killer Buffalo Bill.

At this point Jonathan Demme took a scene originally written and filmed to follow Lecter's transfer to Memphis and inserted it here, in the third act. It whets our appetite for Clarice's ultimate rendezvous with Gumb.

The sequence opens in Gumb's basement with Catherine muttering to herself, "Close enough to touch is close enough to fight. . . ." Fear fueling determination, she baits a chicken bone to the bucket string, tries to coax little Precious to take it. It doesn't work.

The serial killer is in his "dressing room," primping before the mirror, and like some giant death's-head moth opening its wings, Jame Gumb "slowly spreads out his arms, opening his kimono, revealing his naked, utterly hairless body, his rouged nipples, his genitals tucked out of sight between his thighs." He stares at himself in the mirror, "trembling with awe at his own terrible and mysterious beauty."

The transformation, emerging from the cocoon, is almost complete. For both hunter and hunted.

Clarice has located the victim's best friend, Stacy, and questions her about Fredrica, searching for any information she can get her hands on. This little scene, only a few lines in the film, is an excellent example of screenwriting. In this simple transition scene the subtext makes this scene reveal more than any three-page dialogue scene possibly could. What is *not* said is more important than what is said.

Stacy tells us about life in a small town and about Fredrica: "Sewing was her life," she says, and she occasionally worked for a certain Mrs. Lippman. Then Stacy breaks her train of thought and asks Clarice whether working for the FBI is a good job. The question reveals everything we need to know about life in Belvedere, Ohio. "You get to travel around and stuff? I mean, better places than this? Freddie was so happy for me when I got this job. *This*— toaster giveaways, and Barry Manilow on the speakers all day— she thought this was really hot shit. What did she know, big dummy . . . ?" Suddenly "she's fighting tears."

What makes this scene so good is that it says so much with so little. It reveals a young girl's hopes and dreams, her real feelings toward her friend. Many screenwriters, I think, would approach this scene directly: simple questions and answers about Fredrica's life. An expository scene, nothing more, simply another step along the journey to the rendezvous with Buffalo Bill.

Sometimes the screenwriter needs to approach a scene directly: You simply write what the scene's about, like the first scene between Clarice and Crawford. But the screenwriter must always search for another, original way to say what needs to be said, to say it *indirectly,* as opposed to directly; to avoid the obvious. One of the things separating an aspiring screenwriter from a professional is that one writes a scene directly, saying what needs to be said, while the professional looks for a way to say it indirectly. In the craft of writing it's called "playing against the grain of the scene." And Tom Harris is a master at it.

The action cuts back to the cellar where Jame Gumb is selecting a cocoon from his collection, getting ready to "do" Catherine. When he discovers that his precious little Precious is "down here, you sack of shit," he's caught off guard. Catherine holds the little dog up for him to see and threatens it. It's his one weak point, his Achilles' heel, and she knows it. When she yells that the dog's in pain and needs help, he replies, "You don't know what pain is." Interesting answer.

Now we start cooking. Three streams of action begin to intercut with each other, like musical themes, heightening the tension, the suspense. One, Crawford arrives in Calumet City, setting up his FBI team; two, Gumb is trying to get his dog back safely; and three, Clarice is looking for the family of Mrs. Lippman.

This cross-cutting between three parallel streams of action is totally cinematic, a complete departure from the book. I asked Tally how he approached this in the adaptation, and he replied, "There's a hint of that in the book: Gumb opens the door, and Clarice is standing there. The book doesn't stage the FBI raid with Crawford at the wrong house; it was simply implied. From the beginning I thought, Well, this is a real opportunity to cross-cut and build suspense. So I cross-cut between three little segments in the first draft. When Jonathan read it, one of the things he said was, 'This will work; I can sustain this. You can do more with this, this will build. Let's go farther with it.' So I had to invent more action with the SWAT team. We knew the SWAT team hitting the wrong house was a little 'sleight of hand,' but it works well and is effective."

As the SWAT team moves into position in Calumet City, Jame Gumb tries to get Precious away from Catherine. The flower van pulls up to a house. A man gets out, walks to the front door as Crawford and the others move into position. Back and forth we move between the two scenes. The delivery man pushes the buzzer, and the doorbell goes off in Gumb's house. The doorbell rings incessantly as the FBI team readies to make its move.

The doorbell rings again, loud, irritating, as we cut to Clarice ringing the doorbell in Belvedere. When Gumb swings the front door open, we expect to see the flower delivery man followed by Crawford and the SWAT team.

Instead we see Clarice. All of us in the audience that day literally jumped out of our seats, totally linked in the "community of emotion." It is filmmaking at its finest.

"Good afternoon . . . I'm looking for Mrs. Lippman's family," Clarice says, smiling to an uptight Jame Gumb. She's polite but firm, and insists on talking to him.

Notice the situation here: The audience knows he's the killer; Clarice doesn't, of course. The tension comes from the audience wanting the character to know what it knows; this technique generates the tension; it made Hitchcock's films such a treat. This situation is called an "open" story: The audience knows what's going on, but the character doesn't. In a "closed" story, the audience learns what's happening at the same time the character does.

Gumb tells her his name is Jack Gordon, and no, he didn't know Mrs. Lippman. We see he's uptight, but he's cool, casual, in control of the situation. As she follows him inside, her training teaches her to be observant, so she casually looks around, checking it all out. She notices a box of thread, spools of thread in a box, and as she watches, a death's-head moth lands on a spool right in front of her. She freezes. "A beat of pure fear," the script reads. "A terrible struggle to keep her voice calm." This is the way Tally wrote it, and while it was trimmed and thinned in the movie, it's all here.

Very carefully, she drops her notebook back into her bag, lowers the bag to the floor. With her fingertips she brushes back the edge of her coat, loosening its drape.

MR. GUMB

turns back to her cheerfully, holding out a business card.

> MR. GUMB
> Ahhhh . . . here's that number.

CLARICE

keeps her distance. They are about ten feet apart.

> CLARICE
> Good, thank you. Mr. Gordon, can I use
> your phone, please?

MR. GUMB

is about to reply when the moth suddenly flies up from behind him, flutters past his face. He turns, looking at it. He looks back at Clarice, his mouth still open.

HER EYES

are unmoving, locked on his.

HIS EYES

stare back at her, widen. And they know each other.

> MR. GUMB
> (softly)
>
> Yes. It can use my phone. . . .

She pulls her gun, but he ducks behind a door and is gone. Notice that "she" becomes an "it." If you look at a screenplay from the screenwriter's perspective, we've spent the entire screen-play preparing for this moment: the madman hunting the girl in the basement. The rest of the movie is a chase sequence. That's why Tally said that as soon as he could get her into the basement, he's "home free."

Cautiously, she descends into the cellar of Buffalo Bill. She locates Catherine, tells her she'll be back, and continues her hunt for Jame Gumb. This is a natural situation to build and develop tension, as befits a great thriller. Clarice tries to acclimate herself to the surroundings of the cellar. We follow her step by step, until the lights go out and we cut to the "eerie green light" we saw once before, in the abduction of Catherine.

INT. MR. GUMB'S WORKROOM—DAY (Green Light)

Clarice emerges from the bathroom in a half-crouch, arms out, both hands on the gun, extended just below the level of her unseeing eyes. She stops, listens. In her raw-nerved darkness, every SOUND is unnaturally magnified—the HUM of the refrigerator, the TRICKLE of water, her own terrified BREATHING, and Catherine's faraway, echoing SOBS. Moths smack against her face and arms. She eases forward, then stops again, listens. She eases forward again, following her gun, and creeps directly in front of, and then past—

MR. GUMB

who has flattened himself against a wall, arms spread like a high priest, Colt in one hand. He wears his goggles, and over his chest—draping down over his naked arms like some hideous mantle—his terrifying, half-completed suit of human skins. This is an exquisite moment for him—a ritual of supreme exaltation. She moves beyond him, pauses again.

PAST CLARICE'S FACE—

we watch as he steps out behind her, in utter silence. His free hand reaches slowly out, covetously, as if to stroke her skin, his fingers floating delicately through the air, just an inch or so away from the side of her face. And then, as he steps back he slowly, almost reluctantly takes his gun in both hands, raising it—then, in the excruciatingly suspended instant—she senses his presence. He's here—in this room. But where?

CLOSE ON

the Colt Python as—in SLOW MOTION—his thumbs cock the hammer, the SOUND registering as a LOUD METALLIC CLICK, and

CLARICE

spins, still in SLOW MOTION, flame already leaping from her gun muzzle, as we see—

THE TWO FIGURES

almost at point-blank range, guns ROARING hugely, one FLASH from Mr. Gumb, and onetwothreefour FLASHES from CLA-RICE, overlapping his, and then, as the ECHOES crash deafen-ingly—

CLOSE ON CLARICE—LOW ANGLE

as the side of her face hits the floor, and she is gasping, stunned by the noise and flames; there's blood on her cheek, an ugly, pitted powder burn, but she ignores them, twisting to yank her speed-loader from her jacket pocket, locking it blindly onto her gun's cylinder, reloading, right in front of her face, then rolling onto her stomach, aiming her gun upward again, blinking her dazzled eyes, straining to locate him in the darkness. Then, as the ECHOES finally fade, she hears something else—a tortured sucking, WHIS-TLE from perhaps eight feet away.

MOVING

as Clarice crawls forward, on her elbows, following her gun, until it bumps against Mr. Gumb's shoulder. He is lying on his back, his chest a bloody mess. He doesn't move. . . . Then a final, ghastly groan, his hand drops, he is dead. Clarice feels for a pulse at his neck, making sure. Then and only then does she permit herself to roll over, collapsing onto her back.

OVERHEAD ANGLE—

down at the two faces—intimately close together, like lovers on their pillow. Then as we PULL SLOWLY AWAY, we see that her staring eyes, and his dead gaze, are both locked onto—

A DEATH'S-HEAD MOTH

perched on a lightbulb overhead, its wings pumping slowly. SOUND UPCUT—wailing SIRENS, many excited VOICES, as we . . .

dissolve to the ambulance outside the Gumb house; Clarice walks down the steps, and Crawford is there and cradles her protectively. Her transformation is complete: She has emerged from the cocoon of an incomplete childhood, from the nurturing protection of school, into the harsh and often brutal world of the professional; and she's passed with flying colors. The dragon has been slain.

School's out, Starling.

In the next scene she's at graduation, her transformation officially complete. Clarice receives her diploma and is now a full-fledged agent of the FBI. At the celebration party Ardelia tells Clarice there's a phone call for her. After saying good-bye to Crawford, she picks up the receiver and hears the voice of Hannibal Lecter on the other end.

Remember, this story point is still unresolved at the end of Act II; before we can walk out of the theater, we have to know that she completes her relationship with him, however that may be accomplished.

In the novel, the relationship is resolved another way. In the last chapter in the book, a man checks into a nice hotel, orders a bottle of fine wine, sits down, looks out the window, and writes a note to Clarice: *"I have windows,"* he writes, *"and Orion is above the horizon now, and near it Jupiter, brighter than it will ever be again before the year 2000. (I have no intention of telling you the time and how high it is.) But I expect you can see it, too. Some of our stars are the same, Clarice."* It's signed, "Hannibal Lecter."

Not a strong scene, nor does it resolve their relationship satisfactorily or cinematically. Tally had to find a way to resolve the script in a filmic way that is not anticlimactic. So Tally added the phone call from Lecter to Clarice.

"Well, Clarice," Lecter says over the phone, "have the lambs stopped screaming?" She asks where he is, but he ignores her. "Your lambs are still for now, Clarice, but not forever. . . . I have no plans to call on you, Clarice, the world being more interesting with you in it. Be sure you extend me the same courtesy." He ends with, "Good-bye, Clarice. . . . You looked—so very lovely in your blue suit." Here's the way the script ends.

EXT. THE MOONLIT PATIO

Dr. Lecter sighs, sets his phone down, then rises. Popping an orange section into his mouth, he turns toward the brightly lit house. Stepping delicately over the sprawled body of a uniformed security guard, he walks in through open French doors.

INT. A BOOK-LINED STUDY

In a swivel chair, amid the wreckage of his papers and books, is the bound, writhing figure of Dr. Frederick Chilton. His screams are muffled by tape, but he stares at Lecter like a rabbit trapped in headlights.

DR. LECTER

Considers him for a genial moment, then raises the little penknife. His eyes are twinkling.

DR. LECTER
Well, Dr. Chilton. Shall we begin?

"That was the ending I first wrote," Tally said, "and it survived three drafts. But Jonathan was always uncomfortable with it; he liked the idea that Lecter calls her up in the end. He liked the idea of Lecter going after Chilton; that made sense to him. But Jonathan said, 'You know, as much of a slimebag as Chilton is, he's a human being. And it's so squirmy to know that he's trapped, he doesn't have any chance whatsoever of escape. It's too close-ended.'

"So for the final draft I said, 'Well, if Chilton thought Lecter was going to come after him, then maybe he could escape somewhere, drop out of sight. And maybe Lecter would guess where he was going.'

"That freed me up," Tally said, "the fact that Chilton was not yet trapped and caught, and I felt I could have some fun with it. It was more open-ended as well. Something else I learned is that if you can end a movie without tying up all the loose ends, it's better. If you can leave it open-ended, it will live in the audience's imagination better. They're more engaged that way. They will continue the story in their own minds when they leave the theater.

"This was a perfect opportunity to do that, because you could end one part of the story but leave another one alive and open. It's not always possible to do it that way, but it's more lifelike not to be too tidy. I'm sort of a logic freak and I'm probably too worried about making everything too tidy, too logical; a little sloppiness is more real."

"Life is never logical," my mentor, the late, great French film director Jean Renoir used to say. The things that don't work often show you what does work. It's part of the learning process. And Tally came up with a wonderful solution.

INT. TROPICAL AIRPORT TERMINAL—NIGHT

Dr. Lecter is speaking on a pay phone as he watches the arriving passengers drift past. He is immaculate in a crisp khaki suit and

Panama hat. His appearance is quite altered—a mustache, glasses, lighter hair, a deep tan.

He continues his phone conversation with Clarice as originally written; Lecter bids her good-bye, then sees something off-camera that makes him quite happy. "I really wish we could chat longer, but I'm having an old friend for dinner," he says and hangs up. Clarice is left only with a dial tone.

ANGLE ON DR. LECTER

as he turns away from his phone, watching

DR. FREDERICK CHILTON—

now a haunted fugitive, sweating under the weight of four bulging suitcases. He stops to wipe his sunglasses on the tail of his flowered shirt while casting furtive glances around at his fellow travelers. Then he grips his bags again and staggers off down the concourse, past the steel band.

DR. LECTER

smiles, his eyes twinkling.

MOVING ANGLE

the CAMERA pulling slowly AWAY, then UP, as Dr. Lecter begins to follow Chilton. We watch the two men for just a bit longer, before finally losing them both in a blur of pastel cruisewear and goofy hats and sunburned faces while the dreamy, romantic MUSIC throbs on and the tropical moon smiles down. . . .

Simple, clean, precise, unforgettable. The scene resolves their relationship for the time being; when Lecter says that the world is "more interesting with you in it," we know she doesn't have to fear him—at least for now. It certainly leaves us with something to think about. It is an open ending. Perhaps there will be a sequel.

At this writing, there have been rumors circulating in Hollywood about a sequel, so I asked Tally if he had heard anything about it. "No," he replied; "Tom is writing another book, and no one knows at what stage of development this book is because he's very secretive, and none of his friends would even dare pry. But he's in a separate world, wherever he is, in Paris right now, and eventually he will come out with a book. To what extent it will be a sequel in the Hollywood sense, I don't know, because he doesn't feel bound to honor Hollywood's agenda.

"Whatever it is, it'll be a terrific book. I can't wait to read it."

Neither can I.

Dances With
Wolves

21

Trail of
Many Tears:

Dances With Wolves

Dances With Wolves is an epic film. In terms of scope, it is a tale that spans time and memories, birth and death, a time of history and change, the dawning of a new era.

Before the Civil War, "the West" (defined as anything west of the Mississippi River) was an unlimited frontier of plains and prairies that spread across the land as far as the eye could see. For the white man, the West meant expansion, freedom, and liberation. There were no fences, no restrictions, no law. The West was the frontier, as open and vast as the universe is to us now. It wasn't long before the white man started settling and colonizing, intruding into territory that had been Native American tribal lands from the very beginning.

When the Civil War ended, in 1865, it left the people in its wake dissatisfied and disillusioned, restrained by new rules and a new way of life. In the South, the economy shifted daily; men who once wore the Confederate uniform with pride and dignity were now obligated to sign loyalty oaths, pledging their allegiance to the very principles and ideals they had fought so hard against.

The war changed things. The consciousness of the people had changed, and they were caught in a maelstrom of unrest and dissension. People moved West to make a new start.

Native Americans had always honored the land by taking care of it, as the Great Spirit had dictated. They were the caretakers of the land, its guardians and custodians, but as the white man pushed forward relentlessly, driven by greed and his "manifest destiny," the destiny of Native Americans became enclosed within the fences of the reservation, their dignity lost along a trail of broken promises.

This transformation of the land signified the end of one era and the beginning of another. The white man came; the Native American left. One way of life gave way to another.

This is the period of the mythic Old West as we know it from the movies, when the outlaw gangs of Jesse James and Billy the Kid and the Younger brothers rode the range. For a screenwriter, this particular era is a perfect example of a time when the drama of the "outsider," the "outlaw," can be staged most effectively.

Think of those classic Westerns we've seen since we were kids. They star the loner running from his past, a man with strong morals, an unshakable sense of honor, and humble dignity: *Shane* (A. B. Guthrie, Jr.), *The Gunfighter* (William Bowers and William Sellers), *High Noon* (Carl Forman), *Red River* (Borden Chase and Charles Schnee), *Butch Cassidy and the Sundance Kid* (William Goldman), and most recently *The Unforgiven* (David Webb Peoples). All of these movies dramatically portray the Western hero fighting against the injustice of the system; he is the true individual, true to himself and his ideals, unbending in spirit, unyielding in the belief of freedom.

This is the historical arena that Michael Blake wanted to explore in his novel *Dances With Wolves,* the story of a solitary idealist cast adrift after the Civil War, an unchanged man in a changing land.

In mythological terms, there are two types of challenges the hero must overcome during his time of trial. One is the physical challenge, which requires the hero to perform a courageous act during battle, like saving a life, or an entire village. In *Dances With Wolves,* John Dunbar meets two physical challenges: at the very beginning of the story when he inadvertently leads his Army unit into battle, and once more when he protects his Sioux family against the marauding band of Pawnees. One deed comes from desperation, the other from nobility.

The other heroic challenge is the spiritual challenge, an adventure during which the hero experiences the transformation of consciousness and becomes "realized," then returns with an ancient and profound message that has echoed through time, like "see God in each other."

The irony of Dunbar's actions, however, of wanting to end his life, but becoming a hero instead, leads to a second chance, and this is what drives Lieutenant John Dunbar (Kevin Costner) West; "I want to see the frontier before it's gone," he says to the mad captain at Fort Hayes. The officer gracefully grants his boon and sends him to the farthest edge of the frontier. Then the mad captain commits suicide.

"To see the frontier" is Dunbar's dramatic need; it drives the story line simply and directly.

Dunbar's journey to the fort becomes "the mythic journey," the rite of passage that ultimately leads him to the discovery of his own self, his own destiny. Dunbar's search for "the frontier" is really the metaphoric search for self.

It is an epic journal, like Don Quixote or the search for the Holy Grail, and Dunbar, like all the others before and after him, shares the same urge for freedom and independence.

During the late '80s in Hollywood, the Western was dead. There had been only a few made during the decade, and they were not critically or financially "boffo" movies. The people in Hollywood didn't want any "dust" pictures.

When I heard that *Dances With Wolves* was shooting, I thought how amazing that this movie was being made at all, at the dawn of a new decade. How appropriate, I thought, even though I didn't know anything about it except it was "a Western," a "dust" picture.

Needless to say, I was very anxious to see it.

When it opened, I went to a five-o'clock screening on a Sunday afternoon. The theater was filled; word of mouth was strong, and I could feel an air of excitement and expectation in the audience. We all wanted a good movie experience.

When it began, the first images of Kevin Costner lying on that bloody kitchen table surrounded by a mound of boots and sawed-off limbs grabbed me immediately. We were all hooked, joined in the "community of emotion." As the tale unfolded in images of visual grandeur, it became a story of power and feeling. And when it was over, I was surprised that the picture was well over three hours long. It was a good "movie experience."

Very few movies have kept me riveted in the seat for this long (my butt is my most accurate critical guide), so when I left the theater I started thinking about the story in terms of growth and character change. As I contemplated the lieutenant, I saw that John Dunbar was on a journey of transformation, much like the characters in *Thelma and Louise, Terminator 2,* and *Silence of the Lambs.*

But there was something else I responded to, which brought the script to another level, another dimension, and that was the spiritual dynamic. "Of all the trails in this life," says Kicking Bird, "there is one that matters more than all the others. It is the trail of a true human being. I think you are on this trail and it is good to see." Those words penetrated my heart and brought tears to my eyes. Isn't that what we all want, to be true in thoughts, words, and actions? To belong to something larger than ourselves that we can trust and believe in?

And then there were all those *silences* in the film, long, panoramic scenes of breathtaking beauty (Dean Semmler was the cinematographer) that captured the profound majesty of the land and made it echo so loudly in the heart. Silence can be such a profound moment in film, as the great filmmakers of the past constantly remind us.

The actual running time is three hours, ten minutes. There's a lot of concern about the length of a movie in Hollywood these days. In most cases the studios have a clause built into their contracts that the movie delivered by the producer should be in three acts and no longer than two hours and eight minutes. On the surface this seems to be a pretty silly way to make movies, but studios have inserted this clause for a specific reason.

For the producer the two-hour, eight-minute clause offers another way to control the enormous cost of movie production. In terms of dollars and cents it means substantial savings. As of this writing, it costs about $100,000 to $150,000 per day to shoot a major Hollywood film, so each fifteen minutes of film that are shot and not used add about $1.5 million to the budget. In most production schedules about a minute and a half's worth of usable film is shot a day. If a filmmaker shoots thirty minutes of film that's not used, the producer figures it's about $3 million down the drain.

So it's not necessary to shoot a two-hour, forty-minute film if all you need is two hours, eight minutes. That forces the budget down. And, says Jake Eberts, executive producer of *Dances With Wolves,* "You can't go off half cocked and shoot and shoot and shoot, and hope that sometime after you finish shooting you can cobble together all the pieces and get a film out of it."

Jake Eberts is one of the most individual and independent producers in Hollywood. Some of the films he's been involved with include *A River Runs Through It* (Richard Friedenberg), *Driving Miss Daisy* (Albert Uhry), *Dances With Wolves* (Michael Blake), *Emerald Forest* (Rospoe Pallenberg), *Gandhi* (John Briley), *Chariots of Fire* (Colin Welland), *The Killing Fields* (Bruce Robinson), and *The Mission* (Robert Bolt). It's quite an impressive list.

He's a man who believes in his intuition and follows it, regardless of the studio mentality. "There's so many layers of people trying to protect themselves in this town," he says, "that the urge to say 'no' is almost overpowering.

"When you get to the top level you don't want to be seen as a failure because you're at the top. And all along the way you have this built-in negativism, which I don't have. I don't have to consult with anyone. If I take a loss, I take a loss; it's my own fault. And that gives me great flexibility.

"I don't have to fill a pipeline, I don't have a huge overhead to cover, I don't have a lot of bodies to feed and talk to and nurse along and keep busy. If I don't find anything for a year, then I'll just trundle along until I find something that inspires me.

"It's different for a studio. They have to make twenty-five pictures a year. They have to say 'yes' twenty-five times a year, which means committing at least $25 million to produce a film and at least $15 million to market it, so each time the head of the studio says 'yes,' it's $40 million. Twenty-five times forty, you're talking about a huge amount of money: That's $1 billion, or more, in commitments every year.

"That guy probably has a tough time sleeping. Furthermore, of the twenty-five times he said 'yes,' he probably had to deal with people he didn't like in twenty-two of those cases. He doesn't like them, he doesn't want to be with them, he doesn't have any interest in their personal welfare, whereas I only do business with people I really like. So I search for guys who are passionate, attractive, appealing and intelligent, amusing, and have good ideas and are bright and energetic. The same characteristics you look for in a friend. And then if you're lucky enough you can do business with them!" He laughed.

I first met Jake Eberts when I was working with Roland Joffe on *City of Joy,* and was immediately struck by Jake's sharp intelligence and sincerity. He was straight, candid, direct; he seems to be a man you can take at his word. There are not many of these men left in contemporary Hollywood.

When I chose *Dances With Wolves* as one of the films I wanted to include in this book, I asked Jake if we could talk about his involvement in the project, and how the whole thing happened.

I met him on a cold and rainy Sunday afternoon in his room at the Beverly Hills Hotel. He'd been working extensively with Roland on the final touches of *City of Joy* and was leaving for London the next day. Bags were open and half packed, and the phone rang constantly. In the next room his son was watching a video of *A River Runs Through It,* which he had worked on as a production assistant.

We started talking about *City of Joy,* and then I asked how he became involved with *Dances With Wolves.*

"It's a good story," he began. "A producer I know had optioned *Dances With Wolves* from Kevin Costner and had worked on developing the project for about a year. The producer was going through some financial difficulty at the time and couldn't put up all the money, or maybe couldn't put up any money, I don't know.

"I was getting ready to leave for London, so he sent me a copy of the script and told me Kevin wanted to direct his first picture. At the time Kevin Costner was not a major star, but he was obviously a very, very attractive guy onscreen, and a lot of people thought he was going to become a major star.

"I read the script on the plane that night and was completely mesmerized by it. I'd been trying for ten years to do a movie about the North American Indians, but nothing I came across was really good enough. But this one totally captivated me, absolutely mesmerized me.

"So the next day I faxed the producer, telling him that I adored the screenplay and that I had mentally committed to doing it. There were a few minor points about the screenplay I wanted changed: I didn't want the wolf to die, for example, and I wanted to make sure that people could understand what was going on in places where we didn't use subtitles—that the dialogue would be clear enough in Lakota (the Sioux language). I didn't want to put subtitles under every single line.

"Basically, I was prepared to go ahead on that screenplay. And I wrote a wildly enthusiastic letter back to the producer. But I guess I was a little too elaborate in my praise, because he thought maybe he should try to do the whole thing himself; that's what he did, and it ended up that there was a problem getting the deal done, and his option lapsed. I didn't hear from him for a while, so I called him and he told me the script was back with Kevin. I let him know that I was very interested in pursuing it directly with Kevin, even though he had brought it to me.

"The next thing I heard was that Kevin had done a deal to finance the whole picture through Island Records. They were going into the film business, and this was going to be one of their projects. They had signed, or were about to sign, a contract, and the money was due on the thirty-first of January 1990.

"So I called up Island to see if I could get involved in the foreign rights but they told me they were going to take care of it themselves. So, sadly, I lost the deal.

"Early February rolled around and I read in the paper, or someone told me, that the option for *Dances With Wolves* had lapsed because Island had not put up the money. So I called Jim Wilson, Kevin Costner's producer. I'd never met him before, so I introduced myself on the phone, voiced my interest, and he said, 'Jesus, I wish you'd called earlier, but it's too late. A friend of Kevin's from Chicago, who made a lot of money in real estate and wanted to get in the film business, wants to do it.' He thanked me for my interest, but it was 'Thanks, but no thanks.' So I told him if the deal fell apart, please let me know. I had never been thwarted three times.

"By this time I was beginning to feel like I was jinxed. I just seemed to miss it all the time. But the story wasn't over yet. The competing deal didn't work out because the Chicago real-estate investor wanted a bank commitment; he wanted someone else to guarantee that he wouldn't lose money on the film. His proposal was essentially a financing deal, not a risk deal.

"After I found out about this, I called back a few days later, and Jim told me that he didn't think the deal was going to happen, and could I come over. So I left London the next day, it was a Thursday, and immediately went to see Kevin and Jim.

"I met them at the Raleigh Studios, and it was one of the most impressive meetings I'd ever been to, with anybody. Kevin was totally informed. He knew precisely which costumes and what props he wanted to use and what angle to shoot at and what lens to use; he was absolutely and totally well versed.

"Kevin really knew what he was talking about. He's a charismatic guy, and I felt that if he said he was going to do something, by God, he was going to do it. And if he said he would shoot that damn thing in so many days and within a certain budget, you knew that you've got the guy who would get the job done. Also, Jim Wilson is the most impressive nuts-and-bolts producer I've ever met."

When I asked Eberts if there was any one thing that confirmed his gut reaction to go ahead with the picture, he replied, "You could tell by the way Kevin talked and the way he described the scenes that there was a lot of humor in the movie. It was more than simplistic humor, like bumping your head, or whatever; it was like the coffee grinder scene (the scene where Dunbar is grinding coffee for his Sioux guests as they wait patiently); he played that for me in the office, and I could just see it. Kevin has that lightness and mirth about him, and I think that's very important, especially in this business."

He paused for a moment, smiling slightly, watching a large cumulus cloud forming on the horizon. "I came away from that meeting saying to myself that these were two of the most attractive guys I'd ever met. I had no doubt, no hesitation; I was totally committed. We discussed the deal that day, and completed the negotiations with Kevin's lawyer and agent three days later, on a Sunday. We had to hammer out some details, because the lawyer was not really aware of the way I operate; my contracts are usually no more than a page or two long. [This is quite unusual; the simplest legal agreements in Hollywood are usually seven to nine pages long.]

"We signed the deal on Sunday afternoon at four o'clock, and the money started flowing on Monday. The whole thing took four days."

"The films that are going to get made, get made," is an old Hollywood expression. That's true. But it takes a lot of work, a lot of effort and will to pull the whole thing off. Jake Eberts says it was just "luck" that he happened to be in the right place at the right time. But the Hollywood landscape is flowered with stories of great producers and directors and writers working on their scripts for years before they finally see them brought to the screen.

Oliver Stone told me that he spent more than ten years waiting for someone to respond to *Platoon,* and he had reached a point where he had literally given up on ever having that script made during his lifetime.

As I left the Beverly Hills Hotel that day, I couldn't help but think about Michael Blake. How did he fare during all of this? During the years it took to write the book, he must have known this was going to be an "impossible sell." Even to think about this material as a movie would have been naive and idealistic.

I knew nothing about Michael Blake in terms of his previous work, but I knew that writing *Dances With Wolves* had to have been a difficult task, a test of time, faith, and courage, a trail of many tears, just like the test John Dunbar had to endure during his quest to transform himself into a "true human being" at the "farthest edge of the frontier."

22

The Writer's
Journey:

Michael Blake

In 1990, *Dances With Wolves* received Academy Awards for Best Picture, Best Director, and Best Screenwriter, but I knew nothing about the man who conceived and inspired it. As I watched Michael Blake receive his Academy Award on television, I was impressed by two things: one, his mental "toughness," fueled by a sense of dedicated and strong-willed idealism. The second was the compassion, and humility he expressed when he accepted the Award and waved the Oscar above his head, sharing his joy with "his brothers," while declaring that "the dream is not dead."

Heady stuff. But I loved it. Deep down, I felt a tug within myself and identified with everything he said. Any person who worked this long and this hard against all the obstacles confronting him, deserves everything he gets.

What happened to Michael Blake is every writer's dream. He is one of those rare writers who looks deep inside himself, and searches for his own Truths in life, then speaks from the heart, letting nothing interfere with his vision.

"Being is intelligible only in terms of becoming," declares the poet T. S. Eliot.

I had seen the film and read the book before I read the screenplay, and I saw immediately that there were changes: Some new scenes were written, others were dropped; the entire first act of the script, for example, is found in a few pages buried in the fifth chapter. But while the novel explores the points of view of the different characters, of Dunbar, Kicking Bird, and Stands With A Fist, the screenplay had to be anchored with a stronger narrative line, just as in *Silence of the Lambs*. So the movie's story always stays focused on John Dunbar; we follow and discover and share his relationship with the Sioux. In other words, we follow his journey in a linear story line.

The hero's journey, as mentioned, is one of death and resurrection, leaving one way of life and journeying forth to find another source of life that brings him into a "richer, more mature condition."

The hero becomes self-realized. In mythological terms, the hero often sets out to perform a deed. Go find your father is an example; the quest for the father (either physical, or spiritual father) is a major hero adventure (beginning with *The Odyssey*). Sometimes it becomes an adventure of finding out what your destiny is in terms of life and career—in other words, finding your own truth, who you really are.

That's the situation that Lieutenant John Dunbar encounters. It's easy to see "the quest of Dunbar" in all of us—wanting to belong, wanting to live in harmony with the land and his "brothers and sisters."

"He took his time," reads the novel after the buffalo hunt, *"pausing often to look at the river, or at a branch as it bent in the breeze, or at a rabbit nibbling at a shrub. Everything was unconcerned with his presence.*

"He felt invisible. It was a feeling he liked. . . . When he stopped to look up at the moon, he would lift his head, turn his body full into the face of its magical light, and the breastplate would flash the brightest white, like an earthbound star."

In writing *Dances With Wolves* Michael Blake had a personal vision, and he was determined to follow it like that "earthbound star" no matter the cost. To be a writer and stand alone in the face of no agreement is truly a test of faith and courage.

It is the writer's journey.

Blake lives in what he calls his "sanctuary" near a national park in Tucson; it's the "first home I've ever had," he said, and he called it a spiritual place because "the desert's very spiritual. Everything here is left to its own devices; no animals are killed, no construction is done, no stores put in. Everything's pretty much as it was made. And it's a constant inspiration."

Blake was born in an Army hospital in Fayetteville, North Carolina. His father worked for the telephone company and got transferred almost every year. The family moved to Southern California when he was two, and he "grew up like an upper-middle-class migrant," he said, living all over the Southern California area. "I never had a home base," he shared, "and I was forty-six before I owned my first home."

He studied at the University of New Mexico, majoring in English literature and Russian history, then dropped out his senior year. "I had enough education," he declared.

He went back to L.A. and started working as a journalist. "I did publicity for some of the record companies as a free-lance writer, and finally got a job as a reporter with the *L.A. Free Press* [a counterculture paper in Los Angeles during the '60s and '70s], and was the associate editor when it folded. I mainly did investigative reporting, and I was writing for *Cream, Mother Earth News, Boston, Phoenix,* all the counterculture papers.

"I worked in radio as well," he continued, and "went back and forth between the West Coast and New Mexico. I tried to find someplace to fit into journalism during that time but never could. I did public affairs programming for radio stations. I had my own production company and produced commercials for rock concerts. I had a monthly art supplement for one of the big weeklies in New Mexico. I ran a movie theater, a small movie house in Albuquerque for about a year. And all the time I was trying to write, but without success."

Finally he realized he wasn't going anywhere, so he decided to enter film school in Berkeley, California, in a program that Antioch College had and "where I got the idea that maybe I could write for films. I wanted to get my hands on a camera and see how it worked, to try editing, hold film in my hands, see what happens. But about halfway through the program I realized maybe I should write for films. So I wrote my first screenplay; it was based on a story by Ambrose Bierce (an American short-story writer), and it took place during the Civil War."

Blake was thirty-one. When he finished it, "I didn't know anyone in Hollywood; I was living in Oakland and driving a bus part-time. But when I was at the *Free Press* I wrote a review of *McCabe and Mrs. Miller* (Robert Altman and Brian McKay). I admired it greatly, and as a result I had a couple of phone conversations with the producer, Mitchell Brower (producer of Peckinpah's film *The Getaway,* with Steve McQueen and Ali McGraw, among others). I called around and found he was working at Columbia at the time, so in my innocence I just sent him the screenplay.

"About two weeks later, the phone rings, and Mitch is on the phone. I thought this was it, the phone call 'from Hollywood,' and he told me I wrote a pretty good screenplay, but what was I doing up in Oakland? I told him I'm writing and driving a bus, and he said, 'Oh, you're living in splendid isolation. If you want to write films you'd better come down here. I'll try to help you if you do.' And that was the end of our conversation.

"So about a month or two later I left for L.A., moved into a garage in Santa Monica, where I lived for a year and wrote another screenplay." When I asked what it was about, he replied, "It's a screenplay I'm still working on. I started it in 1979, a Western called *Slade,* and it's something that won't go away from my life, that seems to want to be made so badly that we're exploring the possibilities of making it now."

Since his affinity for the West seems obvious, I asked if he had written any other kinds of stories, specifically contemporary stories, and he replied that his new novel *Airman Mortensen* deals with young people in the mid-1960s and how important their lives are. He's just finished adapting the screenplay, and he will direct it.

I asked if he'd always had this special "feel" for the West.

He paused a moment, then replied, "I'm a person whose antecedents are rooted in western history. My great-grandfather came to Arizona when it was a territory in 1880, a lieutenant in the 6th Cavalry. He chased the Apaches around. My grandfather came to New Mexico for his health and ended up meeting his wife in a strange little town before the turn of the century. My uncle wrote Western books and met his wife in a play in Sante Fe. There must be some kind of vibe, some kind of connection that runs through the collective unconscious of our family."

How *Dances With Wolves* came into being is also a fascinating journey of the creative process. When I asked Blake how it had come about, he told me, "I started to read a lot when I was at the *L.A. Free Press,* and I read *Bury My Heart at Wounded Knee.* I was so taken and moved by it that I asked the book editor to let me write a review.

"That was it. I didn't pick up the book again until I reread it ten years later, and that started me on a couple of years' worth of reading. About halfway through this reading period I read a book called *Plains Indian Raiders,* about the Kiowas and Comanches and their wars with white people. And during the course of reading that book I happened to read an anecdote that talked about a wagon driver who had driven out to resupply an outpost in western Kansas. But when he got there he found that no one was there, and the only sign of life was a piece of canvas flapping in the breeze.

"That image somehow moved me, and I started thinking about it, filling it in with other images. I thought to myself, well, what if I was on that wagon, and that was going to be my post, what would happen then?

"That was about as far as I got.

"I met Jim Wilson in film school in 1977, and we became friends. In 1981, I wrote a script for him called *Stacy's Knights,* and Crown International was producing it. We were casting the lead, and this skinny kid comes in, and we felt he was absolutely right for the part, so we cast him. His name was Kevin Costner.

"One night I went out to his house and had dinner with him and his wife while all this was germinating. After dinner the three of us were sitting around talking, and I told them about this vision I had, and said to Kevin, 'Wouldn't that make a great movie?'

"Kevin looked at me and said, 'Don't you dare write a movie about that.'

"I understood why he would say that, because at that time my 'career' in Hollywood had been an absolute disaster. I was living like some parody of a Dostoyevski character: Everybody wanted to see me do better than I was doing. So I knew he said that to me out of love; all he wanted for me was to make a living. Kevin was very adamant about it that night. He wanted me to write this, but he said he wanted me to write it as a book, not a screenplay. I mean, he put his face right in my face when I left the house that night.

"I'll never forget it. He said, 'Write a book.' He was like a drill sergeant. So I went home and started thinking about it, and thought, Hey, that's a great idea. I think I'll start writing a book.

"I got so involved writing the book that I couldn't pay my rent, so I lost the place where I was living. I drove around town in my car and continued to write *Dances With Wolves*."

The first words of the novel deal with the journey of John Dunbar to his new post: *"Lieutenant Dunbar wasn't really swallowed. But that was the first word that stuck in his head.*

"Everything was immense.

"The great, cloudless sky. The rolling ocean of grass. Nothing else, no matter where he put his eyes. No road. No trace of ruts for the big wagon to follow. Just sheer, empty space.

"He was adrift. It made his heart jump in a strange and profound way."

I was curious about the character of Dunbar, so I asked Blake if he was modeled or inspired by a historical figure. After thinking about it for a moment, he replied, "I come from the school of writing that doesn't really create characters so much, as much as trying to share their experience with people. That's what I did with John Dunbar; I was Lieutenant Dunbar. It was a way for me to have these experiences that I wanted so much to have. I had discovered so much spirituality in the lives that were being led at that time by the Indian people that I really wished I could have participated. So the only way I could participate was in a fictional way."

His dogs, Pal and Bear, started barking at that point, and after quieting them, he commented, "The life of a writer is a big process, and the life of a reader is a big process. I was interested in classical fiction for a long time, and certain people in contemporary fiction, and those were the kinds of things that I was reading."

This brought up the question of research. What did he do? I wondered. And how much did he do? The novel and the script seemed so accurate I thought he must have spent a lot of time with the Sioux. He told me, "What I read was mainly first-person accounts to get a feel of the time and place. You have to go to the library to look that stuff up. So I'd spend hours going through the stacks, looking for something that looked like it was interesting, maybe something that was written by someone who experienced something. I'm always fascinated by first-person accounts.

"One of the books I found became a very important book for me," he continued, "the biography of Crazy Horse, written by a white woman, Mary Sandoz. She's dead now, but she wrote a lot of books about Indians, and this book about Crazy Horse was probably the most inspiring thing for me during the years it took to write the book. Crazy Horse was an Oglala Sioux and probably one of the greatest people who ever lived in this world. He was a lot like the great religious leaders, like Jesus, or Muhammad, or the Buddha—a great, great Being."

There are times when you're writing a historical screenplay and you have to write within the constraints of history while remaining true to the characters you are creating. That means it is up to the screenwriter to create incidents and events that reflect the emotional arc in the journey of the character.

In other words, it may be necessary for the writer to change things in the historical perspective to meet the dramatic needs of the story. If that happens to be the case, you don't really have to be true to history, you have to be true to the *facts* of history—the events that actually happened. But when you're filling in the blanks of history, when you're revealing the emotional and dramatic needs of your characters, you may have to create incidents and events that support the story regardless of whether they were true or not. It doesn't matter. A screenplay is a work of *fiction,* even if you're writing about a true event.

For example, when I first saw the movie, I knew John Dunbar's relationship with the Sioux was obviously researched and graphically presented. The action took place within the Sioux Nation. But as I reread the novel, I was surprised to see that the narrative line was about Dunbar and his relationship with the *Comanche,* not the Sioux. Why was it the Sioux in the movie, and the Comanche in the novel?

"We had the constraints of history on us," Blake replied. Jim Wilson went down to Comanche land (now Texas and Oklahoma), and the Comanche language is not in very good shape, it's probably going to die. The Comanche people have done very well, but they're not numerous. There wasn't going to be the pool of people that we needed to fill these roles.

"Besides, there's no buffalo down there. So from a production point of view, it meant that if we didn't do the movie where there were buffalo, we would have to move a whole company of people from one place to another, and we didn't want to do that. South Dakota had the people, the buffalo, and the land; it was perfect. South Dakota fit the bill in every conceivable way.

"But no matter what the differences between the Sioux and the Comanche, the spirituality of it is pretty much the same. And that's what I was writing about—the spiritual aspects of the way these people lived."

The ceremony of the pipe, for example. All the Native American nations honored the pipe, and it plays a prominent role in their life and culture. "When a Sioux Indian would take the pipe," Joseph Campbell says, "he would hold it up stem to the sky so that the sun could take the first puff. Then he'd address the four directions; always. In that frame of mind, when you're addressing yourself to the horizon, to the world that you're in, then you're in your place in the world. It's a different way to live."

So even though there is a great difference between the Sioux and the Comanche people, it really didn't make any difference in terms of the story; it was their way of life, their spirituality, that was important.

As I read the book, I thought back to the movie and wondered whether Blake had any problems adapting his own novel into a screenplay. Did he have enough objectivity to transpose the inner journey of John Dunbar into a visual experience?

"Well," he answered, "there are always a lot of problems adapting a novel into a screenplay. I like screenwriting because there's so much engineering involved."

Engineering? I had never heard that term applied to screenwriting before, so I asked what he meant by it. "Taking things that work in a novel and adapting them into a screenplay is very, very challenging," he explained. "In *Dances With Wolves* there were sequences I wanted to write, but felt I couldn't because they weren't appropriate for the movie.

"There were two very important dream sequences that shed a lot of light on Lieutenant Dunbar and what makes him tick. But I felt, and Kevin felt, that those kinds of sequences never worked very well in movies. Dream sequences just seem to be flops. They were left out even though they were important.

"As a novelist, I like to work in broad strokes, and pay close attention to dialogue and character development. But I have a certain way of writing as a novelist that I don't have as a screenwriter. When I'm writing a script, I prefer to write in a linear way from the main character's point of view. I do some cross-cutting from time to time, but basically I just try to tell the story.

"Writing a movie is a much more linear process, and *Dances With Wolves* is less an epic book than it is an epic movie. As a film it's this big giant thing that plays all over the world, whereas the book is like a little gem. Kevin and I both felt that the only way we could present the book in movie form was as an epic, something larger than life.

"I try to make my screenplays readable. I never approach them as a blueprint for a movie, I approach them as a piece of work in itself. One complete chapter in the book may only be a couple of sentences in the screenplay.

"Screenwriting is a craft," he continued; "it's something that has to be learned just the way a person learns how to be a lead guitarist. You learn the instrument and you play gigs and you get a lot of rejection and you have a lot of self-doubt and you think about giving up all the time. You go through all this stuff and you try to have a life at the same time. It's a discipline, it's not something you can just jump into and expect immediate rewards and gratification."

When I asked how supportive Kevin Costner had been during the writing of the book, he laughed and declared, "Kevin never read any of the stuff I was working on." When I asked why, he replied that when he was writing he "stayed at Kevin's house a couple of times and I remember reading a little of it to him one day, but he didn't want to hear any of it. He never wanted to read *Dances With Wolves* because he was afraid he would like it. And if he liked it, he knew it would be an enormous struggle to make it. So he avoided it as long as he could."

Was it the same with Jim Wilson? I asked. "I shared most of it with him while I was writing," he replied. "There was a time I stayed at Jim's house and I got into this habit of going up to their bedroom, and he and his wife would get in bed and I would read them a chapter from *Dances With Wolves*. They would close their eyes while I read, and I was always concerned that they had fallen asleep. But every time I finished they would open their eyes immediately and say something like, 'And what happened then?' So I knew it was having an effect, which was reassuring.

"I really didn't know what was going to happen; I had no idea. I didn't have a dime. I didn't know what was going to happen to me, let alone the book. Writing really has a life of its own, that's what's so exciting about it. That's why I extol writing wherever I go. I make a lot of appearances now, and I extol writing because it's a way for everyone to participate. Everyone can write a letter to a friend or keep a journal or write a story, or a piece of poetry. I encourage people everywhere to do that, because I guarantee that it will enrich their lives if they do it." He chuckled, then added, "That's a guarantee I haven't had to make good on. No one's come back and said it didn't enrich my life.

"Movies are so important in people's lives that we have to find some way to make them better than they are. And we have to start from the beginning, with the words we write. That's where it all starts, and that's where it has to get better."

23

The Strangeness of Life:

Stranger in a Strange Land

"The strangeness of this life cannot be measured," John Dunbar reflects in the opening scenes of *Dances With Wolves*. "In trying to produce my own death, I was elevated to the status of a living hero."

So begins our introduction to the man called Lieutenant John J. Dunbar and his station in life—a man caught in a war he cannot tolerate or understand. Sick of being an outsider, an outcast, an outlaw, sick of being alone, he yearns for the repose of freedom to rest his weary spirit.

Setting up this kind of character is easier in a novel than in a screenplay because a novel is very much like a tree, always climbing upward, spiraling off in different directions. The trunk is the main idea, the theme, the force that drives the story line forward. But it branches off into other branches, and then branches off from those branches into other branches. We follow the main character, the trunk, and branch off into different characters and situations. Everything is attached to the trunk, but they go off in varying directions.

Not so in a screenplay. The action is focused, linear; the story is always moving forward. In *Dances With Wolves* the main character is isolated and alone, internal; the situation affords him no opportunity to talk to another person, to share his thoughts and feelings. This works for the novel but not the screenplay—a story told in pictures.

So what does the screenwriter do with this type of dramatic situation? First, the writer must find an image, or a picture, and an arena of action that *shows* us this character. And there're only a few pages—about ten, to be exact—in which to do it.

As mentioned, Act I is a unit of dramatic action approximately twenty-five or thirty pages long and held together with the dramatic context known as the Set-Up. It starts at the beginning of the story, page one, word one, and ends at the Plot Point at the end of Act I. By itself, this first ten-page unit of dramatic action is perhaps the most important element in the entire screenplay.

The writer has to "grab" the audience and find a scene or action that gets us involved. As an audience we can determine whether we like a movie within the first ten minutes. You may not be aware of it, but the next time you're watching a movie, pay attention to these first few minutes. When the credits end, the story begins, and we begin to focus our attention on the screen.

There are only two ways to open the screenplay effectively: Either you create a dynamic action opening that grabs us immediately, as in the opening of *Terminator 2,* or you spend time creating character, as in *Thelma and Louise* or *Dances With Wolves.* Action or character, depending on what kind of story is being written. The *genre* (the kind of story: love story, action-adventure, period, romantic thriller, comedy, etc.) usually dictates the best way to open the screenplay, and it varies from script to script.

A good opening determines whether a reader continues reading or an audience stays in the theater. This is nothing new, of course. It's the same now as it was in Shakespeare's time: You start either with action or character. In Shakespeare's time the playwright had to grab the attention of the groundlings in the pit, who were almost always rude, drunk, and boisterous. To do that, he either had to write an interesting action sequence, such as the ghost parading on the parapet in *Hamlet,* or the witches in *Macbeth,* for example, or set up the characters and arena of action like the chorus does in the Prologue to *Romeo and Juliet,* when it proclaims the plight of these "star-crossed lovers."

Because of the introspective nature of the novel, Michael Blake had to introduce John Dunbar in a way that visually reveals his character yet grabs our attention at the same time. In the novel, Blake describes Dunbar as a *"man who possessed a certain strength of character that allowed for working hard when he had very little."*

But we have to *see* that. Every picture tells a story.

So he opens on a black screen; then "we HEAR the SOUND of a knife cutting through boot leather," then see the stricken face of John Dunbar lying on a table waiting to have his foot amputated. From the pile of boots lying in the corner, we see the surgeons must have had a pretty rough time. Their smocks are bathed in blood, and they're so tired they can hardly see. "Well, I can't saw if I can't keep my eyes open. Time to coffee up," one of them says, and they leave, thus sparing the young man.

LIEUTENANT JOHN J. DUNBAR is the young man, his features sharp and handsome. With effort, he lifts his head and searches the room.

His eyes come to rest on the form of a legless man lying in blood-soaked sheets. He's whimpering like a child.

Dunbar comes to a sitting position on the operating table. As his eyes move around the room they come to rest on a crate filled with the boots of men who have lost their legs.

A cane travels through space and deftly hooks one of the boots.

Lieutenant Dunbar brings the boot onto the operating table. He tries to pull it on his mangled foot, but the pain makes him cry out. Deliberately he breaks the cane and sticks a piece of it between his teeth.

Tears of pain are rolling down his face. A sweat has broken out on his forehead and with great determination he pulls the boot on.

What does this show us? That Dunbar, wounded, must confront and overcome a tremendous amount of excruciating pain; it is an extreme test of strength and character, so we *see* he is a man of strength and will.

I'll say it again: The screenwriter needs to set up the story from page one, word one, so he or she must choose an image, a picture, a sequence, or an event that establishes the character within the context of the story.

Though Dunbar is a man of strength and courage, we see (in the next scene) that he is a man who wants to die. In the novel, Blake explains that Dunbar's pain of living was so great that "the lieutenant wanted nothing more than to die. When the opportunity presented itself, he took it."

This is the "opportunity" that sets the book and the screenplay apart. In the opening of the novel, Dunbar is already on his journey to Fort Sedgewick, the "farthest point of the frontier." His character is explained: *"Lieutenant Dunbar had fallen in love. He had fallen in love with this wild, beautiful country and everything it contained. It was the kind of love people dream of having with other people; selfless and free of doubt, reverent and everlasting. His spirit had received a promotion and his heart was jumping. Perhaps this was why the sharply handsome cavalry lieutenant had thought of religion."*

For the screenplay, Blake had to create an entirely new opening, so he took a little incident out of Chapter Five (about two and a half pages) and used that to illustrate Dunbar's character in the opening scene.

In the script we have to see he is a survivor, but at the same time that he wants to die. When Dunbar returns to his unit, he finds the Union and Confederate forces facing each other across St. David's Field in Tennessee; it is a "standoff." Outside of some sniper fire, nothing is happening. So Dunbar leaps on a horse and charges into the middle of the field, drawing Confederate fire. This is the "opportunity" he's been waiting for.

"Looks like a suicide," observes the commanding officer, perched on top of the hill.

As he gallops in front of the Confederate troops, like a target in a shooting gallery, they pepper him with bullets, yet miraculously he avoids being hit. They stand there taunting him to come back, to give them another shot, and Dunbar hesitates only a moment before he mutters "Forgive me, Father," spreads his arms open like the Christ figure, then "digs his heels into the buckskin's flanks" and flies into the face of enemy fire.

His action spurs the Union soldiers forward, their voices loud and their guns blazing. And when it's all over, the battle has been won and Dunbar's action is seen as heroic.

Action is character; what a person does is what he is, not what he says. Film is behavior.

"The strangeness of this life cannot be measured," Dunbar says in a voice-over. "In trying to produce my own death, I was elevated to the status of a living hero."

These two actions of Dunbar's—pulling his boot on, then trying to end his life—lay down the foundation of the entire screenplay; the purpose of these first ten pages is to set up the dramatic forces that reveal character, premise, and situation. Dunbar is a man who wants to die but is reluctantly forced back into life.

That is John Dunbar's journey; it is a physical as well as a spiritual journey. His arrival at Fort Hays is the dramatic hook, or inciting incident of the screenplay.

The sequence at the fort leads us into the second ten-page unit of dramatic action, where we focus on the main character, expanding our knowledge and understanding of who he is. Dunbar dismounts, and enters the fort headquarters. The stage directions read that the fort "has a slackness that echoes the dreariness of this post." But that's only a stage direction; we need to *see* it.

We discover it as Dunbar discovers it; something is wrong here, and it is embodied by the commanding officer, Major Fambrough, "an Army lifer passed over too many times for promotion and right now does not look like a well man."

"Indian fighter?" the major asks immediately, and when Dunbar hesitates, he comments, "Your orders say you are to be posted on the frontier. The frontier is Indian country. I quickly deduced that you are an Indian fighter." Then he adds, "I did not ascend to this position by being stupid."

Strange. When Dunbar explains, "I'm here at my own request. . . . I want to see the frontier . . . before it's gone," he states the dramatic premise of the film. As mentioned, the dramatic premise is what the story is about, and his simple declaration of wanting to "see the frontier" is what drives this story forward.

"Such a smart lad coming straight to me," replies the mad major. He draws himself up, then somberly states: "Sir Knight, I am sending you on a knight's errand. You will report to Captain Cargill at the farthermost outpost of the realm."

The major signs the order sheet with a childish flourish, then folds the orders over and over and over again before he hands them to Dunbar. Dunbar looks at the crumpled paper in his hands then asks, "Sir, how will I be getting there?"

"You think I don't know?" the major questions. But then he relents, and since "I'm in a generous mood, I will grant your boon," and points to the teamster outside: "You will be going with him." Then he stands, and says very formally, "Sir Knight . . . I just pissed in my pants . . . and nobody can do anything about it."

As Dunbar walks outside, the major stands framed in the window and toasts "the Indian fighter" with a glass of wine: "To your journey," he says. Then he turns and toasts himself: "To my journey." Then he blows his brains out.

Welcome to "the frontier."

So end the first ten pages of *Dances With Wolves*. In this ten-page unit of dramatic action, information has been revealed to set up the story. We know the main character, John Dunbar; the dramatic premise, what the story is about ("I want to see the frontier"); and the dramatic situation, the circumstances surrounding the action (Dunbar wanted to end his life, but all he succeeded in doing was ending one way of life and beginning another).

Death and resurrection: the hero's journey.

As Dunbar journeys to the "farthermost point of the frontier," we are introduced to the frontier at the same time he is. Character and audience are connected and we see what he sees, experience what he experiences.

In a screenplay, most of the characters are created when you need them. They are functional, put there to move the story forward. In *Dances With Wolves* the driver was written simply to get Dunbar from Fort Hays to Fort Sedgewick, to move the story forward. Normally, a minor character such as Timmons (played wonderfully by Robert Pastorelli) is written in a direct and straightforward manner. But the frontier is a lively and colorful place, and Blake accentuates Dunbar's introduction to the frontier by pairing him with Timmons, "quite possibly the foulest person I have ever met," the lieutenant observes.

Dunbar says this in voice-over narration, and we see him writing in his diary; we accept his voice-over commentaries and observations without any hesitation. "I felt from the beginning," Blake says, "that a journal was very important for Dunbar, because he spent so much time by himself. I wanted to be able to get into him and see how he really feels, and I felt a voice-over was essential in doing that."

A word about voice-over. Many screenwriters I work with often confess they don't know whether to use a voice-over narration in their screenplay.

I tell them a voice-over (where a character's voice is played over the picture, so we see one thing but hear another) works best when you have a main character who is by himself or herself most of the time, who is isolated and alone, a character with few friends or family. To keep the story moving forward, there has to be someone for the main character to talk to, someone who can provide enough information so the reader and audience know what's going on. *Dances With Wolves* is a story that places the character in a strange and foreign land, so he becomes "a fish out of water," a stranger in a strange land. The journal lets us know Dunbar's thoughts and feelings. We discover things as he discovers them: "We have been gone four days now and still we have seen no signs of life. Only earth and sky."

We see that life on the frontier is both beautiful and harsh; when they find the bleached-out bones of a settler with arrows stuck through them, Timmons laughs; "Somebody back East is sayin', 'Why don't he write?' Stupid bastard."

At this point in the screenplay Blake cuts away to a sequence with Captain Cargill, the commander of Fort Sedgewick and who, at this very moment, is marching back to Fort Hays. In the novel it was explained why Fort Sedgewick is empty when Dunbar arrives. Cargill and his men, stuck without supplies and rations for weeks, maybe months, had to burrow into the earth like animals and were living in caves. They had nothing. Cargill and the men at the fort were waiting for the supplies Timmons is bringing. Unable to wait any longer, Cargill strikes out for Fort Hays, and this is the sequence Blake had written into the script. Costner knew it was too much information and was really unnecessary.

The focus is always on Dunbar; he is the main character, the man whom this story is about.

Dunbar's journey helps establish his character, and those magnificent shots of the wild and untamed frontier are intercut with the necessary dialogue essential to move the story forward. When Dunbar asks about the Indians, Timmons tells him that the "Goddamn Indians you'd jus' as soon not see, lessen the bastards're dead. Nothing but thieves and beggars."

That, of course, is *his* point of view, but basically it's our point of view as well. Simplistic though it is, that's the way most white men looked upon the Native Americans. That's what we've been told, and that's what we believe; it is a perception that Blake wants us to overcome.

When Dunbar asks, "How come we haven't seen any buffalo?" Timmons replies, "You can't figger the stinkin' buffalo. Sometimes you don't see 'em for days, sometimes they're thick as curls on a whore."

Those two things—Indians and buffalo—are key elements in the story, and are set up now to pay them off later.

When the two men finally reach Fort Sedgewick, there's nothing there; the only sound is of the canvas flapping in the breeze. "Everybody's run off . . . or got kilt," Timmons observes.

Dunbar goes through the fort, feeling its mystery, then tells Timmons to unload the wagon; he's staying. When Timmons resists, Dunbar threatens him and he reluctantly begins unloading the supplies.

The job done, Timmons wishes Dunbar luck, and the wagon pulls out. In a shot that seemingly goes on forever, we watch with Dunbar as the wagon disappears into the setting sun.

John Dunbar is alone.

That is the Plot Point at the end of Act I, the incident, episode, or event that "hooks" into the action and spins it around in another direction, in this case Act II. It is not a big, dramatic moment, as it is in *Thelma and Louise, Terminator 2,* or *The Silence of the Lambs;* it is a moment of silence and solitude, a moment of contemplation. The Plot Point at the end of Act I, or Act II, does not have to be a major dramatic scene or sequence. It is what it needs to be; it serves the story and moves it forward.

At this point in the story John Dunbar is at the farthermost point of the frontier, alone, without anybody or anything except his guns and his horse to guide or comfort him.

That night, before he goes to sleep, we hear his thoughts in a voice-over narration: "Have arrived to find Fort Sedgewick deserted. Am now waiting for the garrison's return or word from headquarters. Post is in exceedingly poor condition. Have decided to assign myself clean-up duty beginning tomorrow. Supplies abundant. The country is everything I dreamed it would be. There can be no place like this on earth."

Then he settles back for his first night on the frontier. His boon has been granted, his dramatic need fulfilled.

Now the story can really begin.

24

First Encounters:

A New Life

It's dawn when John Dunbar is awakened by the sound of a strange footfall outside his quarters. It takes a moment for him to get his bearings; then, suddenly alert, he yanks his gun out and points it at the door. Silence. Then a shadow falls across the threshold and "Cisco's big buckskin head" pokes through the doorway and looks at Dunbar as if to say, Well, what's going on?

So begins the resurrection of John Dunbar. It's a new life; he's starting over with the slate wiped clean, and now he must learn to adapt to the ways of the frontier. In studio talk he's "a fish out of water."

The First Half of Act II seems very musical in structure, almost like a sonata (introduction, development, and conclusion), and executed in three movements: In the beginning he adapts to the land; in the middle he establishes his relationship with the Sioux; and at the end he is accepted into the tribe. That's the flow of the story, the "linear engineering" that Michael Blake spoke about.

Dunbar's first action in Act II is to explore his surroundings, to do what's necessary to set up his living quarters. This is pure visual exposition, and Blake doesn't create a long series of scenes. A few short scenes reveal the conditions of Fort Sedgewick: the river polluted with dead animals, caves dug into the hillside, garbage and filth everywhere. We discover Fort Sedgewick the same way Dunbar does; audience and character are connected by the "community of emotion."

Blake establishes his point of view here: The whites are seen as the polluters of the land. We see this over and over throughout the screenplay, and it serves a specific dramatic function: to heighten Dunbar's awareness (and ours as well) of the life and culture of the Native American, to contrast their way of life with our own. The good guys and the bad guys. To show this, Blake exaggerates it, and weaves it throughout the script like a thread through a tapestry.

Dunbar cleans up the area (you might say he's cleaning up his life), then "fastens the last of the traces to a pile of garbage spread out on a sheet of canvas, picks up a set of long reins, clucks to Cisco, and they start up the steep back with the load."

When he puts a match to the pile of debris, he watches in horror as a wall of smoke climbs into the sky, alerting everyone in the area that he is there; it is a beacon, a signal.

Lesson number one.

Blake uses the smoke visually as a natural transition to lead us into the next scene. He cuts to "four fantastic faces" watching the smoke of another fire. Timmons, the teamster, is gobbling up hot bacon when he takes an arrow in the thigh, another in the chest, then another and another and another, and we watch in horror as he is scalped.

These scenes illustrate life on the frontier visually; each little incident sketches in some of the obstacles John Dunbar will be confronted with, and sets up his encounter with the Sioux.

Dunbar's first encounter is set up with a stage direction:

PLEASE NOTE: ALL INDIAN DIALOGUE WILL BE IN NATIVE DIALECT AS INDICATED BY TRIBE. SUBTITLES WILL BE USED.

Sometimes a situation like this poses a problem for the studio and distribution people. It is generally believed in the inner circles of Hollywood that a film with subtitles is not successful at the box office, as Jake Eberts observes in Chapter Twenty-one. It is just one of the obstacles that Costner, Wilson, and Blake had to overcome before they could get this picture made.

The subcontext of the First Half of Act II is adaptation: John Dunbar has to *adapt* to his new way of life. The *story line* is held together with the concept of Dunbar adapting to the land and the Indians. It is the engine that powers the First Half of Act II to the Mid-Point.

"There is a wolf who seems intent on the goings-on here," Dunbar observes in his journal. "He does not seem inclined to be a nuisance, however, and aside from Cisco has been my only company. He has appeared each afternoon for the past two days. He has milky white socks on both feet. If he comes calling tomorrow I will name him Two Socks."

Dunbar's relationship with the wolf is introduced here and becomes a key element in the story. From the very beginning, we have seen that John Dunbar is isolated and alone, a loner adrift in a troubled world, just like the wolf. Shakespeare said the artist must "hold the mirror up to Nature," and the wolf is a good example of that. It reflects Dunbar's emotional state.

A passage of time bridges the action: "Almost a month and no one has come," Dunbar writes in his journal. "The longer this condition persists, the less inclined I am to believe that anyone will. . . . It is the loneliest of times . . . but I cannot say that I am unhappy."

"The loneliest of times" leads into developing the second movement of the First Half of Act II, Dunbar's first encounter with the Indians. It is a transition as well, and we cut to "a real Indian: tough, wild, and free. He has a special maturity. He radiates wisdom and is a man of responsibility in his community. He is a Sioux medicine man. His name is Kicking Bird." (Graham Greene.)

Dunbar's first encounter with Kicking Bird is amusing, and displays the humor that is so much a part of this screenplay. Dunbar is washing his clothes at the stream, naked save for his hat, when we see Kicking Bird looking "thoughtfully at the 'new' Fort Sedgewick: the tidy grounds, the great awning, the repaired corral, the beautiful buckskin standing inside."

Dunbar watches as Kicking Bird gently coaxes Cisco toward

him, then reacts and yells "You there!" and the Indian freaks. "He turns and runs, tearing through the corral fence as if it were made of twigs. He leaps onto his horse and quirts the pony into full gallop."

In a few quick shots we see Dunbar hiding supplies as we hear him in voice-over narration as he writes in his journal:

> DUNBAR (VO)
> Have made first contact with a wild Indian.
> One came to the fort and tried to steal my
> horse. Do not know how many more are in
> the vicinity but I am taking steps for another
> visitation. Am burying excess ordnance, lest
> it fall into enemy hands.

The last square of sod is placed carefully on the surface of the earth. Dunbar drives a bleached rib bone into the ground at an angle just in front of his cache. Dunbar steps back from his work. The replaced sod is invisible. The guns will not be found.

EXT. PRAIRIE—DAY

The lieutenant sits atop Cisco, scouting along the bluff. Fort Sedgewick lies in the background.

INT. QUARTERS—DAY

Dunbar's journal lies open on his bunk. We hear a digging sound in the background. The lieutenant is facing the wall of his quarters. Using a bayonet as a cutting tool, he has carved a window out of the sod. He's nearly finished and is just tidying up.

> DUNBAR (VO cont'd.)
> Have made all the preparations I can think
> of. I cannot mount an adequate defense but
> will try to make a big impression when they
> come. Waiting.

He pauses, then comments, "The man I encountered was a magnificent-looking fellow."

Then we cut to the Sioux sitting in council.

The last line of one scene leads us directly into the next scene. Ten Bears (Floyd Red Crow Westerman) and Kicking Bird discuss the coming of the white man, and it sets the tone of the relationship between the village elder and the medicine man.

"It's a funny thing about signs," the elder begins in a scene that was cut from the film. "They are always flying in our faces. We know when they are bad or good but sometimes they are strange and there is no way to understand them. Sometimes they make people crazy, but a smart man will take such a sign into himself and let it run around for two or three days. If he is still confused he will tell somebody. He might come to you or to me and tell it. A smart man always does that."

Kicking Bird replies, "I have seen such a sign. . . . I saw a white man." Ten Bears is silent, then replies, "We will council on this."

Blake cuts directly into the council scene (enter late and get out early) as the council discusses this "white man." The council is a place where each man can speak freely, expressing his point of view. Different points of view, as stated earlier, generate conflict, and the conflict between Kicking Bird and Wind In His Hair is established immediately. What's to be done? Wind In His Hair has a simple solution: He declares that "we will ride to the soldier fort. We will shoot some arrows into this white man. If he truly has medicine, he will not be hurt. If he has no medicine, he will be dead."

Kicking Bird disagrees; he feels the white man may be some kind of a sign, or signal, about what the future may hold for the Sioux.

When Ten Bears concludes the meeting we see three Indian boys slide out of the tepee and spur their horses into the night. The boys are used as a transition to take us back to Dunbar. The creative choice here is to find a realistic (not contrived) story element that will keep Dunbar in contact with the Sioux and continue moving the story forward.

That link is Cisco. A horse is a valuable asset on the frontier, and the Sioux want it. The three boys set out to steal the animal, but when Dunbar hears them "he runs through the door and forgets to duck under the wooden crossbeam. His skull cracks resoundingly against the overhang and Dunbar slumps onto his back . . . out cold."

As the three Indian boys gallop into the night, laughing about their escapade, Cisco suddenly stops in his tracks; the boy holding the reins is jerked forward to the earth and lies dazed and hurt; Cisco turns around and gallops back to the fort.

When Dunbar finally comes to, it is daybreak, and he sees Cisco pawing for breakfast.

There are several humorous bits like this in *Dances With Wolves,* and each one becomes an attractive element in the story. In Hollywood there's always a question about why one film gets made and not another. There are so many variable factors—schedules, star availability, script, budget considerations—that these little bits of humor add to the texture and salability of the script. It was one of the things that caught Jake Eberts's eye when he read it, and may have been one of the reasons he committed to it immediately, in an emotional sense, even though the property was owned by somebody else.

Dunbar is sitting naked, shaving, when he notices the wolf, Two Socks, staring into the distance. Then Two Socks disappears over the horizon. Dunbar knows how to read signs on the frontier a little better by now, and as he scrambles up the incline to see what's going on, we hear the thundering sound of hoofbeats and see five mounted warriors, "their faces streaked with colorful designs, their weapons slung around their shoulders, their nearly naked bodies all sinew and bone. They are the full and breathtaking glory of war."

This is our first introduction to Wind In His Hair (Rodney Grant) as written in the script:

He sits for a moment on his whirling pony, trying to decide if he should confront this white god.

He makes a warrior's choice. Wind In His Hair shouts to his fellows to go on and charges down the slope . . . straight for Dunbar.

Dunbar's eyes are fixed on the closing horseman. He can't move.

Wind In His Hair is coming flat out, his lance extended. At the last moment he pulls up so hard that the black pony skids to a sit. The horse is up quickly and hard to manage. He pitches back and forth only a few feet in front of Lieutenant Dunbar.

> WIND IN HIS HAIR
> I am Wind In His Hair. Do you not see that I
> am not afraid of you? Do you see?

Wind In His Hair suddenly turns his pony and whips after his comrades.

Dunbar stares after the disappearing horse and rider. He feels the weight of the gun and lets it drop to the ground.

For two or three steps he staggers toward the quarters, but his legs give way and he falls face first in a dead faint.

EXT. PRAIRIE—DAY

Wind In His Hair is riding hard and happy. He really fixed that white god. But as he clears the brow of a rise, a riderless horse blows past him, running in the opposite direction.

Cisco's running back to the fort at full speed, the lines of two ropes flying behind him.

For Dunbar it becomes another lesson in his education: "I realize now that I have been wrong. All this time I have been waiting. Waiting for what? For someone to find me? For Indians to take my horse? To see a buffalo?"

For the first time since he's been at Fort Sedgewick, John Dunbar is dramatically active; until now he's been reacting to the situation. That makes him passive. Action is character; what he does is what he is. The trials of the hero are always designed to see whether the potential hero should *really be* a hero. Is he a match for the task? Can he overcome the dangers? Does he have the courage, the knowledge, the capacity to enable him to serve?

"Since I arrived at this post," Dunbar says in voice-over, "I have been walking on eggs. It has become a bad habit, and I am sick of it. Tomorrow morning I will ride out to the Indians. I do not know the outcome or the wisdom of this thinking. But I have become a target, and a target makes a poor impression. I am through waiting."

In the next few shots we see him polishing his buttons, brushing Cisco, shining his boots. This turnaround of character, from reaction to action, is the emotional link that leads us to Dunbar's encounter with Stands With A Fist and the Sioux village, which is Pinch I in the line of dramatic action.

As Dunbar rides toward the Sioux, his buttons sparkling in the sun, Blake sets up Pinch I, that sequence in the First Half of Act II that keeps the story on track, heading toward the Mid-Point.

Pinch I in *Dances With Wolves* is Dunbar's first face-to-face encounter with the Sioux. It begins under the shade of a lonely cottonwood, as Stands With A Fist (Mary McDonnell) sits in a pool of her own blood. She sees the white soldier "sitting on a horse, with a sword, a bright uniform, and a red sash. And most amazing of all, no face," read the stage directions. "A shift in the breeze has wrapped the popping red, white, and blue flag around his head. One of the soldier's hands is trying to claw it away from his face."

Frightened, she turns to flee, but she's too weak to run, and there's nowhere to hide, and she falls in the grass. Dunbar slips off Cisco and forcefully holds her. "She struggles mightily, twisting onto her back. She lashes out at his face but he grabs her hands, holding them tight. They're nose to nose." That's when she says "Don't . . ." and can't believe she said it. "She spits out a stream of Sioux curses, throws her head back, and wails like a wolf. Then she passes out."

This is the first part of the sequence showing Dunbar's encounter with the Indians. We pick him up entering the Sioux village, cradling Stands With A Fist in his arms. It is a dramatic entrance as pandemonium spreads throughout the lodges; women and children scream, flee in terror.

Dunbar is confronted by a line of warriors. He dismounts and offers Stands With A Fist to the Sioux. Wind In His Hair strides toward the white man, war club in hand. When he sees Stands With A Fist he tears her out of Dunbar's grasp, drags her across the ground, drops her unceremoniously, then strides back to Dunbar. "You're not welcome here," he says in Sioux, and though the white man doesn't understand the words, he understands the message. Dunbar leaves, "his head down and his shoulders slumped. It is a sight that makes Kicking Bird's head turn."

In the novel, *"The lieutenant felt the spirit run out of him. These were not his people. He would never know them. He might as well have been a thousand miles away. He wanted to be small, small enough to crawl into the smallest, darkest hole.*

"What had he expected of these people? He must have thought they would run out and throw their arms around him, speak his language, have him to supper, share his jokes, without so much as a how-do-you-do. How lonely he must be. How pitiful he was to entertain any expectations at all, grasping at these outlandish straws, hoping hopes that were so far-flung that he could not be honest with himself. He had managed to fool himself about everything, fool himself into thinking he was something when he was nothing."

It is a nice insight into John Dunbar, something the novel does very well, but not the screenplay. All we can reveal in the script is the "slump" of his shoulders.

After he has gone, the Sioux discuss the white man in council. Kicking Bird wants to establish contact with Dunbar because "I see someone who might speak for all the white people coming. I think this may be someone with whom treaties could be struck."

But Wind In His Hair has other ideas:

WIND IN HIS HAIR
When I hear that more whites are coming
. . . I want to laugh. We took a hundred
horses from these people, there was no
honor in it. They don't ride well, they don't

WIND IN HIS HAIR (cont'd.)
shoot well, they're dirty. They could not
even make it through one winter in our
country. And these people are said to flourish? I think they will all be dead in ten years.

I asked Blake how he developed the characters of the two Indians, and he replied that during his reading he found that "Kicking
Bird was a Kiowa medicine man. And it's widely believed that he
was assassinated, poisoned, because he was a very effective warrior, but he straddled the time when these people were wild and
the time they were on the reservation. He tried to be a mediator
and work with both sides. Eventually he paid for it politically and
was assassinated. I used him as the inspiration for Kicking Bird.

"For Wind In His Hair the inspiration probably came from
some of the Sioux warriors I read about. I've known a lot of people that are like Wind In His Hair. They're people that you don't
always agree with, but you always listen to them, because you
might have some real trouble if you don't allow them the opportunity to speak. There's a point where Dunbar says in his journal
about Wind In His Hair that he hopes he never has to fight him,
because he's a rough customer. You have to respect that."

At the end of the council meeting, Ten Bears announces that
both Kicking Bird and Wind In His Hair will go visit the white
man, and in the last descriptive line in the stage directions Blake
writes that Ten Bears takes a bite of meat and begins chewing.
Then he cuts to:

Dunbar chewing bacon. As a transition it works nicely and
leads us into the next scene. He offers a piece to the wolf sitting
only a few feet away, but the animal, while obviously tempted,
will not come farther. The lieutenant finally tosses the bacon to
him, and the animal scampers toward the river.

That's when he sees six Sioux warriors sitting on top of the
ridge. Kicking Bird and Wind In His Hair come toward him in
their first friendly encounter. It's a nice scene, laced with humor as
they explore a way to communicate with each other. Dunbar offers them coffee, and they sit stoically as he grinds the beans in his
primitive coffee grinder. When they don't drink, he offers them

sugar, and when Wind In His Hair licks it and discovers its sweetness, a barrier is removed. You can't explain sugar; you have to experience it: words and pictures.

Dunbar asks about the buffalo, then tries to "show" them in a farcical game of charades, but Wind In His Hair thinks "his mind is gone." But as Kicking Bird watches, he understands what the white man is trying to communicate, and they find the first word to bridge their understanding: buffalo.

As Dunbar observes the Sioux over the next few visits, he understands that "nothing I have been told about these people is correct. They are not beggars and thieves. They are not the bogeymen they have been made out to be."

Once the relationship between the white man and the Sioux has been established, the stage is now set to advance the story; the focus shifts to the Sioux and the importance of Stands With A Fist. We learn she is a white woman whose parents were killed by the Pawnee when she was a child. She was found and raised by the Sioux.

This information is conveyed as Kicking Bird asks her to recall the white language and act as interpreter for the white man, but she is hesitant. "I am afraid the whites will try and take me away," she confides. He tells her he will not let that happen, but when he tries to force her to remember "the talk," she reacts and runs out of the lodge.

We follow her to the river, and then, "as if shocked by some unseen force, her eyes spring open," read the stage directions. "Wide and unblinking, her eyes stare deeply into space. Someone is calling. The voice is so faint at first that the words can't be heard. But the calling grows and suddenly the word is upon her."

And we hear the word "Christine," which leads us directly into a flashback; we see the incident that led to Stands With A Fist being found by the Sioux. Three Pawnees attack the family, and the little girl flees to safety.

The flashback leads us to the Mid-Point, that link in the chain of dramatic action that connects the First Half of Act II with the Second Half of Act II. The incident that does this in *Dances With Wolves* is the buffalo hunt. Because Dunbar "brings" them the buffalo, he is honored and rewarded, allowed to enter the inner circles of the Sioux, accepted as one of their own. But this acceptance does not come easily.

EXT. SEDGEWICK—NIGHT

The moon is full. As we look down on the fort we can hear a new sound coming off the prairie. A light rumbling.

INT. QUARTERS—NIGHT

Lieutenant Dunbar is asleep in the moonlight. The rumbling is getting louder. It wakes him. He gropes about, lights the lantern, and listens to the strange, powerful sound.

Something's in the air. He holds the lantern toward the ceiling. Particles of dirt and dust are being shaken from the roof. It's the earth that's trembling.

EXT. SEDGEWICK—NIGHT

Dressed in only pants and boots, Dunbar walks along the bluff above the river, his lantern held out in front of him. The sound is tremendous now. Dunbar stops as a great wall of dust rises before him.

At the same time, he realizes something is alive behind the wall of dust, he recognizes the sound . . . the sound of thousands of hoofbeats.

He sees one veer out. And now another. And another, darting briefly from the great cloud of dust. The most powerful force on the prairie now seems like the most powerful force on earth as it thunders by.

The buffalo.

Dunbar charges into the Sioux village during the buffalo dance, upsetting the entire village. Dunbar manages to convey his discovery to Kicking Bird, and "for a fleeting moment there is shocked silence. Then the Sioux explode with excitement. Dunbar is pulled to his feet. The people are surging in around him with yelps of joy."

Dunbar joins the Sioux on the trail of the buffalo, and once again we see the horrible curse the whites have brought to the land: Carcasses of slaughtered buffalo have been left rotting on the prairie. "Dunbar looks queasy. The lieutenant glances at Kicking Bird riding next to him. He looks sick, too. Dunbar looks away. The entire column is stretched along the killing ground, looking.

"A naked cow, covered with birds, lies on her side. Her newborn calf, doomed to death, cries for his dead mother. And next to the calf, Dunbar sees something else. He sees wagon tracks and the booted footprints of white men."

Dunbar says in voice-over: "Who would do such a thing? Only a people without value and soul, without regard for Sioux rights. . . . It could only be white hunters. These buffalo were killed only for their tongues and the price of their hides."

When the Sioux do find the buffalo "by the thousands," the script reads (it's a producer's nightmare to read that), the hunt begins, a forceful and dynamic sequence that captures the excitement and tension of the chase. We see Dunbar handling himself well, killing a few buffalo, and when he saves a young warrior, he further adds to his stature.

When it's all over, Wind In His Hair comes to him with a buffalo's "liver, still warm and steaming. He sticks the fresh liver in his mouth and happily bites off a chunk, letting the juices run from the edges of his mouth. Now he figures the lieutenant knows what to do, and hands the liver to him. . . . Tentatively, Dunbar bites off a small piece and chews it thoughtfully. It's good. He takes a man-sized bite. Shrill Sioux voices rise all around him as they cheer the lieutenant. Dunbar holds the liver triumphantly over his head."

With this one gesture, Dunbar has become one of them, a member of the Sioux community; he has literally been reborn. *"Like many people, Lieutenant Dunbar had spent most of his life on the*

sidelines, observing rather than participating," reads the novel.
"At the times when he was a participant, his actions were distinctly independent, much like his experience in the war had been.

"It was a frustrating thing, always standing apart.

"Something about this lifelong rut changed when he enthusiastically lifted the liver, the symbol of his kill, and heard the cries of encouragement from his fellows. Then he had felt the satisfaction of belonging to something whose whole was greater than any of its parts. . . .

"The Army had tirelessly extolled the virtues of service, of individual sacrifice in the name of God or country or both. The lieutenant had done his best to adopt these tenets, but the feeling of service to the Army had dwelled mostly in his head. Not in his heart. It never lasted beyond the fading, hollow rhetoric of patriotism.

"The Comanches were different. . . . But the facts of their lives had grown less important to him. They were a group who lived and prospered through service. Service was how they controlled the fragile destiny of their lives. It was constantly being rendered, faithfully and without complaint, to the simple, beautiful spirit of the way they lived, and in it Dunbar found a peace that was to his liking.

"He did not deceive himself. He did not think of becoming an Indian. But he knew that so long as he was with them, he would serve the same spirit."

25

Dances With Wolves:

The Trail of a True Human Being

After the Mid-Point, the buffalo hunt, we see a definite shift in the action; Dunbar has been transformed from the total outsider, the loner, into an honored guest of the Sioux. All night long they feast, celebrating the victorious hunt.

Wind In His Hair will not let Dunbar alone. He has now taken it upon himself to host the white man; he wants him to eat, eat, and then eat some more. Everywhere the white man goes, people in camp welcome him like a hero, and he is forced to repeat his tales of the hunt over and over again.

When the hero sets out on his quest, searching for the Holy Grail, or the Fountain of Youth, it usually ends with the discovery of his own self; it is a journey of self-discovery. This is what happens to Dunbar. By losing himself he has found himself. It's this acceptance by the Sioux that provides the subtext for the Second Half of Act II. This subtext holds the Second Half of Act II in place. Everything flows through the theme of his acceptance, and it is this that keeps the story moving forward toward the Plot Point at the end of Act II.

"Lieutenant Dunbar's course in life shifted," the novel reads. *"There was no single, bombastic event to account for the shift. He had no mystic visions. God did not make an appearance. He was not dubbed a Comanche [Sioux] warrior.*

"There was no moment of proof, no obvious relic of evidence a person could point to and say it was here or there, at this time or that.

"It was as if some beautiful, mysterious virus of awakening that had been long in incubation finally came to the forefront of his life. . . .

"Every day begins with a miracle, he thought suddenly. . . .

"Whatever God may be, I thank God for this day."

It's a major shift in the way he sees the world, a transformation. There's a scripture from an ancient Hindu text called *The Yoga Vashsita* that says, "The world is as you see it." What we believe to be true, *is* true. The world—what's inside our heads, our thoughts, feelings, memories, emotions—is reflected outside in our everyday life. How we see the world is how we experience it. Our life is like a giant mirror reflecting our beliefs and experience.

Blake reveals this theme in a scene between Wind In His Hair and Dunbar in which they engage in a trading ritual. Each gives something he cherishes to the other. When Dunbar sees the Indian admiring his Army jacket, he offers it to him (a metaphorical gesture that shows Dunbar giving away his old way of life), and Wind In His Hair reciprocates by offering Dunbar his breastplate, something of great value and significance. "The breastplate is craftsmanship at its finest," Blake writes in stage directions; "a good deal has been struck."

The Second Half of Act II reflects the expanding bond of friendship and respect between the two. The Sioux treat him like a brother.

He is one of them. He belongs.

From the very first scene in the script, Michael Blake has focused on getting inside the character of John Dunbar. A few paragraphs in the book add a little more insight into his character. After the hunt, Wind In His Hair leads him into a card game with some of the other warriors, and Dunbar wins three ponies. Not really needing them, the first thing he does is give them to Kicking Bird, and in his own personal gesture, Kicking Bird gives one of the ponies back to him. So the white man takes it and presents it to

Ten Bears as a gift of friendship and appreciation. The old man is very pleased, the novel reads. *"Comanche tradition called for the rich to spread their wealth among the less fortunate. But Dunbar reversed that, and the old man was left with the thought that this white man was truly extraordinary."*

Action is character, and these little actions establish why he is being accepted into the village as a Sioux, not a white man. Film is behavior. What a person does is what he is. Dunbar has been born again, given a second chance in life, like the phoenix rising from the ashes. This movement ends with Kicking Bird making the decision that the first thing Dunbar needs is a "real name."

Lonely at the fort, Dunbar is riding back to the Sioux when he sees Two Socks trailing him like a devoted dog. When Dunbar tries to "chase" him back to the fort, the wolf turns around and chases him, even nips his heels playfully, sending Dunbar sprawling to the earth.

Kicking Bird observes this little dance on a knoll a short distance away. As he watches, *"he remembered the old names,"* the novel reads, *"like The Man Who Shines Like Snow, and some of the new ones, like Finds The Buffalo. None of them really fit.*

"As he watched the white man and the wolf scampering back and forth, he felt certain that this was the right one. It suited the white soldier's personality. People would remember him by this. And Kicking Bird himself, with two witnesses to back him up, had been present at the time the Great Spirit revealed it.

"He said it to himself several times as he came down the slope. The sound of it was as good as the name itself.

"Dances With Wolves."

As we become more involved in the relationship between Dances With Wolves and the Sioux, we learn more about the Sioux. For example, one of the sacred traditions of the Native American is the smoking of the pipe. Michael Blake explained it this way: "The concept of the pipe is so simple, so straight, so direct. If I wanted to borrow something from you, like a tool, or lawnmower, or truck, and we were Indians living in those times, I would invite you over and have you sit in a place that was very comfortable. I'd get out my pipe and we'd have a smoke. Then we'd smoke for however long it took us to make small talk and get really comfortable with each other. The whole idea would be to get ourselves centered so we could have an honest exchange. The Indians believed that pipe smoke went to heaven, and it took your thoughts and your ideas and your feelings straight to God. Straight to the Great Spirit. So if you smoked the pipe first before you got down to business, your business would be right.

"It was a system that worked. What was revered in their society, what was worshiped and honored, was being able to talk straight. The word of a human being was something worshiped by the Indian people."

When we are introduced to the pipe, "it's being smoked," reads the script. "Kicking Bird puffs a few times and hands the pipe to Dunbar. The lieutenant, aware the pipe is something special, handles it with care," the stage directions read.

When Stands With A Fist enters Kicking Bird's lodge, we learn she will become the bridge connecting Dances With Wolves with the Sioux. We already know her background, set up in the flashback earlier, and she becomes an integral part of the story.

Time passes, and in voice-over, Dunbar comments on this first meeting with Kicking Bird and Stands With A Fist. We see him in a montage, walking and talking with Kicking Bird and Stands With A Fist. What's interesting is to look at the subtext, the growing attraction between Dunbar and Stands With A Fist, and the words he is saying:

> DUNBAR (VO)
> I try to answer all of Kicking Bird's questions but I know he is frustrated with me. He always wants to know how many more white people are coming. I tell him that it is impossible for me to say. When he persists I tell him that the white people will most likely pass through this country and nothing more.

Kicking Bird and Stands With A Fist are walking away from Dunbar, who takes a few steps in the opposite direction before paus-

ing. Toward the end of the following speech he glances back at
them, and Stands With A Fist glances back at him.

> DUNBAR (VO cont'd.)
> But I am speaking to him in half truths. One
> day there will be too many, but I cannot
> bring myself to tell him that. I am sure that
> Stands With A Fist knows.

That one reference visually sets the stage for their relationship.
What can we do to set up the love story between them? That's the
question the screenwriter must deal with. The answer? To create a
situation where they must spend time alone together.

When a Sioux war party gets ready to go against the Pawnee,
Dances With Wolves volunteers to go with them, but Kicking Bird
flatly refuses: "The Sioux way of being a warrior is not the white
way. You are not ready." But he does ask the white man to look
out after his family while he is gone. It is a great honor.

If we take apart and analyze the purpose of this war party, we
see it's put in for one reason only: to give Dunbar and Stands With
A Fist time to be alone together, to advance their relationship in a
natural, dramatic, and uncontrived way. It is here that he is called
Dances With Wolves, and for the first time he feels that he belongs.
Lieutenant John Dunbar has died, been reborn as Dances With
Wolves, and is starting out on the trail of a new life. That's the
theme Antonioni was exploring in *The Passenger,* with Jack Nicholson. But the Nicholson character did not return; he died because
he was harboring another man's identity and had to accept the
destiny of the other person.

It's different in the spiritual journey of Dances With Wolves. He
embodies the eternal quest of the classic hero: "departure, fulfillment, return." In all mythological quests, Campbell says, the hero
leaves one condition (the Civil War) to find another, a new and
deeper experience of life (the Sioux) that will bring him into a
"richer, more mature condition."

Transformation.

With the war party gone, Stands With A Fist begins to educate
him in the Sioux language and tradition. As the two become closer

and closer, the attraction between them grows. And soon the fires of passion are ignited.

When the white man asks Stands With A Fist how she got her name, she tells how it happened, posing another choice for Michael Blake: Does he show how she gets her name in flashback, or not? He had previously shown how she came to be with the Sioux in flashback, so showing how she got her name could easily have been shown in flashback.

This is the kind of creative choice that screenwriters debate over and over again. If you're thinking of using a flashback, ask yourself why you're using it. What do you hope to achieve with it? What do you want to reveal? There are only two basic reasons to use a flashback: to learn more about the character, and to provide more story information. If you decide to use a flashback in a situation like this, you have to make sure it doesn't intrude, or impede the action, that it doesn't get in the way. As we've seen in *The Silence of the Lambs,* inserting a flashback in the middle of the scene between Hannibal Lecter and Clarice Starling would simply have detracted from the action, not added to it.

In flashback, if you can say it, you don't have to show it.

At this point the relationship between Dances With Wolves and Stands With A Fist is more important than seeing how she got her name.

Names are important to the Native American because a person's name reflects who that person is—his or her true nature. A child's name is usually *revealed* to the child's parents.

When Stands With A Fist first came to the Sioux, there was a woman who kept abusing her, until one day the little white girl got fed up and punched her out. From that day on she was called Stands With A Fist. She is tough and strong, a person who stands tall.

When Dances With Wolves asks why she isn't married, why she's not with a man, Stands With A Fist bolts and runs away. Later we find out her husband had been killed, and she is still in mourning. That's when Dances With Wolves first found her, wounded and bleeding on the prairie.

Now separated from Stands With A Fist, Dunbar returns to Fort Sedgewick but feels isolated, alone, a stranger. As he sits on his bed, reading through his journal, he writes an entry that tells us what we already suspect: "I love Stands With A Fist." Then he signs it with his new name: Dances With Wolves.

Their romance is like a dream; we don't need a lot of scenes, or lines to be spoken to tell us how they feel about each other. We know who they are, and that they've been brought together by background, temperament, and fate. In the novel we share her feelings about this newfound love in her life. Stands With A Fist *"could not deny it. She saw herself in him. She saw that they could be one. . . . The rarest of all things in this life has happened, she thought. The Great Spirit has brought us together."*

Blake constructs this romantic interlude by cross-cutting between them after Stands With A Fist has run away. Now he brings them together. One scene is all that's needed.

EXT. RIVERSIDE—DAY

Stands With A Fist is wading through the water, her mind far away.

In a moment there is a shift in the wind. The rustling of the trees alerts her to a presence she had not thought to feel before.

Gradually she raises her eyes to see the figure of a man moving through the trees . . . Dances With Wolves.

Stands With A Fist walks slowly out of the water. He opens his arms and she melts into them, letting her head rest against his chest.

> STANDS WITH A FIST
> I am in mourning.

> DANCES WITH WOLVES
> I know. . . .

She presses her body full against his, feeling all of him. She climbs higher into his arms for a moment. Then, supporting each other, the lovers move into the cover of the willow breaks along the river.

The dialogue works against the scene; the subtext, their passion is what's important here, not the words said. Subtext is a very powerful tool in the writer's toolbox. The *subtext,* what is *not* said in a scene, is more important than what *is* said.

The relationship between Stands With A Fist and Dances With Wolves is Pinch II. In this case, as in *Thelma and Louise,* Pinch I and Pinch II are related. Pinch I, if you recall, had Thelma picking up the hitchhiker; Pinch II is when the police pick up the hitchhiker after he has stolen the money from them. In *Dances With Wolves,* Pinch I has Dunbar finding Stands With A Fist and making contact with the Sioux. Pinch II is when they make love.

"They stare across at each other," the stage directions read. "Dances With Wolves walks slowly to her and they embrace lightly. Stands With A Fist starts to slip out of her dress."

But their passion is interrupted by a surge of noise and pandemonium outside, and we learn that a war party of Pawnee is nearby, and "they come for blood," Stone Calf tells the white man. Dances With Wolves tells him there are guns buried at Fort Sedgewick, and after a hurried council with Ten Bears, he convinces the elder that "guns will make one warrior like two," and he is given permission to return to the fort. He takes the young boy Smiles A Lot with him.

A sequence, remember, is a series of scenes connected by one single idea with a beginning, middle, and end. Look at the forces working in this sequence. The Pawnee are nearby, so there is an urgency to go to the fort, retrieve the guns, and return as soon as possible. They don't have much time. To create this sense of urgency, the visual elements of the action are written in a fast pace and rhythm; the tempo of the scenes gets shorter and shorter, faster and faster, until the sequence explodes into a frenzy of action.

Here's the way it begins. Dances With Wolves and the Indian boy Smiles A Lot race to the fort. But a driving rainstorm makes it almost impossible to find the bone that Dunbar had left as a marker. Again, the simplicity of the rainstorm is a physical conflict that impedes the action and creates tension; all that is needed is a few shots of the two men searching the area for the marker, finding it, then Dances With Wolves digging with his hands. That's the beginning of the sequence, finding the guns. The pictures that set up the sequence give us visual information, one, two, three; that's all we need to establish.

From Dances With Wolves digging in the earth, we cut to the Sioux village. The guns are passed out, but only Dances With Wolves knows how to use them. What would the white soldier do? Ten Bears asks. "I would let the enemy think we are asleep . . . let him come close. Then we would shoot together and run to fight them, drive them into the river, and kill so many that they would never trouble us again."

We cut to the village at dawn, when everything is quiet and peaceful. As the Pawnee slink through the brush toward the village, we see "a war party at its fiercest, painted and feathered and armed to the teeth." After a few moments, a Pawnee war cry goes up and then all hell breaks loose and we're into a three-page action sequence.

The canvas of this action is savage, but the focus is always on Dances With Wolves, running, fighting, killing the Pawnee. He is more Sioux than white at this point. The sequence ends when "Dances With Wolves climbs to his feet and discovers that the battlefield is quiet. The fighting has stopped. It is a scene of carnage and joy. The Pawnee attackers lay where they fell."

For Dances With Wolves, it is a sobering experience.

> DANCES WITH WOLVES (VO)
> It was hard to know how to feel. I had never been in a battle like this one. This had not been a fight for territory or riches or to make men free. This battle had no ego. It had been fought to preserve the food stores that would see us through winter, to protect the lives of women and children and loved ones only a few feet away. I felt a pride I had never felt before. . . . I had never really known who John Dunbar was, perhaps because the name itself had no meaning. But as I heard my Sioux name being

> DANCES WITH WOLVES (VO cont'd.)
> called over and over, I knew for the first
> time who I really was.

When Kicking Bird returns, he must release Stands With A Fist from her vow of mourning, and he does this in a gruff but lovable way. Here's the way it's written—short, direct, to the point:

EXT. INDIAN VILLAGE—DAY

Stands With A Fist is walking through the village with Kicking Bird's youngest child. They're both carrying armloads of firewood.

Here comes Kicking Bird. He's out of breath.

> KICKING BIRD
> Stands With A Fist.

> STANDS WITH A FIST
> Yes.

> KICKING BIRD
> You are no longer a widow.

Kicking Bird turns abruptly and stalks off, leaving Stands With A Fist to ponder the meaning of his curt announcement. A smile gradually works onto her face.

It's no longer necessary for the two lovers to hide their feelings for each other. It's only natural that Dances With Wolves and Stands With A Fist will marry.

Gifts must be given. In the process, the relationship between Dances With Wolves and Wind In His Hair is further developed. There's a nice scene where Wind In His Hair tells Dances With Wolves that "the man she mourned for was my best friend. . . . He was a good man. It's been hard for me. I am not the thinker Kicking Bird is. But I think he went away from her because you were coming. That is how I see it now." It is a touching moment in the lives of these two men.

During the ceremony, Dances With Wolves says in voice-over, "I had never been married before. I don't know if all grooms have the same experience . . . but my mind swam in a way that shut out everything but her. The tiny details of her costume. The contours of her shape. The light in her eyes. The smallness of her feet. I knew that the love between us would be served."

After the ceremony, Blake makes a nice visual transition to indicate the passing of time. When Dances With Wolves and Stands With A Fist disappear into their lodge after the ceremony, "the flap is dropped and there it stays. The light begins to change, growing darker, the wind comes up, blowing leaves against the door. In the distance there is thunder."

We cut to "the lodge flap still closed. But now it is covered in sunshine," and the Sioux are "bundled against the chill of oncoming winter."

At this point in the screenplay Blake wrote a sequence that was cut out of the movie. Kicking Bird and Dances With Wolves are riding together to visit a sacred grove where "the trees shelter every animal the Great Spirit has made. It is said they hatched here when life began and constantly return to the place of their birth."

Costner decided to keep only the front part of the scene, the lead-in, where Kicking Bird and Dances With Wolves are riding across the prairie. The transformation, that character arc that began with Lieutenant John Dunbar then merged into Dances With Wolves, is now complete. "The medicine man keeps looking at his protégé," the script reads. "There is virtually no semblance of Lieutenant Dunbar left."

KICKING BIRD

I was just thinking that of all the trails in
this life, there is one that matters more than
all the others. It is the trail of a true human
being. I think you are on this trail and it is
good to see.

Dances With Wolves doesn't reply, but if Lieutenant Dunbar could put into words what he has been searching for his entire life, perhaps it is this, to be "a true human being." This search has been at the very root of his character, something so simple, yet so profound.

It is a moment of completion, of acceptance. In one sense, the film really could end here. Dunbar's achieved everything he set out to achieve, has accomplished his dramatic need. But the story isn't over yet. All drama is conflict; without conflict, there's no action; without action, there's no character; without character, there's no story; and without story, there's no screenplay.

We still have to set up the Resolution, the *real* story—what happens to Dances With Wolves against the backdrop of the Native Americans losing their land, then their identity, to the invading whites.

We see this in the omitted sequence. Kicking Bird and Dances With Wolves ride into the sacred grove. "It is said," Kicking Bird tells Dances With Wolves, "that all the animals were born here . . . that from here they spread over the prairies to feed all the people. Even our enemies say this is a sacred place."

As they enter this almost magical, spiritual grove, the medicine man stops, sensing something is not right. As they ride farther into the area:

Just ahead the forest opens into an incredible cathedral-like expanse. Sunlight streams down onto the floor in beautiful pools.

But still there is a deathly quiet, and Dances With Wolves can see now that this remarkable place has been horribly desecrated.

Trees have been felled everywhere, most of them left to rot for no explicable reason.

At the same time he sees this destruction, Dances With Wolves realizes that the strange buzzing sound is not coming from overhead but from the forest floor.

The insects are not bees. They are flies, and they are swarming over dozens of carcasses strewn over the ground—badgers, skunks, squirrels, and other small animals, nearly all of them killed merely for target practice.

The two men are silent as they contemplate the scene in front of them. There is no need for words. What can they say? The art of screenwriting is finding places where silence works better than words. We know who's responsible for this carnage. We don't have to say it, we just have to show it. It's true it's a little heavy-handed and was probably omitted because we've seen it before on the buffalo hunt.

As they ride back to the village, Blake sets up the Plot Point at the end of Act II. Dances With Wolves and Kicking Bird are sitting by an open fire when the white man tells Kicking Bird what he has been holding back all this time. "You have asked me," he begins, "about the white people. . . . You always ask how many more are coming. There will be a lot, my friend, more than can be counted." When the Indian asks how many, Dances With Wolves replies, "Like the stars." We hold for a long moment, then we're with Ten Bears in his lodge, showing the two men with an old rusted Spanish helmet from the time of Cortez. "The men who wore this," the elder explains, "came in the time of my grandfather's grandfather. Eventually we drove them out. Then the Mexicans came. In my own time the whites came . . . the Texans. They have been like all the others who find something they want in our country. They take it without asking. I have always been a peaceful man, happy to be in my own country and wanting nothing from the white people. But I think you are right: I think they will keep coming. When I think of that, I look at this bundle. Our country is all that we want. We will fight to keep it."

Then he adds, "We will strike the village and go to the winter camp." This sets up Plot Point II, Dances With Wolves's capture by the white soldiers who have returned to Fort Sedgewick.

The Sioux are packing, almost ready to move, when Dances With Wolves remembers that he has left the journal at the fort; he must return to get it because "the words in the book are like a trail for people to follow. It tells everything about my life here. I must get it." He leaps on his horse and spurs his faithful Cisco back to the place where he began his journey. The journal has been set up and used throughout the script, and now we're ready for the payoff.

The white soldiers are everywhere at Fort Sedgewick. Before

Dances With Wolves can stop and retreat, the soldiers "scramble for their rifles and scream out the alarm: 'Indians!' " And before we know what's happening, Cisco is shot several times and falls to the ground, dead. The white soldiers pounce on Dances With Wolves, and after a struggle, he is knocked unconscious and dragged into the stockade.

A prisoner. Neither white man nor Sioux.

Plot Point II.

26

The Wheel of Life:

The Passing of the Way

"You turned Injun, din'cha?"

Those are the first words Dances With Wolves hears when he regains consciousness, and they reflect the point of view of the white soldiers. Dances With Wolves straddles two worlds here, but the soldiers see only what they see and have no understanding or compassion for him or his situation.

For them it's simple: He's a traitor, an outlaw, and no matter what he says or does, he cannot convince or persuade them otherwise.

How quickly the wheel of life turns.

With Dances With Wolves captured, two things have to be resolved by the screenwriter: First, what's going to happen to him? Is he going to live or die, honor the uniform of the Army and his country, or escape with the help of the Sioux? And second, what's going to happen to the Sioux?

Act III deals with Dances With Wolves's reintroduction to the white world. It's not easy, nor is it pleasant. When I first saw the movie it was very hard for me to sit through this part. It was too "black-and-white"—the white soldiers are portrayed as the "bad guys," and I thought it was a little too obvious, too direct.

If we look at the structure of *Dances With Wolves,* we see that

Act I, the Set-Up, deals with Dunbar's life as a soldier and his search for a better way of life. In Act II he finds it with the Sioux, and in Act III he's forced back into his old way of life.

Departure, Fulfillment, Return.

In the novel, his capture by and escape from the whites is only a few pages long, but in the script it's almost the entire Third Act. I asked Blake why he exaggerated the destructive behavior of the whites so much. He replied that he wanted to make a point, to create a "dramatic reality"; this story is about Dances With Wolves and his relationship with the Sioux, and it's told from his point of view.

"The world is as you see it," says the *Yoga Vashsita*.

It doesn't take long for Dances With Wolves to figure out that the only way out of this predicament is to escape and to hope his Sioux brothers find a way to help him.

After the soldiers interrogate him, repeatedly beating him, he's informed, "Your status as a traitor might improve should you choose to cooperate with the United States Army." He replies, "There is nothing for you to do out here." Asked more questions, he withdraws into himself and repeats in Sioux, "I am Dances With Wolves. . . . I have nothing to say to you. You are not worth talking to."

With an Army escort he's transferred back to Fort Hays, and as the wagon bounces across the prairie, one of the soldiers sees Two Socks running along the ridge following the wagon. They start shooting at the wolf, using him for target practice. Instead of trying to escape, the wolf continues following the wagon, his loyalty to his captured friend obvious. When Dances With Wolves tries to stop their sport, he receives a brutal rifle butt to the head. Two Socks is hit, and whimpering in pain, finally succumbs and lies motionless.

The white soldiers have no respect for any living thing, especially animals. The relationship between Dunbar and the wolf is something we've seen from the beginning. "How we relate to animals is an important part of living to me," Michael Blake says. "When we pick up the gun and destroy first, that's a mistake. It makes it harder for the human race to progress when it has a destructive policy toward other forms of life."

[As] the CAMERA continues over the hill, Two Socks's body is nowhere in sight. Instead, the Indian war party of six is waiting silently in ambush. Frustrated, they will try again.

To set up and establish the ambush sequence takes only two shots. Nothing has to be explained; if you set it up, then you pay it off. As the wagon crosses the river, the lieutenant takes an arrow in the chest, and the action sequence of rescuing Dances With Wolves begins.

While Dances With Wolves throws his handcuffs around the soldier's neck, Bauer, one of the badass soldiers, tries to escape and stumbles upon Smiles A Lot holding the horses. The boy is frozen; the soldier points a gun at his head, pulls the trigger. Empty; he pistol-whips the boy and grabs a horse. But as he tries to mount:

He hears a bone-chilling whoop. Wind In His Hair is coming.

His pony plows through the water at full speed. A skullcracker dangles from one hand. The warrior begins to whirl it around.

Terrified, Bauer turns to run. Before he can take a step, a hatchet buries itself to the hilt. Smiles A Lot is at the other end. But Bauer is not through.

His hands are around the boy's neck, choking him with his last seconds of life. A larger-than-life Wind In His Hair draws even and swings his club. Bauer's head explodes, covering Smiles A Lot in blood—the sergeant's hands cannot be seen.

As the Sioux regroup, we watch Dances With Wolves's journal floating down the river—"lost forever," the script says, but found in the next shot by Smiles A Lot. The Sioux leave the scene, and Smiles A Lot shows Dances With Wolves the journal, the very object that has brought about this death and destruction. For the first time, Dances With Wolves realizes that his presence among the Sioux may be dangerous.

Finding the journal sets up the ending of the film. As they ride back toward camp, there is a scene in the script (that was omitted from the film) that clearly marks a shift in Dances With Wolves's awareness that this bloodshed may be a sign of things to come.

EXT. PRAIRIE—DUSK

The rescue party is cantering across the prairie.

> DANCES WITH WOLVES
> (to Wind In His Hair)
> We go south?

> WIND IN HIS HAIR
> We will ride south for two days . . . then
> turn east. No one must follow.

This doesn't seem to bother Wind In His Hair. But it sets Dances With Wolves to thinking.

At this moment, Dances With Wolves realizes the Army will hunt him down mercilessly, just the way they will hunt down and eradicate the Sioux and all the other great Indian nations.

The passing of the way. The change in his character is complete.

And that brings us to the ending.

"The book," says Michael Blake, "ends in a lodge, in this wonderful exchange between Dances With Wolves and Ten Bears. It had a lot of power, a lot of drama."

In the novel, Dances With Wolves decides to remain with his wife and the Sioux; whatever happens, happens—their fate will be his fate. He knows the whites will come looking for him: *"I have not been among you for very long,"* he tells his friends in the novel, *"but I feel in my heart that it has been all my life. I'm proud to be a Comanche. I will always be proud to be a Comanche. I love the Comanche way and I love each of you as if we were of the same blood. In my heart and spirit I will always be with you. So you must know that it is hard for me to say that I must leave."*

When their reaction subsides, he explains the soldiers *"think I'm a traitor because they think I have betrayed them. In their eyes*

I am a traitor because I have chosen to live among you. I do not care if they are right or wrong, but I tell you truly that this is what they believe."

He pauses, then continues, *"White men will hunt a traitor long after they have given up on other men. To them a traitor is the worst thing a soldier can be. So they will hunt me until they find me. They will not give up."*

Ten Bears replies that if the Army comes looking for him, they will not find him, *"they will only find a Comanche named Dances With Wolves."* And the two friends sit together and smoke Dances With Wolves's new pipe because *"it's good to pass the time this way."*

That's the end of the book: Dances With Wolves remains with the Sioux. But there's a little epilogue written that sketches in the future: *"A new camp was set up that year, far from the old one near Fort Sedgewick. It was a good spot with plenty of water and grass for the ponies. The buffalo came again by the thousands and the hunting was good, with very few men getting hurt. Late that summer many babies were born, more than most people could remember.*

"They strayed far from the traveled trails, seeing no white men and only a few Mexican traders. It made the people happy to have so little bother.

"But a human tide, one that they could neither see nor hear, was rising in the East. It would be upon them soon. The good times of that summer were the last they would have. Their time was running out and would soon be gone forever."

Warm, sad, thoughtful.

"That ending could have been done on film," Blake declares, "but Kevin wanted them to leave, and that changed the entire focus of the ending."

In the screenplay, Dances With Wolves and Stands With A Fist leaving the Sioux created structural problems for Blake. How does he keep the feeling and tone of the book, yet open the story up visually to enrich it and make it more powerful? By introducing a new element. If they're going to leave, we have to *see* the reason they're leaving. So we show the Army hunting and tracking the Sioux, and intercutting between them. The Army, intercut with the farewell of Dances With Wolves, create tension and intensity in the story.

Cinematically, the cross-cutting between the two streams of action heightens the tension. When you write this kind of sequence, you begin with longer scenes; then, as the action continues, the scenes get shorter and shorter, the pace faster and faster.

"It was difficult for me to think of cramming all this pursuit by the Army and all this flight by the Indians into a sequence that really doesn't last any time at all in the movie," says Blake.

Here's the way Blake sets it up in the screenplay. A lot of information has to be jammed into a very tight space. After the rescue of Dances With Wolves, the return to camp is joyous. But in their lodge that night, "Dances With Wolves is combing Stands With A Fist's hair. It's something he is doing with care and affection. She is loving it as much as he. They are as together as two people can be and yet it is a hard time."

The scene opens after the conversation has taken place. "You have nothing to say?" Dances With Wolves begins. "What can I tell you?" she replies. "We have decided. You are my husband. I am your wife. That is all I know." Dances With Wolves lays his forehead on her back. He sighs. Then he pulls away, slips a robe around his shoulders, and walks out of the lodge. Sadly, she watches him go.

As Dances With Wolves walks in the snow, we cut to "a pair of boots walking in the snow," and the Army tracking him; they discover a fire still smoking, examine it, and then we "follow the smoke and the steam as it rises," and cut to a "warm column of smoke spiraling out of Ten Bears's lodge." Back and forth, smoke to smoke, action to action, into the next scene. The transition is smooth and visual.

INT. TEN BEARS'S LODGE—DAY

Several men are gathered around Ten Bears's fire, including Kicking Bird, Wind In His Hair, and Dances With Wolves.

All the men are draped with blankets. The wind is howling outside. The men are engaged in small talk as the pipe goes around the circle. The pipe comes around to Dances With Wolves, and the man next to him must nudge him to attention. Dances With Wolves takes the pipe and begins to smoke.

Ten Bears watches him closely.

TEN BEARS
(to Dances With Wolves)
Dances With Wolves is quiet these days.

He does not reply. He smokes a little more and passes the pipe.

TEN BEARS (cont'd.)
Is his heart bad?

Dances With Wolves glances at the men around the fire.

DANCES WITH WOLVES
Killing the soldiers at the river was a good thing. It made me free, and my heart was big to see my friends coming to help me. I did not mind killing those men. I was glad to do it.

He searches for the right words.

DANCES WITH WOLVES (cont'd.)
But the soldiers hate me now like they hate no other. I am more than an enemy to them. I am a traitor. They will hunt for me. They will not give up. And when they find me they find you and that cannot happen.

Objections break out all around the fire. Wind In His Hair jumps to his feet, and even Kicking Bird is protesting.

The sound of their objections takes us to the column of marching soldiers singing "The Battle Hymn of the Republic," the relentless and unshakable force of the future. It's a nice sound cut, a nice transition that bridges time and takes us to Dances With Wolves saying good-bye.

The first good-bye is with Ten Bears. As they sit by the fire, Ten Bears tells the white man:

> TEN BEARS
> You are the only white man I have ever known. I have thought about you a lot, more than you know. . . . You have always spoken with your heart. And like all of us, you are a free man and can do anything you like. When I look across this fire, I do not see a white soldier. I see only a Sioux named Dances With Wolves. And there is nothing they hate so much as a Sioux.

This statement by Ten Bears is really the payoff to the whole screenplay. In the beginning, John Dunbar is seeking a better way of life, and he finds what he's looking for with the Sioux. He has reached his goal, his dramatic need is satisfied, his transformation complete. The old man is right: Lieutenant Dunbar will never be found.

We cut back to the soldiers following the trail, just one shot, then cut back to the Sioux, where Kicking Bird and Dances With Wolves say farewell. It's done with the pipe; if the smoke goes to heaven, and the heart is open and true, surely the Great Spirit must see the love and feelings these two men have for each other.

This is another good example of subtext in a screenplay; what is not said becomes more important than what is said. The situation is all.

EXT. WINTER CAMP—DAWN

Carrying the pipe he made, Dances With Wolves walks through the village. Suddenly he stops. Kicking Bird is standing in the middle of the empty avenue.

Like gunfighters, the two men approach each other at a slow and deliberate walk.

Gradually they realize that each has selected the same parting gift. It's heartbreaking. Kicking Bird tries to cover with a casual question, but it's all fake.

> KICKING BIRD
> You've finished your pipe? How does it smoke?

> DANCES WITH WOLVES
> I'm told it smokes well.

Dances With Wolves moves to make the exchange. Kicking Bird does the same. From one hand to the other. Men couldn't be closer.

> KICKING BIRD
> It doesn't seem possible that we could come this far.

> DANCES WITH WOLVES
> You were the first man I ever wanted to be like. I will not forget you.

Neither can speak. There is only good-bye.

And we cut back to the column of soldiers marching. We know it's only a matter of time before they find the Sioux.

Cut back to Dances With Wolves and Stands With A Fist outside their lodge, the horses loaded. Every cross-cut between them bridges time and action, so only the most important and dramatic scenes of the farewell are needed. As Dances With Wolves and Stands With A Fist walk the trail leading out of camp, we hear the pain of Wind In His Hair saying his good-bye, the only way he knows how, from the top of the cliff, as far away as possible. It's heartrending to hear him yell out, "Can you not see that I am your friend? . . . Can you not see that you will always be my friend?"

His voice hovers throughout the canyon. Then we cut to the troops moving quietly through the trees, their sabers drawn.

EXT. CANYON RIM—DUSK

The rest of the troops have moved to the edge. They, too, are quiet. Down below, the Pawnee scouts are milling about looking for signs.

The soldiers from the canyon floor are silently arriving on the scene. The Pawnee look to the lead scout on the canyon rim. They have no answer, and the lead scout has nothing to say to the general at his side. Ten Bears's village is gone.

EXT. CANYON RIM—DUSK

Wind In His Hair and several other warriors are just drawing back from unseen vantage points on the canyon rim. Wind In His Hair glances back and hesitates, as though waiting for someone. A great, yellow full moon has just appeared above the opposite rim of the canyon. The yellow is brilliant, a great spotlight of golden color.

A wolf steps into the light on the opposite rim. He's walking in the backdrop of the moon. The wolf suddenly arches his back, sticks his muzzle in the air, and produces a spine-tingling howl. The SOUND bounces all over the canyon.

Dances With Wolves is at the canyon's rim. He listens a long time, fully entranced by the wolf's howl. He is still listening when it is gone. A whisper floats out of the night behind him.

> WIND IN HIS HAIR (VO)
> Dances With Wolves . . .

Dances With Wolves shrinks back from the canyon's rim, turns, and trots off into the darkness, following his friends.

The image freezes, and "Thirteen years later" is written over the end credits. "Their homes destroyed, their buffalo gone, the last band of Sioux submitted to white authority at Fort Robinson, Nebraska. The great horse culture of the plains was gone and the American frontier was soon to pass into history."

It is a very strong and moving ending. To save the people he loves, he must leave them. It is a perfect example of unconditional love—an act of heroism, like that of the Terminator, because he sacrifices his life for the good of others.

Michael Blake has succeeded in capturing the passing of the way, a change of life where the old gives way to the new. The Native Americans have followed their trail, their destiny has been written. But the culture and the knowledge of these people have not been lost, and we can learn about the world we live in the same way John Dunbar learned.

To the Native American, all life is connected: the trees, the stones, the earth, the sky. The earth is just one giant, wondrous, living organism, and everyone and every living thing on this planet are connected. We are all the same, and must honor ourselves and each other, whether human, animal, or plant. In the ancient path of Siddha Yoga, the Scriptures say: "See God in each other."

Astronauts who have flown the space shuttle remark that as they leave the earth's environment, they can see the cities, the states, and the countries, all the boundaries the human race has imposed upon the earth. But as they orbit the earth from space, their perspective changes and all they see are the continents, the oceans, the sun, the moon. They see no boundaries, no lines of demarcation.

Only the planet earth.

"If we can think of ourselves as coming out of the earth," Joseph Campbell says, "rather than having been thrown in here from somewhere else, you can see that we are the earth, that we are the consciousness of the earth. These are the eyes of the earth. And this is the voice of the Earth."

One planet, one world.

Scientists call it the Gaia Principle.

In 1852 the President of the United States wrote to Chief Seattle and inquired about the possibility of buying some of the tribal lands to house the massive amounts of people flooding into the United States. The chief's reply is an extraordinary letter that captures a universal truth in the wheel of life, a seed of thought that transcends time and place, a philosophy that we need to water, nourish, and care for:

> The President in Washington sends word that he wishes to buy our land. But how can you buy or sell the sky? The land? The idea is strange to us. If we do not own the freshness of the air and the sparkle of the water, how can you buy them?
>
> Every part of this earth is sacred to my people. Every shining pine needle, every sandy shore, every mist in the dark woods, every meadow, every humming insect. All are holy in the memory and experience of my people.
>
> We are part of the earth and it is part of us. . . . The shining water that moves in the streams and rivers is not just water, but the blood of our ancestors. If we sell you our land, you must remember that it is sacred. The water's murmur is the voice of my father's father.
>
> If we sell you our land, remember that the air is precious to us, that the air shares its spirit with all the life it supports. The wind that gave our grandfather his first breath also receives his last sigh. So if we sell you our land, you must keep it apart and sacred, as a place where man can go to taste the wind that is sweetened by the meadow flowers.
>
> Will you teach your children what we have taught our children? That the earth is our mother? What befalls the earth befalls all the sons of the earth.
>
> This we know: The earth does not belong to man, man belongs to the earth. All things are connected like the blood that unites us all. Man did not weave the web of life, he is merely a strand in it.

One thing we know: Our God is also your God. The earth is precious to him and to harm the earth is to heap contempt on its creator.

Your destiny is a mystery to us. What will happen when the buffalo are all slaughtered? The wild horses tamed? What will happen when the secret corners of the forest are heavy with the scent of many men and the view of the ripe hills is blotted by talking wires? Where will the thicket be? Gone! Where will the eagle be? Gone! And what is it to say good-bye to the swift pony and the hunt? The end of living and the beginning of survival.

When the last red man has vanished with his wilderness, and his memory is only the shadow of a cloud moving across the prairie, will these shores and forests still be here? Will there be any of the spirit of my people left?

We love this earth as a newborn loves its mother's heartbeat. So if we sell you our land, love it as we have loved it. Care for it as we have cared for it. Hold in your mind the memory of the land as it is when you receive it. Preserve the land for all children and love it, as God loves us all.

As we are part of the land, you, too, are part of the land. This earth is precious to us. It is also precious to you. One thing we know: There is only one God. No man, be he red man or white man, can be apart. We *are* brothers after all.

All things are One.

The '90s are a time of great change and upheaval. The crosscurrents of all this turbulence constitute a fertile environment for the screenwriter. More than at any other time in our history, the contemporary screenwriter is in a position to influence our behavior, to forge new ways of looking at the world, no matter what country or culture.

Movies have become so important in people's lives that we must find a way to make them better than they are. And there's only one way to do that, only one place to start.

With the word.

Appendix:
Casts and Production Credits

THELMA & LOUISE

Directed by	RIDLEY SCOTT
Written by	CALLIE KHOURI
Produced by	RIDLEY SCOTT AND MIMI POLK
Released by	MGM-PATHÉ

CAST

Louise	SUSAN SARANDON
Thelma	GEENA DAVIS
Hal	HARVEY KEITEL
Jimmy	MICHAEL MADSEN
Darryl	CHRISTOPHER McDONALD
Max	STEPHEN TOBOLOWSKY
J.D.	BRAD PITT
Harlan	TIMOTHY CARHART
Lena, the Waitress	LUCINDA JENNEY
State Trooper	JASON BEGHE
Truck Driver	MARCO ST. JOHN
Albert	SONNY CARL DAVIS
Major	KEN SWOFFORD

East Indian Motel Clerk	SHELLY DE SAI
Waitress	CAROL MANSELL
Surveillance Man	STEPHEN POLK
Plainclothes Cop	ROB ROY FITZGERALD
I.D. Tech	JACK LINDINE
Silver Bullet Dancer	MICHAEL DELMAN
Girl Smoker	KRISTEL L. ROSE
Mountain Bike Rider	NOEL WALCOTT

TERMINATOR 2

Produced and Directed by	JAMES CAMERON
Written by	JAMES CAMERON AND WILLIAM WISHER
Co-Producers	B. J. RACK AND STEPHANIE AUSTIN
Executive Producers	GALE ANNE HURD AND MARIO KASSAR

A Pacific Western Production in association with Lightstorm Entertainment

CAST

The Terminator	ARNOLD SCHWARZENEGGER
Sarah Connor	LINDA HAMILTON
John Connor	EDWARD FURLONG
T-1000	ROBERT PATRICK
Dr. Silberman	EARL BOEN
Miles Dyson	JOE MORTON
Tarissa Dyson	S. EPATHA MERKERSON
Enrique Salceda	CASTULO GUERRA
Tim	DANNY COOKSEY
Janelle Voight	JENETTE GOLDSTEIN
Todd Voight	XANDER BERKELEY
Twin Sarah	LESLIE HAMILTON GEARREN
Douglas	KEN GIBBEL
Cigar Biker	ROBERT WINLEY

Lloyd	PETE SCHRUM
Trucker	SHANE WILDER
Old John Connor	MICHAEL EDWARDS
Kids	JARED LOUNSBERY
	CASEY CHAVEZ
Bryant	ENNALLS BERL
Mossberg	DON LAKE
Weatherby	RICHARD VIDAN
Cop	TOM McDONALD
Jocks	JIM PALMER
	GERARD G. WILLIAMS
Night Nurse	GWENDA DEACON
Lewis, the Guard	DON STANTON
Lewis as T-1000	DAN STANTON
Attendant	COLIN PATRICK LYNCH
Hospital Guard	NOEL EVANGELISTI
Girls	NIKKI COX
	LISA BRINEGAR
Danny Dyson	DE VAUGHN NIXON
Vault Guard	TONY SIMOTES
Jolanda Salceda	DIANE RODRIGUEZ
Infant John Connor	DALTON ABBOTT
Pool Cue Biker	RON YOUNG
Tattoo Biker	CHARLES ROBERT BROWN
Gibbons	ABDUL SALAAM EL RAZZAC
Moshier	MIKE MUSCAT
SWAT Team Leader	DEAN NORRIS
Police Chopper Pilot	CHARLES TAMBURRO
Pickup Truck Driver	J. ROB JORDAN
Tanker Truck Driver	TERRENCE EVANS
Burly Attendants	DENNEY PIERCE
	MARK CHRISTOPHER LAWRENCE
SWAT Leader	PAT KOURI
Cyberdyne Tech	VAN LING
Mr. Schwarzenegger's Stand-In	PETER KENT

Ms. Hamilton's Stand-In	MARY ELLEN AVIANO
Mr. Furlong's Stand-In	RHONDA MILLER

THE SILENCE OF THE LAMBS

Directed by	JONATHAN DEMME
Produced by	EDWARD SAXON
	KENNETH UTT
	RON BOZMAN
Screenplay by	TED TALLY
Executive Producer	GARY GOETZMAN
Based on the Novel by	THOMAS HARRIS
Edited by	CRAIG McKAY, A.C.E.
Director of Photography	TAK FUJIMOTO
Production Designer	KRISTI ZEA
Costume Designer	COLLEEN ATWOOD
Music by	HOWARD SHORE
Casting by	HOWARD FEUER
Associate Producer	GRACE BLAKE

CAST

Clarice Starling	JODIE FOSTER
FBI Instructor	LAWRENCE A. BONNEY
Ardelia Mapp	KASI LEMMONS
Agent Burroughs	LAWRENCE T. WRENTZ
Jack Crawford	SCOTT GLENN
Dr. Frederick Chilton	ANTHONY HEALD
Barney	FRANKIE FAISON
Friendly Psychopath	DON BROCKETT
Brooding Psychopath	FRANK SEALS, JR.
Miggs	STUART RUDIN
Dr. Hannibal Lecter	ANTHONY HOPKINS
Young Clarice	MASHA SKOROBOGATOV
Clarice's Father	JEFFRIE LANE
Mr. Lang	LEIB LENSKY
Mr. Lang's Driver	RED SCHWARTZ

TV Evangelist	JIM ROCHE
Catherine Martin	BROOKE SMITH
Jame Gumb	TED LEVINE
Boxing Instructor	JAMES B. HOWARD
Mr. Brigham	BILL MILLER
Agent Terry	CHUCK ABER
Oscar	GENE BORKAN
Sheriff Perkins	PAT McNAMARA
Lamar	TRACEY WALTER
Dr. Akin	KENNETH UTT
Roden	DAN BUTLER
Pilcher	PAUL LAZAR
"Precious"	"DARLA"
TV Anchor Woman	ADELLE LUTZ
TV Anchor Man	OBBA BABATUNDE
TV Sportscaster	GEORGE MICHAEL
Senator Ruth Martin	DIANE BAKER
FBI Director Hayden Burke	ROGER CORMAN
Paul Krendler	RON VAWTER
Lt. Boyle	CHARLES NAPIER
Senator Martin's Aide	JIM DRATFIELD
1st Reporter	STANTON-MIRANDA
2nd Reporter	REBECCA SAXON
Sgt. Tate	DANNY DARST
Officer Jacobs	CYNTHIA ETTINGER
Officer Murray	BRENT HINKLEY
Airport Flirt	STEVE WYATT
Sgt. Pembry	ALEX COLEMAN
Spooked Memphis Cop	DAVID EARLY
Tall Memphis Cop	ANDRE BLAKE
Distraught Memphis Cop	BILL DALZELL III
SWAT Commander	CHRIS ISAAK
SWAT Communicator	DANIEL von BARGEN
SWAT Shooter	TOMMY LaFITTE
EMS Attendant	JOSH BRODER
EMS Driver	BUZZ KILMAN
Mr. Bimmel	HARRY NORTHUP

Stacy Hubka	LAUREN ROSELLI
Flower Delivery Man	LAMONT ARNOLD

DANCES WITH WOLVES

Directed By	KEVIN COSTNER
Produced By	JIM WILSON and KEVIN COSTNER
Executive Producer	JAKE EBERTS
Screenplay By	MICHAEL BLAKE
	Based on His Novel
Edited By	NEIL TRAVIS, A.C.E.
Director of Photography	DEAN SEMLER, A.C.S.
Production Designer	JEFFREY BEECROFT
Costume Designer	ELSA ZAMPARELLI
Music Composed and Conducted by	JOHN BARRY
Casting by	ELISABETH LEUSTIG, C.S.A.

CAST

Lieutenant Dunbar	KEVIN COSTNER
Stands With A Fist	MARY McDONNELL
Kicking Bird	GRAHAM GREENE
Wind In His Hair	RODNEY A. GRANT
Ten Bears	FLOYD RED CROW WESTERMAN
Black Shawl	TANTOO CARDINAL
Timmons	ROBERT PASTORELLI
Lieutenant Elgin	CHARLES ROCKET
Major Fambrough	MAURY CHAYKIN
Stone Calf	JIMMY HERMAN
Smiles A Lot	NATHAN LEE CHASING HIS HORSE
Otter	MICHAEL SPEARS
Worm	JASON R. LONE HILL
Spivey	TONY PIERCE

Pretty Shield	DORIS LEADER CHARGE
Sergeant Pepper	TOM EVERETT
Sergeant Bauer	LARRY JOSHUA
Edwards	KIRK BALTZ
Major	WAYNE GRACE
General Tide	DONALD HOTTON
Christine	ANNIE COSTNER
Willie	CONOR DUFFY
Christine's Mother	ELISA DANIEL
Big Warrior	PERCY WHITE PLUME
Escort Warrior	JOHN TAIL
Sioux #1/Warrior #1	STEVE REEVIS
Sioux #2/Warrior #2	SHELDON WOLFCHILD
Toughest Pawnee	WES STUDI
Pawnee #1	BUFFALO CHILD
Pawnee #2	CLAYTON BIG EAGLE
Pawnee #3	RICHARD LEADER CHARGE
Sioux Warriors	REDWING TED NEZ
	MARVIN HOLY
Sioux Courier	RAYMOND NEWHOLY
Kicking Bird's Son	DAVID J. FULLER
Kicking Bird's Eldest Son	RYAN WHITE BULL
Kicking Bird's Daughter	OTAKUYE CONROY
Village Mother	MARETTA BIG CROW
Guard	STEVE CHAMBERS
General's Aide	WILLIAM H. BURTON
Confederate Cavalryman	BILL W. CURRY
Confederate Soldiers	NICK THOMPSON
	CARTER HANNER
Wagon Driver	KENT HAYS
Union Soldier	ROBERT GOLDMAN
Tucker	FRANK P. COSTANZA
Ray	JAMES A. MITCHELL
Ambush Wagon Driver	R.I. CURTIN
"Cisco"	"JUSTIN"
"Two Socks"	"TEDDY" & "BUCK"

Index